PERGAMON INTER**N**
of Science, Technology, E**n**
The 1000-volume original pape
industrial training and
Publisher: Robert Maxwell, M.C.

Can Governments Learn?

Pergamon Government and Politics Series

Series Editors

Richard Brody
Stanford University

Norman J. Ornstein
American Enterprise Institute for Public Policy Research

Paul E. Peterson
The Brookings Institution

Nelson W. Polsby
University of California, Berkeley

Martin M. Shapiro
University of California, Berkeley

Pergamon Titles of Related Interest

Foreign Affairs AMERICA AND THE WORLD 1984
Leiken CENTRAL AMERICA: Anatomy of Conflict
Nogee/Donaldson SOVIET FOREIGN POLICY SINCE
WORLD WAR II, Second Edition
Spanier/Nogee CONGRESS, THE PRESIDENCY AND AMERICAN
FOREIGN POLICY

Pergamon Government & Politics Series

Can Governments Learn?

American Foreign Policy and Central American Revolutions

Lloyd S. Etheredge
Nelson A. Rockefeller Institute of Government,
State University of New York at Albany

PERGAMON PRESS

New York • Oxford • Beijing • Frankfurt
São Paulo • Sydney • Tokyo • Toronto

Pergamon Press Offices:

U.S.A.	Pergamon Press, Maxwell House, Fairview Park, Elmsford, New York 10523, U.S.A.
U.K.	Pergamon Press, Headington Hill Hall, Oxford OX3 0BW, England
PEOPLE'S REPUBLIC OF CHINA	Pergamon Press, Qianmen Hotel, Beijing, People's Republic of China
FEDERAL REPUBLIC OF GERMANY	Pergamon Press, Hammerweg 6, D-6242 Kronberg, Federal Republic of Germany
BRAZIL	Pergamon Editora, Rua Eça de Queiros, 346, CEP 04011, São Paulo, Brazil
AUSTRALIA	Pergamon Press (Aust.) Pty., P.O. Box 544, Potts Point, NSW 2011, Australia
JAPAN	Pergamon Press, 8th Floor, Matsuoka Central Building, 1-7-1 Nishishinjuku, Shinjuku-ku, Tokyo 160, Japan
CANADA	Pergamon Press Canada, Suite 104, 150 Consumers Road, Willowdale, Ontario M2J 1P9, Canada

For my parents

Copyright © 1985 Pergamon Press Inc.

Second printing 1987

Library of Congress Cataloging in Publication Data

Etheredge, Lloyd S.
Can governments learn?
(Pergamon government and politics series)
Bibliography: p.
Includes index.
1. Central America--Foreign relations--United States.
2. United States--Foreign relations--Central America.
3. United States--Foreign relations--1945-
I. Title. II. Series.
F1436.8.U6E85 1985   327.730728   84-26611
ISBN 0-08-027218-5
ISBN 0-08-032401-0 (pbk.)

Printed in Great Britain by A. Wheaton & Co. Ltd., Exeter

 CONTENTS

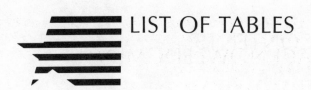 LIST OF TABLES

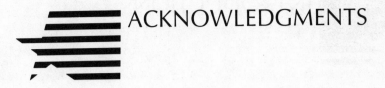 # ACKNOWLEDGMENTS

This book has been made possible by many contributions. Several years ago the National Science Foundation provided support, through grant SOC 77-27240, to begin work on the interdisciplinary study of government learning rates. James Short provided continuing assistance for that project. Chris Achen, Hayward Alker, Henry Brady, Roger Hurwitz, Ithiel Pool, Lucian Pye, and Henry Elonge read the manuscript at different stages, with valuable critical review. Lynn Etheredge has been a continuing source of advice and support. Many others have contributed to preparation of the manuscript, among them: Muriel Bell, Merina Halingten, Bill Hedberg, Maxine Morman, Addie Napolitano, and Anna Tower. I am especially indebted to the staff of the Center for Advanced Study in the Behavioral Sciences, and to its Trustees, for an invaluable year.

# INTRODUCTION

Over the past forty years, since America assumed global responsibility after World War II, it has encountered various types of recurring foreign policy problems. We might expect historical experience to produce learning, a record of increasing intelligence and effectiveness across return engagements. Often, however, such government learning has not occurred, and the purpose of this book is an inquiry into the nature of the problems involved.[1]

My subject will be one recurring problem, American policy toward revolutions which use Marxist rhetoric, receive material aid from the Soviet Union, and are directed against a repressive government that has received substantial material aid and political support from the United States.[2] The case material will be drawn from the history of American policy in Latin America, the 1954 overthrow of a leftist government in Guatemala, the evolution of Cuban policy from 1958 to 1962, and the current repetition of similar policies in the 1980s.[3]

Chapters 1–3 review the history of America's failed Bay of Pigs invasion in 1961, Operation MONGOOSE, and the Cuban nuclear confrontation crisis of 1962. These chapters include discussion of the successful use of the Bay of Pigs model in 1954 (against a government in Guatemala) and the U.S. government's contract with the Mafia to assassinate Premier Castro at the time of the Bay of Pigs invasion. Readers unfamiliar with recently declassified material will, I think, find the invasion to have been more intelligently conceived than earlier explanations credited.

Chapters 4–6 recast the case material and broaden the scope of historical evidence to explain three vectors reflecting the blockage of government learning: (a) the adoption of similar policies across historical encounters; (b) the repetition of collectively self-blocking behavior within the national security decision process; and (c) the repetition of a common syndrome of errors in judgment and perception. Chapter 6 presents a new theory of American foreign policy, identifying a common source to explain the principal features and recurrence of these vectors; it is also, in part, a reflection on the vulnerabilities to which a great (and global) power is prone as an effect of the forms by which the human imagination seeks to understand this role.

Chapter 7 applies this historically based explanation to analyze, and place in a broader perspective, American foreign policy toward Central America in the 1980s. I draw lessons about the weakness in the design of American political institutions which makes it difficult for them to effect and sustain long-term learning outside the Western European arena, and conclude with suggestions to improve the foreign policy learning rate.

My thesis is that these three vectors of blocked learning in American foreign policy reflect imagination-based behavior, specifically a system of hierarchical images used to understand the nature of power. I will develop a case that American foreign policy decisions evidence a "dual track" information processing by which a system of strong imagery (and associated motives engaged within it), used to understand the world, determines policy more consequentially than analytical reasoning. Standard theories of failed analytical brilliance, poor design of bureaucracies, inadvertent flaws in decision-making processes, or simple cognitive errors do not, I will argue, explain the historical record. I will also argue that remedies based on such theories would effect useful changes, but these would be modest at best. And if the reconstruction I propose of these American policies is true generally, then our understanding of international politics might become wiser by the lesson that analytical brilliance and technical rationality are neither necessary nor sufficient conditions for peace. Of desirable qualities, if given modesty and graciousness by all parties we might recognize there to be little basis for armed conflict between nations.[4]

Let me recount a story to introduce the historical discussion which begins in the first chapter.

During the afternoon of June 22, 1954, Allen Dulles, the director of the Central Intelligence Agency, met with President Eisenhower to make an urgent request. The CIA, with Eisenhower's approval, was conducting a covert operation to overthrow a leftist government in Guatemala. Three old bombers had been used to effect psychological warfare against the regime. Earlier that day, two had been shot down; Dulles wanted to resupply the operation with aircraft from America.

At the meeting in Eisenhower's office was an assistant secretary of state for inter-American affairs, Henry Holland, who argued forcefully against the plan. He warned that the resupply could become public knowledge and raise an outcry against America's involvement. Holland also opposed such involvement because it further violated treaties previous United States governments had signed. Among these was the Charter of the Organization of American States, signed by the United States and ratified by a two-thirds vote of the Senate. The United States had formally pledged to respect the principle (Article 15) that:

"No State or group of States has the right to intervene, directly or indirectly, for any reason whatever, in the internal affairs of any other State. The foregoing principle prohibits not only armed force but also any other form of interference or attempted threat . . . "[5]

The assistant secretary thought a legal prohibition clear. The words of the treaty—"directly or indirectly, for any reason whatever"—were as strong a prohibition as language could state.

President Eisenhower asked Dulles to estimate America's probability of success if replacements were sent. "Twenty percent," said Dulles. Without resupply, he estimated the CIA's chance of success to be "about zero." Eisenhower granted his request.

Strong feelings had been expressed. To ease any tensions Dulles might feel, afterward Eisenhower took him aside and kidded him about his "twenty percent" estimate: "Allen, that figure of twenty percent was persuasive," Eisenhower said. "It showed me that you had thought this matter through realistically. If you had told me that the chances would be ninety percent, I would have had a much more difficult decision." Dulles, a grin on his face, replied: "Mr. President, when I saw Henry walking into your office with three large law books under his arm, I knew he had lost his case already."[6]

This brief conversation between two old friends thirty years ago begins a story of repeated American encounters. As we will see, the slightly breathless dramas of daily newspaper headlines are misleading. The people change, but the issues, arguments—and usually the policy decisions—remain the same.

NOTES

1. Current reviews of definitions and theories in the study of government learning are L. Etheredge, "Government Learning: An Overview" in S. Long, ed., *Handbook of Political Behavior*, vol. 2 (New York: Plenum Press, 1981), pp. 73–161 and L. Etheredge and J. Short, "Thinking About Government Learning" *Journal of Management Studies* (1983) 20(1), pp. 41–58. See also G. Brewer and P. deLeon, *The Foundations of Policy Analysis* (Homewood, IL: Dorsey Press, 1983). Discussions central to the field include A. George, *Presidential Decisionmaking in Foreign Policy: The Effective Use of Information and Advice* (Boulder, CO: Westview Press, 1980); C. Argyris and D. Schon, *Organization Learning: A Theory of Action Perspective* (Reading, MA: Addison-Wesley, 1978); K. Deutsch, *The Nerves of Government: Models of Communication and Control* (New York: Free Press, 1963), and his *Politics and Government: How People Decide Their Fate*, 3rd ed., (Boston: Houghton Mifflin, 1974); H. Wilensky, *Organizational Intelligence: Knowledge and Policy in Government and Industry* (New York: Basic Books, 1967). For general work concerning intellectual life and organizational behavior see the work of J. March, e.g., M. Cohen, J. March and J. Olsen, "A Garbage Can Model of Organizational Choice" *Administrative Science Quarterly* 17 (1972): 1–25; and J. March, "Bounded Rationality, Ambiguity, and the Engineering of Choice" *Bell Journal of Economics* 9 (1978): 587–608; E. Jaques, *A General Theory of Bureaucracy* (New York: Heinemann, 1981); K. Weick, "Cognitive Processes in Organizations" in B. Staw, ed., *Research in Organizational Beahvior: An Annual Series of Analytic Essays and Critical Reviews* (Greenwich, CT: JAI Press, 1979), vol. 1; K. Weick and R. Daft, "The Effectiveness of Interpretation Systems" in K. Cameron and D. Whetten, ed., *Organizational Effectiveness: A Comparison of Multiple Models* (New York: Academic Press, 1983); H. Lasswell, "Research in Policy Analysis: the Intelligence and Appraisal Functions" in F. Greenstein and N. Polsby,

ed., *Handbook of Political Science* (Reading, MA: Addison-Wesley, 1975), vol. 6; and Y. Dror, *Design for Policy Sciences* (New York: American Elsevier, 1971). The Club of Rome Report (J. Botkin et al., *No Limits to Learning* (New York: Pergamon, 1979)) is visionary but probably loads too many empirical issues and too much normative content into a single concept.

2. Other recurring problems which, recent history suggests, any new administration should expect to face would include: (a) the threat or use of force by the Soviet Union to defend its hegemony in Eastern Europe; (b) another war will occur between Israel and its neighbors; and (c) there will be a further opportunity for arms control negotiation with the Soviet Union, accompanied by arguments that new weapons systems which will serve as effective bargaining chips.

There are types of "invisible," continuing problems with which a president should be prepared to deal at his own initiative and which would might benefit from institutional memory, e.g., the 15 million deaths each year, worldwide, from malnutrition and starvation.

3. The most recent works on the Guatemala operation are by S. Kinzer and S. Schlesinger, *Bitter Fruit: The Untold Story of the American Coup in Guatemala* (Garden City, NY: Doubleday, 1982) and R. Immerman, *The CIA in Guatemala: The Foreign Policy of Intervention* (Austin: Univ. of Texas Press, 1982).

The most recent work on the Bay of Pigs is P. Wyden, *Bay of Pigs: The Untold Story* (New York: Simon and Schuster, 1979) who supplemented and enriched previous accounts by interviews with both American and Cuban participants. The author's eye for detail has been invaluable for my purposes of reconstruction and improvement of theory. I have reviewed the basic sources, attempted to clarify remaining ambiguities with American participants, and incorporated more recent material. In my interpretation, I place more weight on the intellectual merits and dramatic logic of the invasion plan and on systemic determinants of the decision.

There is substantial agreement about what happened. The lacunae are: (a) the private discussions of Rusk and Bundy with the president; (b) information concerning the specific location of the 2,500 hardcore supporters the CIA believed were in Cuba, and what aid they were expected to provide; and (c) the issue of whether D-Day was intentionally postponed to allow time for a second Mafia attempt on Castro's life.

The Operation MONGOOSE story has fewer published sources. Arthur Schlesinger's account *Robert F. Kennedy and His Times* (Boston: Houghton Mifflin, 1978) is based on access to many still-restricted documents (e.g., Robert Kennedy's private journal). His occasional tendency to attribute virtues to the White House, and "excesses" to the CIA, is at variance with other accounts. The Church Committee investigations (U.S. Senate, Select Committee to Study Governmental Operations with Respect to Intelligence Activities, *Alleged Assassination Plots Involving Foreign Leaders*. Senate Report 94–465, November 20, 1975, Washington, DC: Government Printing Office, 1975); T. Powers, *The Man Who Kept the Secrets: Richard Helms and the CIA* (New York: Pocket Books, 1979); and D. Martin, *Wilderness of Mirrors* (New York: Ballentine, 1981) are also valuable. T. Branch and G. Crile, "The Kennedy Vendetta: An Account of the CIA's Entanglement in the Secret War Against Castro" *Harper's* (August, 1975), pp. 49–63 is still the best descriptive overview. W. Hinckle and W. Turner, *The Fish is Red: The Story of the Secret War Against Castro* (New York: Harper and Row, 1981) introduce a broader range of issues covering the post-1962 period: Further declassifications will be necessary before scholars can be certain of the reliability of the picture they have assembled. A significant problem of inference is that right-wing and expatriate groups have free-lanced against Castro, and CIA agents have often posed as "representatives of American business interests," making it a complicated task to assay what activities against Castro have reflected official policy.

Graham Allison's systematic review of the Cuban Missile Crisis decision, *Essence of Decision: Explaining the Cuban Missile Crisis* (Boston: Little, Brown, 1971) remains the standard work on the American side. Using the information provided at the time (Operation MONGOOSE had not been disclosed in the press), Allison tended to discount the Cuban defense hypothesis. An excellent introduction to current scholarship is N. Lebow's "The Cuban Missile Crisis: Reading the Lessons Correctly" *Political Science Quarterly* 98 (1983): 431–458.

The complex interplay of events and reciprocal interpretations during the early 1960s has yet to be analyzed fully. R. Slusser, "The Berlin Crises of 1958–59 and 1961" in B. Blechman and S. Kaplan, ed., *Force Without War: The U.S. Armed Forces as a Political Instrument* (Washington, DC: Brookings Institution, 1978), pp. 343–439 makes a valuable beginning. Scholars may have understated the benefit, to Khrushchev, of dramatizing a threat to Berlin to deter Kennedy from using American troops against Cuba, a deterrent threat that appears to have worked.

4. I am referring to a reformulated imagination system of decision making *consistent* with modesty and graciousness. Thus, I am not making a simple or authoritative prescription. I will develop this argument in chapter 6. For a related discussion of the "triple need for modesty" see S. Hoffman, "Detente" in J. Nye, ed., *The Making of America's Soviet Policy* (New Haven, CT: Yale Univ. Press, 1984), pp. 231–263, esp. p. 260; also S. Hoffman, *Primacy or World Order: American Foreign Policy Since the Cold War* (New York: McGraw-Hill, 1978).

6. Cited in C. Ronning, ed., *Intervention in Latin America* (New York: Knopf, 1970), p. 14.

7. D. Eisenhower, *The White House Years: Mandate for Change, 1953–1956* (Garden City, NY: Doubleday, 1963), pp. 425–426 tells the story in his memoirs. Note that he expects an American audience to appreciate the humor, his decision criteria, and probably his choice to "ease tensions" with Dulles rather than Holland. Eisenhower and Dulles had known one another since World War II, when Dulles had been involved in Allied spying operations and an attempt to assassinate Hitler. See S. Ambrose and R. Immerman, *Ike's Spies: Eisenhower and the Espionage Establishment* (Garden City, NY: Doubleday, 1981), passim. The story suggests they shared a common sensibility concerning the conduct of international power, and a viewpoint about legal arguments and restraints, which I will discuss in chapter 6.

After the operation succeeded, Eisenhower hosted a briefing and slide show for his cabinet, and included his wife, Mamie, so the CIA could explain how they had pulled off the operation. He beamed with pleasure. The memory of his warm congratulations remained with the same CIA team as they began to design the overthrow of Castro. See Wyden, *Bay of Pigs*, p. 21.

Chapter 1 PLANS, A BATTLE...
AND FAILURE

Mr. President, I know you're doubtful about this, but I stood at this very desk and said to President Eisenhower about a similar operation in Guatemala, 'I believe it will work.' And I say to you now, Mr. President, that the prospects for this plan are even better than our prospects were in Guatemala.
— Allen Dulles to
President Kennedy[1]

In January 1961, President Kennedy and his advisers began to review plans developed by the Eisenhower administration for the military overthrow of Cuban Premier Fidel Castro. In April, Kennedy approved an invasion by 1,200 Cuban expatriates.[2] It failed. With hindsight, a member of the administration described it as "the most screwed up operation there has ever been."[3] Next, Kennedy ordered Operation MONGOOSE, until that time the largest covert operation undertaken by the CIA. That failed, too.

This chapter describes the main events of the Bay of Pigs through the beachhead collapse. It reviews, as part of that description, the Guatemala success (in 1954) which shaped the plans, and it reviews the CIA's contract with the Mafia to assassinate Castro at the time of the invasion.[4]

BACKGROUND

In 1959 the international arena, in American popular and elite conception, was the scene of a cold war: America and its allies were opposed by the forces of the Sino-Soviet bloc. After Castro overthrew the Cuban dictator, Batista, he began, in the eyes of American policymakers, to grow increasingly anti-American and pro-Communist, spurning efforts by Washington to establish good relations.

This official viewpoint is described in a background memorandum provided by the State Department:

> When the Castro regime came to power in 1959, the United States looked upon it with sympathy, recognized it almost immediately, and welcomed its promises of political freedom and social justice for the Cuban people. We made clear our willingness to discuss Cuba's economic needs. Despite our concern at the Cuban regime's mounting hostility toward the United States and its growing communist

1

tendencies, we attempted patiently and consistently from early 1959 until mid-1960 to negotiate differences with the regime.

Elements in the Castro movement engaged in anti-American activities during the revolution against Batista. Soon after it came to power in 1959, the Castro government turned away from its previous promises, permitted communist influence to grow, attacked and persecuted its own supporters in Cuba who expressed opposition to communism, arbitrarily seized U.S. properties, and made a series of baseless charges against the United States. It ignored, rejected or imposed impossible conditions on repeated United States overtures to cooperate and negotiate. In 1960 Cuba established close political, economic, and military relationships with the Sino-Soviet bloc, while increasing the pace and vehemence of measures and attacks against the United States. We did not take measures in our own behalf to isolate Cuba until July 1960.[5]

To American policymakers, Castro, whom many had originally hoped was only a socialist and a nationalist, exhibited his true colors as a Communist revolutionary established in the Western Hemisphere, ninety miles from American shores. He threatened to spread Communist revolution in Central and South America and challenged traditionally claimed (Monroe Doctrine) American hegemony by allying himself with the Soviet Union. The Soviet Union and other Communist nations had agreed to buy Cuban sugar and to supply Cuba with foreign aid and arms.

This evolution did not mean that the American government would attempt, automatically, to overthrow Castro by military force. People who believed that Castro had become an urgent problem that needed a solution, and who had a solution in mind, set out to sell both ideas. The CIA promoted Castro as a serious threat, defined the objective to be his elimination, and proposed the solution (a covert operation directed by themselves).

The key mover at the CIA was its deputy director for plans (the CIA's designation for espionage and clandestine operations), Richard Bissell. In a phrase later coined to describe some of the men in the Kennedy administration, he was an "action intellectual." A former member of the economics faculty at M.I.T. and Yale, he was an unusually gifted man, equally admired for analytical brilliance, his articulate mastery of material, and his ability to get things done. Within "the agency" (as the CIA called itself), he was considered likely to become the next director. He had developed the U-2 spy plane, one of the CIA's major contributions to improved intelligence about the Soviet nuclear threat. He did it in absolute secrecy and in two years (the air force, which had campaigned for the assignment, estimated it would take seven years). He came to government service from an elite background: independent wealth, Groton, Yale. He did not need to be cautious, and he was not there to push papers. He had an abiding intention to use human intelligence to understand the world and to shape history. He had gained experience with this type of work as an outstanding administrator and planner with the Marshall Plan, reconstructing the economies of Europe. He had the sense of mastery to take responsibility for the evolution of Latin America. And he had the intellectual ability and nervous energy to welcome such a challenge: he was constantly pacing, fidgeting with paper clips, moving quickly, flipping through briefing memos at high speed, taking in and recalling it all.[6]

The director of the Central Intelligence Agency was Allen Dulles, another holdover appointment from the Eisenhower administration, where his relationship with his older brother, John Foster Dulles, the secretary of state, had helped to give the CIA and its covert operations a major role in American foreign policy. He had achieved a distinguished record in espionage and counterintelligence during World War II, and he was widely regarded as America's foremost intelligence expert. He loved the details of spying, "tradecraft" as it is known, and would spend major portions of his time reviewing the minute details of the various activities of his individual spies. A quiet man, a pipe smoker, he relished the impression of mystery and of knowing more than he would reveal. Two of the CIA's great successes during his tenure were the overthrow of the Mossadegh government of Iran (replacing him with the Shah of Iran) and the overthrow, in 1954, of the left-leaning government in Guatemala. People in Washington knew Allen Dulles had masterminded both overthrows, but they did not know how these feats were accomplished. The mystique of the CIA's magical power to accomplish such things was one he nurtured. He was not known as a good administrator, nor did he consider this his metier.[7]

Dulles met with President Eisenhower in March 1960 to review CIA-developed options for covert operations against Castro. He was seeking guidance and an official mandate for planning. He presented Eisenhower with a few ideas for minor sabotage which Eisenhower realized, as Dulles knew he would, gave no chance to be more than minor harassment. Eisenhower responded that if Dulles were serious about overthrowing Castro, the CIA should come back with a "program." Thus the instruction to begin became a presidential instruction. This maneuver to induce Eisenhower to initiate the instruction he wanted was not malicious: it was a small, polished detail of the tradecraft of managing presidents, a skill that senior civil servants learn well.[8]

With this mandate, the CIA drafted a four-part proposal to (a) create a Cuban government in exile; (b) mount a propaganda campaign against Castro from secret, covertly funded, transmitters; (c) build covert intelligence and "action capability" networks on the island; and (d) develop a paramilitary force for future guerrilla action. Eisenhower approved the proposal on March 17, 1960.

But the president's attitude was casual, even unenthusiastic. He did not consider Castro a major threat. He was willing for the CIA to develop plans and then to have a look at them.[9]

Vice-President Richard Nixon, who had announced he would run for the presidency, took a strong personal interest in the project and urged Eisenhower to eliminate Castro before election day.[10] Nixon judged rightly the role Castro would play in American politics. The need for greater toughness against Communism did become a major issue in that election: Kennedy, now remembered for initiatives to reduce the dangers of the cold war and increase selective cooperation with the Soviet Union, in fact was a hard-liner in the campaign. He charged the Eisenhower administration had allowed a "missile gap" to develop in the Soviet Union's favor. And he criticized it for allowing a Communist government to come to power in Cuba. Prior to his last televised debate with Nixon, and unaware of the Eisenhower administration's planning, Kennedy's aides issued a statement to toughen his challenge, calling for "strengthening anti-Castro forces in exile . . . who offer eventual hope of overthrowing Castro."[11] Kennedy's aides later claimed he had gone to bed before the statement was discussed with him. It made Nixon furious as he thought Kennedy had been briefed on the CIA plans. (His charge of duplicity, in his *Six Crises*, prompted the rebuttal from the Kennedy White House.) He was unable to breach intelligence to reveal what the Republican administration had been doing and defend himself, and he felt forced to oppose military intervention in their televised debate. The exact phrasing used by a Kennedy aide (Richard Goodwin) may have gone further than the candidate would have gone. But the tone of the campaign, and the statement, exemplified a truth of American politics that Kennedy carried with him in later discussions of whether to abort the invasion: in America, a politician had a good campaign issue if he charged insufficient toughness against Communism by an incumbent administration.[12]

The CIA's plans had grown by the time Allen Dulles and Richard Bissell briefed President-elect Kennedy on November 18, 1960.[13] After the go-ahead from Eisenhower they had tried a great many things. These were not working. Underground networks established by the Cubans were almost always penetrated by Castro.[14] Arms drops were frequently intercepted. As Richard Bissell later described their problem: "I think that every team we sent in was picked up within a few days. . . . [The political exiles in Miami] all claimed large and organized followings on the island. Well, they may have had vague sympathizers on the island, but they had no way of communicating with them securely, no command and control over them, and therefore there were no internal underground cells to which we could send supplies, or with which we could establish communication. It was a mess."[15]

The CIA's covert operations and supplies, together with those provided by private right-wing American groups, might produce several bombings a week in Cuba, but there was no obvious effect save the rate of executions of the traitors and terrorists Castro's police captured. The Castro regime, if anything, seemed able to survive. And Castro's influence appeared to grow: by July 1960, American embassies throughout Latin America were reporting that Castro was exciting interest in revolutionary approaches. The Eisenhower administration countered by beginning (in September 1960 at Bogota, Columbia) a modest program for economic development and social change, funded at $500 million.[16]

With Castro to receive increased arms shipments from the Soviet bloc, including MIG jets, an initiative to overthrow him by a covert operation now appeared to require expanded capability, and this needed to be available quickly. Thus, during the administration transition period, primarily at Bissell's direction, the plan grew, without formal authorization, to envision a concerted military effort. Dulles and Bissell told the president-elect what they were doing. He expressed willingness for them to continue, and even enthusiasm, but he was also unwilling to commit himself until he took office in January.[17]

During a transition meeting on January 19, 1961, Eisenhower spoke favorably to Kennedy about the Cuba project: America had a "responsibility" to "bring it to a successful conclusion." The endorsement was ambiguous but probably contributed to a favorable framework for its initial evaluation. Eisenhower was America's most respected military leader: his judgment on a military matter would carry weight.[18]

The first CIA plan, the Trinidad plan, was presented in outline on January 28, 1961; it called for landing 1,200 troops at the town of Trinidad on the southeast coast of Cuba, a dramatic "shock" invasion in daylight. The Trinidad area was thought to include a large number of disaffected people who would join the invaders to create an impression of momentum.[19] Moreover, the site was near the Escambray Mountains, a natural fallback for guerrilla operations if the assault began to fail. (The Escambray Mountains previously had been used as a base by Castro in his guerrilla war against Batista. In 1960 the mountains were the location of anti-Castro guerrillas being supplied by CIA airdrops.)[20]

The Guatemala Model

To understand the rationale of the Trinidad plan, it is necessary to review the overthrow of Jacobo Arbenz, the president of Guatemala, designed by the CIA in 1954. The CIA intended to repeat this earlier operation, an explicit case of learning from experience: Dulles and Bissell sought to transfer a past success, to draw on their understanding of a low-cost method to topple a Latin American government. Semiofficial historians of Kennedy's decision (Schlesinger, Sorenson) later portrayed the Bay of Pigs as an operation that should never have been approved. They understated the CIA's case. It had sophistication, and a track record that did not depend on battlefield victory or on a spontaneous mass uprising, which the White House hoped to ignite.

To overthrow the democratically elected Arbenz government, the CIA approached several expatriates to consider which to install in his place. It finally struck a deal to support Lt. Col. Carlos Castillo Armas, a former Guatemalan soldier who had been sentenced to death for an unsuccessful coup attempted in late 1950, had escaped from prison, and fled to neighboring Honduras. At the same time, a new American ambassador with experience in anti-Communist work in Greece, John Peurifoy, was dispatched to Guatemala to plan and coordinate covert operations within the country.[21]

The plan was to conduct psychological and political warfare. Secretary of State Dulles and the State Department orchestrated a major propaganda campaign against the Arbenz regime, initiated an Organization of American States resolution opposing Communist influence in the hemisphere, dramatized a shipment of arms purchased by Arbenz from Communist-bloc sources, and signed defense treaties with the governments of Nicaragua and Honduras.[22] By the time the invasion occurred, the Arbenz government and all of Latin America were intended to understand that the power of the United States was committed — although in unknown ways — and to believe the fate of the Arbenz government to be sealed. Preparation also included secret radio transmitters, run by the CIA and broadcasting across the border, carrying fictitious messages to a (nonexistent) large underground. The transmissions were clearly audible throughout Guatemala and were designed to play on the nerves and morale of Arbenz and his key supporters. They did panic the government (which learned of the invasion preparations in Nicaragua as early as January 1954) into mass arrests, torture, and murder of suspected collaborators in the urban middle class, further alienating supporters. (The McCarthy period in the United States, when there was no realistic danger of invasion, provides a basis for grasping the fear the CIA began to generate within the Guatemalan government and among its supporters.)[23]

Technological tricks of psychological warfare were designed to create the impression that a small invasion force was large and ominous. Several bombers, P-47 fighters, and C-47 transports were assembled, and 150 troops trained, in Nicaragua. The small Castillo Armas "army" crossed the border on June 19, 1954 and stopped a few miles inside the country to wait for the government to collapse. Several small bombing raids were directed against Guatemala City targets (e.g., army barracks), and there were leaflet drops over the capital. The propaganda radio stepped up its messages and the CIA adroitly engaged its technological weapons, selectively jammed the communications of the Guatemalan army and fed false orders and reports of a larger invasion over its radio network. Thus, believing his country under major attack, Arbenz found himself unable to learn what was happening or even to control his own troops. The army was not eager to fight, especially faced with the possibility such resistance would only bring invasion by American troops. The early air strikes were taken to be a token of what might follow. Defeat was considered inevitable. With the army in disarray, except for desultory shooting, there was little combat. The main clash, the "Battle of Chiquimula," left a total of seventeen dead on both sides.[24]

Luck was also on the CIA's side. A Guatemalan pilot defected. He refused to broadcast an appeal to his fellow pilots, out of fear of reprisals against his family. But the CIA operatives showed initiative, got him drunk, and persuaded him to talk about what he would say if he felt free to make an appeal. Secretly, they tape-recorded him, then spliced the tape and broadcast it. Arbenz, fearing more defections, grounded the remainder of his air force.[25]

Within eight days the army top command forced Arbenz to resign. The head of a new three-man government, Colonel Diaz, vowed to continue the fight and thus was not satisfactory to the United States. In two days, after the CIA dropped two bombs on the main military barracks and destroyed the government radio station, a meeting with Ambassador Peurifoy produced a more acceptable and staunchly anti-Communist head of government, Col. Elfego Monzon. The ambassador personally negotiated the paperwork of the formal transition to Castillo Armas at a meeting in San Salvador, and Castillo Armas arrived at the capital aboard the ambassador's private plane.[26]

The CIA strategy was to produce a victory by psychological demoralization and political destabilization, not by a military defeat. Faced by an apparently massive invasion, the dimensions of which it could not evaluate, and which was backed by an ominous association with the power of the United States, the Arbenz government—as Richard Bissell interpreted it—"lost its nerve."[27] Scared and demoralized, key elite supporters abandoned Arbenz rather than die for his hopeless cause. American embassy contacts with the military aided the plan, both in the transfer of power and in encouraging them to block a last-ditch Arbenz plan to distribute arms to proregime peasants.

Leaving aside the issue of whether historians will eventually conclude this to be an accurate appraisal of why the CIA won in Guatemala, what is crucial here is that it is what the CIA *thought* happened.[28]

To use this same plan against Cuba did not depend upon history learned secondhand from documents. It was personal knowledge. Allen Dulles was CIA director throughout this period. In 1954 his special assistant was Richard Bissell, later chief Bay of Pigs planner. Frank Wisner, deputy director for Plans in 1954 (the operational head for Guatemala) had resigned in 1958, but his assistant, beginning in April 1954, was Tracy Barnes, who was to be special assistant to Richard Bissell during the Bay of Pigs. The deputy director of the CIA at the Bay of Pigs, General Charles P. Cabell, held the same position during Guatemala. The propaganda operation was run by the same man (David Phillips). E. Howard Hunt (later of Watergate repute) was chief of political action for Guatemala and served in the same capacity for most of the Bay of Pigs operation. The CIA station chief in Guatemala City ("Jake Engler") was Hunt's superior during the Bay of Pigs. In 1960 and 1961 the old team, enthusiastic to repeat its earlier success, went into action again. The speed with which they mounted their new operation reflected this unique and superb institutional memory.

From the Guatemala success several lessons carried forward — in addition to knowledge that this bold and clever plan could work. Each, while not a dramatic lesson, nevertheless confirmed understandings that were to continue in 1961 planning, although to mixed effect.

1. American activity violated several formal treaty commitments made in earlier decades by the United States.[29] But it was apparent that few Americans would be upset by overthrow of a pro-Communist government, whatever international laws proposed.

2. The operation remained "plausibly deniable." No journalist published hard evidence that the CIA was involved. Alert journalists suspected this was more than a patriotic action by the Guatemalans themselves, but they made little effort to prove it, or at least little headway. Eisenhower's official denial was accepted. Such press loyalty did not continue in 1961.

3. Both the United Nations and the Organization of American States proved ineffectual instruments of collective security to safeguard Guatemala's national boundaries against foreign aggression. No one, of course, believed such organizations would be effective, but the United States maneuvered to assure the impotence of the guarantees of international charters and to keep even official inquiries from being launched.[30] And the Soviet Union sent no aid and engaged in no reprisals. In Latin America, the United States was reassured that it could overthrow Communist (or potentially Communist) governments without third parties coming to the aid of the target country.

4. When several of the invader aircraft were disabled or shot down, CIA Director Allen Dulles — as we have seen — gained ready assent from President Eisenhower for emergency resupply from American stores, despite State Department objections.[31] Although it did not in itself determine these same planners' expectations of Kennedy, the experience did not contradict general knowledge that a politician, once committed, might change earlier restrictive guidelines rather than allow such an operation to fail.

5. Eisenhower, and other politicians, learned that covert operations were a useful method for cold war interventions in underdeveloped countries. After the Guatemala success, the role of CIA covert activities in American foreign policy expanded.

Another event after 1954 probably favored use of the Guatemala model and worked against direct introduction of American troops. In the 1950s, Americans prided themselves on their idealism and on their moral superiority to crass power politics, specifically, moral superiority to the Soviet Union. A Soviet invasion of Hungary in 1956, ostensibly in support of liberation, and the creation of a "puppet government" were widely reported: photographs showing Soviet tanks rolling into Budapest and the shooting of nationalist freedom fighters brought outrage in the American press. Privately, Kennedy and his advisers probably favored the Guatemala model as a device to deal with Castro that would avoid charges (and a self-image) of cynically undertaking Hungarian-type suppression with American troops.[32]

Offstage: The CIA Plan to Assassinate Castro

At this point another chain of events, offstage and then unknown to almost everyone, needs to be described. The CIA's plan was that Fidel Castro, and perhaps also his brother Raoul, and Ché Guevara (Castro's military chief), be killed prior to D-Day. Using the Guatemala model alone, Allen Dulles and Richard Bissell felt America had a good chance of success. But with the Cuban government so personalized, and power so dependent on the charisma of one man, they thought they would virtually guarantee the success of the expatriates, with minimal loss of life on both sides, if they effected an assassination prior to the troop landings.[33]

Work on Castro's personal elimination, by nonviolent or violent means, began in December 1959 with what Allen Dulles believed was clear authorization from Eisenhower. Various schemes were invented, for example to spray Castro's broadcast studios with an LSD-like substance and to treat a box of cigars with a similar compound so he would appear publicly disoriented and erratic. Another plan was to dust his shoes with thallium salts to cause his beard to mysteriously fall out and produce heightened mental instability. (I return to this element in their calculations—their psychological assessment of Castro—later.) But these ideas were recognized as more clever than likely to be effective. A box of Castro's favorite cigars was treated with botulism toxin, although it was not delivered successfully.[34]

Planning to use a hit-man or team of hit-men, contract killers, began in July 1960. By August, Richard Bissell was using intermediaries to negotiate a contract with the Mafia.[35]

The Mafia contract was negotiated through Robert Maheu, a former FBI agent whose private investigation firm included among its clients the reclusive multimillionaire Howard Hughes. Maheu contacted John Rosselli. Rosselli had started out in Chicago under the mobster Al Capone: While not a Mafia chief in his own right, he was the syndicate's top man in Las Vegas.

Rosselli put the CIA in contact with Momo Salvatore ("Sam") Giancana, the Mafia chief in Chicago, and with Santos Trafficante, Mafia chief in Florida and former syndicate chief in Havana (under Batista). They agreed to help, but the motives involved were undoubtedly more complicated than patriotism or money ($150,000 was a figure discussed).[36]

Schlesinger has speculated that Trafficante decided to be a double agent; the plans never bore fruit, he suggests, because the Mafia chief struck a deal with Castro to use Cuba for drug smuggling to the United States, earning Castro hard foreign exchange, and the Mafia a substantial profit.[37] By this scenario, Trafficante ostensibly went along with the CIA but was obtaining the best of both worlds. He achieved (he thought) a "hold" over the United States government to ward off future prosecution, plus the smuggling profits. And the longer he tried and failed, the longer the situation worked to his benefit.

It is likely that others in the Mafia had other reasons for their involvement. Schlesinger, uncommonly ingenuous, speaks only of their "grudge" at losing $100 million or more per year because Castro threw them out and closed the brothels and casinos.[38] Obviously, there was not only a "grudge"; they wanted to return to business as usual. Doubtless no government official favored returning the mob to power, or would have made promises to that effect. But it would have been clear that such hopes of the syndicate were part of the context of the discussion.

The Mafia finally informed the CIA that recruiting a human assassin for a gangland slaying was too difficult. Castro's security was tight, and it would be a suicide mission. They requested poison pills, and these were used in two serious attempts to kill Castro prior to the invasion, one in March 1961, the other in April, just before the scheduled D-Day.[39]

Did the president himself know at the time he approved the invasion that the plan included assassination? The CIA says that he did. From everything known about Richard Bissell — and he was widely regarded as an honest man, a gentleman, and a highly professional civil servant — it seems certain he believed he had presidential approval for the assassination. He surmised that it was given in very private, and possibly circumlocutory, discussion between Allen Dulles and the presidents involved.[40] Dulles, of course, was deceased by the time congressional inquiries opened in the mid-1970s, as were the two presidents. There were no written records of such conversations, but it would be standard tradecraft not to put such things into writing, and from this fact no inference can be drawn.

Arthur Schlesinger, Jr., presents the best brief for Jack Kennedy and his brother Robert, arguing that assassination approval was a misunderstanding, one of those odd mix-ups.[41] Everyone would know, Schlesinger says, that a "king can do no wrong" code ("plausible deniability" is the standard term) should govern any discussions. The president always needed deniability and so he could not utter the exact words of approval himself: magically, by this theory, he was not exactly "tied" to what would follow if he communicated what he wanted without saying it in so many words. Knowing the code, no one — as Richard Bissell put it — would "embarrass" a president by asking him directly, thereby compromising him if he said yes.[42] A president and his CIA chief (who, it was understood, would take the rap) could also then testify, under oath if necessary, that there had been no formal approval for such an operation.

By Schlesinger's theory, Allen Dulles played a too-subtle verbal game with the president when they met in private and misunderstood his response. There is no manual for new presidents indicating that when a CIA director says, for example, that he is also discussing alternative ways to "eliminate" Castro by providing financial support to private groups who have that similar purpose (or whatever euphemism might be used), alarm bells should ring in the president's head and he should anticipate that assassination plans will shift into high gear unless he, at that moment, is alert enough to grasp what has just gone past him.

A second route by which President Kennedy may have known of assassination plans was established when Frank Sinatra introduced then-Senator Kennedy to a buxom young woman, Judith Campbell, at a party. It has since come to light that Kennedy started an affair with her that continued while he was in the White House.[43] White House logs show more than seventy telephone calls between them from January 1961 through March 22, 1962, when Kennedy stopped the affair after a private meeting requested by FBI Director J. Edgar Hoover.[44] What was on Hoover's mind was a Mafia connection: Judith Campbell (later Judith Exner) was also the mistress of Sam Giancana, who was sharing her with the president, and may in fact have been using her to have something on the president in case he had trouble with the law. Whether Kennedy knew of assassination plans through this channel is not established.[45]

Another piece of evidence that President Kennedy knew of the assassination plan is that Robert Kennedy later saw — in writing — reference to an assassination plan against Castro. And he said nothing. It seemed not to surprise him or catch his attention, although he was very angry that the CIA was dealing with the mob (and at a time when he was prosecuting them more vigorously than any other administration has wanted to do).[46] Given that he served with Maxwell Taylor on his brother's top secret postmortem commission — and Allen Dulles said nothing to the commission (on the record) about it — he might have been expected to react strongly if this information were a surprise or a shocking piece of knowledge.[47]

If Kennedy did approve assassination efforts, it seems likely that he was ambivalent about them, since the use of Mafia hit-men was not the idealistic Cuban patriot operation he wanted. This would explain why, after the pre-invasion assassination failed, he became more concerned and tried at the last minute to cut back the operation and further reduce its possible cost.

I think the presumption must be that Kennedy did know and approve; the best evidence (necessarily secondhand) by Bissell is that he did. There is also a documented discussion between McGeorge Bundy (Kennedy's national security advisor) and Bissell, early in the Kennedy administration, about the CIA's assassination capability, and Bundy made no effort to turn it off.[48] Moreover, Kennedy is on record as later telling a journalist he was being urged openly to order Castro's assassination, contrary to Schlesinger's theory that such discussions would never occur in the presidential presence.[49] And it seems quite unlikely, given the caution and experience of Allen Dulles, that he would have left such an issue to chance misunderstanding. But the code of "plausible deniability" has worked the way it was designed to work; there is no direct evidence, and on that basis a leap of faith could exonerate Kennedy.

But a definite answer to this question is not necessary for understanding the consensus favorable to the Bay of Pigs decision by the senior advisers. By their testimony, only Dulles, Cabell, and Bissell — among senior advisers — knew this additional element of the plan. And there is no evidence that Dulles and Bissell themselves counted on this element succeeding — but it did offer added hope that, with luck, the invaders might take control easily.[50]

Evolution of the Plan

Go Ahead.

— John F. Kennedy to
Richard Bissell

Drawing upon this background, we can return to the White House meetings that spring with a clearer understanding of the intellectual framework in which the CIA participants operated.

The CIA's Trinidad plan was a Guatemala-like scenario. B-26 bombers would destroy Castro's air force and his microwave and telephone capabilities (perhaps power plants, if that became necessary), forcing Castro to use radio and enabling the CIA both to learn his plans and to fool and paralyze him with the same technologies used in Guatemala. Two "feint" landings would cause Castro to divide his troops and feel attacked from all sides just as his communications started to go out. CIA broadcasts, in disguise on Cuban military radio networks, would make Castro and his troops dash about the island from one presumed center of crisis to another (railroads and roads were deliberately to be left intact so the defenders would more readily exhaust themselves). Castro would be unable to use radio or television to rally his people. After blocking communications from Havana to the outside world, the CIA planned to fly American and foreign journalists to the beach where it would feed them predesigned stories. Their credible foreign radio broadcasts, allowed to reach Cuba without jamming, would strengthen perception within Cuba that Castro's situation was deteriorating and hopeless.[51]

Moreover, with Castro's air force destroyed, B-26 bombers would now roam at will over the island, bombing and strafing troops, barracks, and other targets. Overwhelmed, Castro would lose his nerve, or at least most of his political supporters and the army would consider the cause hopeless. The CIA expected chaos and, with momentum established, popular unrest to organize itself in about a week, with a coup, abandonment, or negotiated settlement to follow.[52]

This Trinidad plan was discussed by the president and his advisers at several meetings in February and March. Kennedy expressed his favorable attitude in principle, but rejected the specific plan because it was public and dramatic, jeopardizing the secrecy of America's role.[53] Moreover, there was no adequate airstrip at the port of Trinidad that could be seized. The CIA proposed to use bombers from Nicaraguan bases against Castro, but to do so would implicate another country in continuing aggression against another Western Hemisphere nation. Kennedy wanted to avoid that; it would create the belief that the United States had given its approval to the other government.[54]

Kennedy, reviewing the plan, asked about infiltrating guerrillas in small bands so their opposition would appear to arise within Cuba, but he later agreed this would be too low-key to effect the desired psychological impact.[55] Instructed to develop other alternatives for a quiet invasion, the CIA proposed three sites, favoring the Bay of Pigs. The Bay of Pigs lies on the coast of south-central Cuba. It is isolated, sparsely populated, and the area included an airstrip that could be seized. Surrounded by the Zapata swamps, it was accessible by only three roads, built on dikes raised above the swamp, which could be easily mined and blocked against attacking forces: an ideal location for defense. Isolation offered hope that the guerrillas could land and secure their initial beachhead quietly, without opposition or detection. The 1,200 men and most of their ammunition and supplies could be put ashore before sunrise. The rest could follow the next night. An American naval task force would escort the vessels to Cuban territorial waters.

Consideration of the revised plan moved quickly.

The CIA pressed for speed because Castro had purchased MIG fighters from Czechoslovakia, and Cuban pilots were expected to be trained and to return by June. Against such weapons a small, "plausibly deniable" invasion was impossible. The exiles could not use jets to battle Castro's jets or to defend the old B-26 bombers because possession of jets would prove American sponsorship. Their old B-26s were the type of plane America had sold to Batista or that might be purchased by expatriates on the black market.[56]

Moreover, the CIA urged a speedy decision because the rainy season was coming, which would make air operations difficult (the exiles needed to bomb all of Castro's planes on the ground, and to see the targets). Nights were becoming shorter and the troops were impatient and could not be trained further in the rainy season. The Guatemalan government was restive and asked that the expatriate troops leave by the end of April.[57]

The CIA probably exaggerated the need for a decision within a few days. But the tactic was useful and showed a sophisticated grasp of how to get things done by setting a deadline. The CIA's strategy had been to set March 15 as D-Day in its January planning document. This later created the mind-set that "D-Day is being allowed to slip" and the president needed to decide. Pressing the case for approval, Allen Dulles was now explicit about a "disposal problem." That is, if Kennedy rejected the plan, 1,200 Cuban expatriates would return to America, violently angry that Kennedy had abandoned the fight against Castro and Latin American Communism — a fact that could not be kept secret.[58] Kennedy would have a serious domestic political problem. It was certain that Richard Nixon would be an aggressive critic: Narrowly defeated for the presidency, an early advocate of the plan, stalking the administration, alert to issues for his 1964 campaign, he was a man with an unerring instinct for the political jugular. And the publicity would send the "wrong message" — of faltering resolve — to the Soviet Union and other countries.

Why Did Kennedy Do It?

CIA will present a revised plan for the Cuban operation. They have done a remarkable job of reframing the landing plan so as to make it unspectacular and quiet, and plausibly Cuban in its essentials.
— McGeorge Bundy,
Memorandum for the President,
March 15, 1961[59]

With this background, we can draw a summary about why Kennedy gave his approval.

A basic psychological truth is that the plan was never fully Kennedy's own plan. He came to office after the camp was established in Guatemala. When, later, he asked rhetorically, "How could I have been so stupid to let *them* (*sic*) go ahead?" he was expressing what had been his attitude all along. This was not *his* operation but a plan designed and presented to him by holdover appointees from the Eisenhower administration.[60] His own instincts were competitive, but fitted most comfortably with initiatives that were his own creation: the Alliance for Progress, the Peace Corps.[61] The decision he faced was not how to get rid of Castro; it was what to do about this package on his desk.

It is important to recall the international pressures. Fidel Castro — openly linked with the Soviet bloc — captured imaginations, gave voice to discontent, proved repressive regimes could be overthrown by guerrilla warfare. It was the height of the cold war, the need to "pay any price, bear any burden" (as he put it in his Inaugural Address) defined Kennedy's view of the American role in history as the responsible "guardian" of endangered freedom.

In favor of the operation was Kennedy's instinctive attention to the drama of single men or small bands challenging powerful forces and, in the eyes of history, succeeding. He wrote *Profiles in Courage*, an appreciation of such men. In his favorite novels (by Ian Fleming) a single hero, the agent James Bond, triumphed against the awesome forces of SMERSH. Kennedy believed in acting "with vigor," and contrasted his administration with the dangerous, somnolent passivity of Eisenhower. This was a drama, too, of his own life:

a grass roots movement challenged the established rulers of his own party for the presidential nomination and he won his presidency at a comparatively young age.[62] While other knowledgeable men disagreed (Senator Fulbright of Arkansas, chairman of the Senate Foreign Relations Committee, wrote Kennedy cautioning that Castro was "a thorn in the flesh, not a dagger at the heart"), Kennedy was youthfully ready to imagine Castro's challenge would ignite idealistic revolution throughout the western hemisphere, and thus was more willing to help a small group of young, patriotic challengers and to believe they might have a chance, acting boldly and with courage, to capture popular imaginations themselves and succeed.[63]

As Kennedy worked to make the operation one he could support, he remained at a distance from it, and skeptical. Soviet premier Nikita Khrushchev had warned publicly that the Soviet Union would support Cuba's independence.[64] Kennedy worried that the USSR might respond elsewhere (in Berlin or Laos), and he thought a nuclear "missile gap" then favored the Soviet Union. The world was dangerous not only because Communist revolutionaries had gained a foothold on a Caribbean island.

At the end, Kennedy decided favorably against a background of personal and political success, the activist mood and style of his administration, and the momentum of events. Activist commitments were reinforced by Kennedy's past success: he won the nomination and the presidency by them, and by advocating them. As the rhythm of events and anticipation quickened, the advisers debated and then said yes. As D-Day approached there was both the reassurance of past success and the almost visceral drive to go forward to bring the drama to life.[65]

Central arguments against? Not many (according to Sorenson) were salient to Kennedy if his expectations were fulfilled. He worked on the plan to minimize every risk he could foresee: secrecy for American involvement (at least enough), the guerrilla option if things turned bad.[66] A quiet landing at a remote spot without press coverage. No overt American military involvement that would provoke the Russians. Ultimately, all his senior advisers approved, and his best experts, with past success at these operations, said it had a good chance. And he thought so too.[67]

But there is still a puzzle, and we will see later that Kennedy may have had deeper, unspoken reservations. Ordinarily cool, analytical, and alert, he later showed strong ambivalence, canceled his own crucial air strike at the last minute, did it without consulting the experts he had relied on throughout, and did so for reasons that were spurious.

Yet even as he considered the plan, his mood varied. At times he was tough and assertive: "We can't go on living with this Castro cancer for ten years more" he declared to one aide.[68] At another time, when another aide asked him what he thought of the plan, he replied, "As little as possible."[69] His personal decision process was to try on different postures, experiment to see how he felt, and search for a plan that would integrate satisfactorily his different reactions and instincts.[70]

We can probably infer that Kennedy was restive about being an "aggressor." As we will see in the next chapter, he worked hard to change the plan so he could see it in other terms.

Perhaps other reservations were not spoken aloud. Wyden speculates that Kennedy and his new advisers resented Ike's remaining influence over them. They resented being trapped by his plan now when, having defeated him and what he stood for, they had obtained power. They could not be rid of the plan directly, but they could distance themselves, withhold the personal involvement that would make it their own and make it work, and allow it to screw up.[71]

Another unspoken reservation may have been that Kennedy felt a degree of ambivalent identification with Castro: the passionate, idealistic guerrilla fighter with Kennedy's own spirit who had overthrown a government and spoke, Marxism aside, for many of Kennedy's own ideals. Perhaps, too, Castro stirred jealousy and competition: given a choice, would the Cuban people prefer Castro — or Kennedy and his band of American liberal reformers? ("We're the true revolutionaries," Richard Bissell, a liberal with an affinity to Stevenson and Bowles, told his staff after discussion of the new land reform and social action programs the administration intended to see implemented.)[72]

Typical analyses of major government decisions do not propose that sexual connotations affect policy choices. Yet it should be acknowledged that sexual metaphors were used openly by these men to discuss their decisions. Kennedy said privately that the advisers who opposed intervention and sent forth a verbal cloud of idealistic objections "lacked balls."[73] And later, telling Sorenson that the last-minute equivocators were trying to protect themselves, he said, "everyone is grabbing their nuts on this."[74] Richard Bissell used sexual metaphor to discuss the secrecy issue: so long as the United States retained a "fig leaf," any outcry would dissipate.[75] Kennedy's resistance to being drawn in had its analogue in the case of a man being tempted by an affair but unwilling to find himself exposed, naked in public.[76]

A summary of the factors in Kennedy's decision is provided in Table 1.1. An asterisk appears before crucial but erroneous beliefs to be analyzed more fully in the next chapter.

I will return to a detailed discussion in later chapters, but for purposes of this overview the following key events are important: all of Kennedy's senior advisers favored the plan at a final large meeting on April 4.[77] On April 5, Kennedy met privately with Dean Rusk, Dulles, and Robert McNamara to underscore his prohibition against American involvement.[78] Kennedy approved the plan, but he then severely reduced a first (D-2) air strike against Castro's planes (from sixteen to six) and did so at the last minute; he abruptly canceled (again at the last minute) all air strikes for the morning of D-Day.

Table 1.1. Why Kennedy Said "Go Ahead"

Situational Effects

1. Castro, as an activist and Marxist sympathizer, was perceived as a threat in the Western Hemisphere, a threat likely to grow rather than diminish, and a threat linked to a powerful and dangerous worldwide Soviet threat.

2. Plans and operational capabilities were already developed, waiting approval. He had to do something with them.

3. The American government had achieved previous success by this model.

*4. American journalists, and elite opinion, would accept this type of operation and cooperate to retain its covertness.

5. The Soviet Union and other potential allies of Cuba were unlikely to render effective aid.

6. The Soviet Union was unlikely to retaliate by military action elsewhere if the operation retained its "plausible deniability."

Personal Predispositions of Kennedy

1. Kennedy perceived stronger themes of achievement and competition than did others, and was attracted to support dramatic adventures.
   a. He had a history of personal activist success that produced a faith that his, and perhaps others', activist commitments would succeed.
   b. He judged Castro a more dangerous and effective competitor in Latin America than did others.
   *c. He was personally attracted to support of idealistic, activist Cubans.
   *d. He was ready to believe that the Cuban masses would rally to assure the success of the exile challengers' "New Frontier" cause.

2. He had residual deference to military and CIA expertise for those issues where he had no expertise.

3. He tended to discount idealistic advisers who opposed effective action by worrying about morality.

Key Assumptions About the Plan

1. No downside risk to Kennedy (or U.S.)
   *a. Secrecy
   *b. While the plan had some military risk (perhaps a ⅔ chance of success), the men could "go guerrilla" if momentum was not established and a decisive, visible defeat could be avoided.
   c. No American military involvement would be required.
   d. Soviet reprisal was unlikely given secrecy and no American military involvement.

*2. America was in a secondary, support role to patriotic Cubans who were eager to attempt the job even without American military involvement.

*3. The Cubans were "New Frontier" reformers and idealistic patriots who would promote *Fidelismo sin Fidel*.

*4. Castro's military response would likely be ineffective.

*5. A mass uprising was expected because many Cubans opposed Castro's "sellout" of a nationalist revolution to Communism and probably would prefer a Kennedy-style leader.

6. Assassination of Fidel Castro would, if successful, assure low-cost success.

7. There was a serious "disposal" problem if the plan were aborted, with certainty of Republican attacks, especially from Nixon, possibly supported by Eisenhower and Dulles. It would send the "wrong message" internationally.

(continued)

Table 1.1. Why Kennedy Said "Go Ahead" (*continued*)

Adviser Support

1. He believed all senior advisers supported the plan.

2. The most qualified experts in American government (Dulles, Bissell, and the Joint Chiefs of Staff) endorsed the plan and had (Kennedy thought) the clear understanding that no American forces would be used. The past success of the same CIA team with a similar model in Guatemala lent credibility to their judgment.

*3. "Bonsai" enthusiasm of final troop readiness and morale report.

4. Kennedy believed Eisenhower endorsed the plan.

Time Pressures — "Last Chance"

1. MIG pilots, due soon, would abort a mission. This was the last chance to mount a small, low-cost, volunteer operation. Later, a president would have to do the job with the air force and the marines.

2. A rainy season was approaching, thus visibility would be reduced and additional training would soon be impossible.

3. Troop morale, at a peak, was likely to deteriorate with further delay.

4. The Guatemala government asked that troops leave by the end of April.

5. Growing momentum of the planning process.

BATTLE NARRATIVE

I will now turn to the overthrow attempt itself.

Air strikes were launched from "Happy Valley," a base in Nicaragua. The first strike, early on Saturday, April 15, sent two B-26s against each of the three military airfields where U-2 spy plane photographs showed Castro's planes to be based: Camp Libertad outside Havana, Antonio Maceo Airport in Oriente Province, and San Antonio de los Banos. Mario Zuñiga flew directly from Nicaragua to Miami International Airport to provide a CIA cover story that he and three other pilots, disenchanted with Castro, had defected and dropped the bombs before they fled. His plane was painted with Cuban Air Force markings (as were all Brigade planes); bullets were fired into it before he left Happy Valley; thirty minutes from Miami — according to plan — Zuñiga opened his cockpit at 1,500 feet, and sought to enhance his story by firing his revolver into one of his engines and feathering it.[79]

Castro, altered by the raids to anticipate imminent invasion, implemented standby plans for immediate police roundup of suspected members of the underground and others whose loyalty was in doubt. He was not sanguine in estimates of his potential opposition: between 100,000 and 200,000 people were arrested and detained.[80]

To coincide with the first raids, the CIA planned a diversionary landing on the east coast of Cuba, in Oriente Province. This feint, carried out near a naval base the United States retained in Cuba (under a long-term lease) at

Guantanamo Bay, was intended to be misinterpreted as the main invasion and to draw Castro's forces.[81] But the expatriate commander, to preserve security, was not told how vital his role was to be. He believed he was resupplying guerrillas and that many others would be involved in similar actions at other points around the island. When he judged he did not have a clear path through the breakers to a landing site, and that he might have been spotted and would face fire if a landing were attempted, he aborted the operation. (Ten men equipped with radio were to have marked the landing site. But four days earlier the team leader, conducting hand grenade instruction, accidently set off a grenade and blew up himself and his team.) Unknown to the ship's commander, four American destroyers were also in the vicinity to strengthen the ruse by appearing on Cuban radar. That extra trick failed, too: the Cubans did not have radar installations in the vicinity.[82]

The initial D-2 raids on Saturday morning took place at dawn and were completed by about 6:30 A.M. At 10:30 A.M. the United Nations General Assembly began a regular session. Dr. Raul Roa, Cuba's foreign minister, was in New York City to begin a debate, scheduled for Monday, of Cuba's charges that America was planning an invasion (Cuba was requesting collective security assistance). The United States, as it had during the Guatemala case in 1954, was already implying such charges were blatant Marxist propaganda to discredit the United States falsely. Dr. Roa requested, and received, a special session for that afternoon.

Ambassador Adlai Stevenson, caught by surprise, checked with the State Department, which checked with the CIA, and it sent back assurances the defector was genuine. Stevenson delivered a ringing defense in the world's most public forum, dictated to him over the telephone, acting with assurance that the facts had been "carefully checked."[83] His photograph, holding aloft a picture of the Miami plane, appeared, together with his denial, on the front page of papers around the world.

But meanwhile, the American press set to work on the cover story, and it began to fall apart.[84] The plane had a metal nose cone (Castro's B-26 force had Plexiglas nose cones). One reporter walked close enough to the plane to observe that its machine guns had not been fired. The pilot's name was not released — odd if he were a genuine defector, for Castro would already know it — a mark of a potential CIA cover story. In New York, enthusiastic Cuban expatriate leaders issued statements implying more prior knowledge of the operation than they would have if the cover story (of a spur-of-the-moment defection) were valid.

Stevenson's staff pressed ahead, on Saturday and Sunday, to assemble the technical detail needed to refute totally the baseless Cuban charges when U.N. debate resumed on Monday. No one in Washington called Stevenson directly to inform him the story was a lie. A member of his staff, asking for more facts, was told simply that it "wouldn't be worthwhile to pursue that line of inquiry any longer." That's when Stevenson concluded he had been set up. A proud man, twice the presidential candidate of his party, his anger made itself felt later that Sunday in a cable to Dean Rusk which gave Rusk an additional basis to urge on the president concern for the "international noise level" problem in New York.[85]

At 1:45 P.M. Sunday, Kennedy gave final approval for the invasion; the ships, south of Cuba, moved to final rendezvous. The CIA fleet consisted of two converted landing craft of its own, the *Blagar* and the *Barbara J.*, plus old merchant boats owned by a Cuban expatriate firm in New York and operated by the firm under contract (the *Houston, Caribe, Atlantico*, and the *Rio Escondido*).[86] The crews on the civilian boats were not military volunteers: when told their destination they were given a chance to leave the boats before this final run. They remained on assurance that it would be a night landing, uncontested, and that American ships would be there and "not let them fail."

The ships had moved toward their rendezvous by zigzag routes, to minimize chance of detection. They were shadowed by ships of an American naval task force. Under precisely drawn rules of engagement these American ships were to monitor the invasion craft from a distance, refrain from radio contact, render any navigation assistance needed, defend them and immediately escort them back to a Central American port in the event of attack in international waters.[87]

The principal ships of the American naval task force were seven destroyers, the carrier *Essex* (with an augmented amphibious assault force of 1,200 marines plus a squadron of jet fighters), and the LSD (Landing Ship Dock) *San Marcos*.[88] The *San Marcos* carried seven smaller boats (three LCUs – landing craft utility and four LCVPs – landing craft vehicles-personnel) loaded with tanks, trucks, a bulldozer, and other heavy equipment. These seven craft were off-loaded and turned over to the Brigade in international waters three miles off the Cuban coast.

When the *San Marcos* off-loading was completed, the boats started forward and paused while teams of frogmen proceeded to the beaches. The frogmen teams were led (against Kennedy's orders) by the two senior CIA operatives with the force, "Rip" Robertson and Gray Lynch. At one of the three landing sites the frogmen's rubber raft hit the off-shore coral reef the CIA's U-2 photo interpreters had thought to be seaweed. Members of a Cuban militia patrol saw the raft coming in and, thinking they were fishermen, drove down to the beach to flash the headlights of their jeep to warn of the reef. The CIA man opened fire with his machine gun (the first shots fired at the Bay of Pigs were fired by an American), his men opened up, and the two Cubans who had come to offer assistance died in a hail of bullets. In the confusion and excitement the order for the full landing to proceed was flashed without remembering to mention the reef. Filled with anticipation, and with their outboards at full throttle, the first two contingents roared in, puncturing the double bottoms of both boats.[89]

The CIA men now obeyed President Kennedy's order and returned to their boats offshore. There, at 1:00 A.M., a brief message arrived from CIA headquarters: "Castro still has operational aircraft. Expect you to be hit at dawn. Unload all troops and supplies and take ships to sea as soon as possible."[90]

The message did not tell the complete story. Probably to avoid upsetting the men, Bissell did not tell them the reason for this urgent order: There would be no D-Day strike.

The message produced some speed up, but not much. Without knowing the reason for the message, the CIA men only thought headquarters was being cautious. Everyone assumed Castro might have planes that survived the D-2 strikes: That was why a D-Day strike was planned. The men on the scene thought the D-Day raids, coming at dawn, would finish Castro's air power and assure their safety. They saw nothing new in the message.[91]

It is doubtful they could have unloaded rapidly in any case. The hulls were punctured on two small boats, and these were out of action. The outboards on eight new fiberglass boats to ferry the men gave problems. When, at the last minute, Kennedy shifted the invasion site from Trinidad (which had a harbor), these boats were airlifted in, but in the rush of events they had not been tested. Now, two refused to start and the propeller of one dropped off and fell to the bottom of the ocean as soon as it was put in the water. The other outboards gave out, at various points, in the middle of the bay: Soon, only two were usable.[92]

The reef also delayed operations because it required the LCUs and the LCVPs to stop 150 yards offshore and their cargo to be off-loaded by men wading in chest-deep water. Not until almost daybreak did high tide, and a route through the reef finally charted by frogmen at 6 A.M., make it possible to begin off-loading the heavy equipment.[93]

Contrary to expectations, Castro had watchers posted along his beaches, and he had equipped them with microwave. At a second landing site the invaders were also spotted, and from here an alarm was flashed to Castro just after 1:00 A.M.[94] He moved swiftly, ordered his remaining planes to attack at dawn, and began moving 20,000 troops toward the invader's position. Ramon Fernandez, the first commander on the scene, was to do a first-rate job: He had learned infantry tactics at the U.S. Army Field Artillery School, Fort Still, Oklahoma.[95]

Castro's senior pilot scored his first kill at 6:30 A.M. Monday when rockets from his British-built Sea Fury sank one of the invader ships, the *Houston*. Most of the men got ashore, but supplies, including the field hospital, were lost. Just after 9:00 A.M., a rocket from the Sea Fury ignited 200 barrels of aviation gasoline on the *Rio Escondido*. Within minutes the ship blew, sending flames 100 feet into the air, and it went to the bottom along with ammunition, other supplies, and the communications van. For the remainder of the invasion there were virtually no communications between air and ground forces. The dispersed ground forces, whose hand radios had become wet and inoperative when the men were forced to wade ashore because of the reef, were without effective radio communications.[96]

With off-loading stalled, under air attack by Castro's planes equipped with machine guns and rockets, and without American jet support from the carrier offshore, the civilian crews of the *Atlantico* and the *Caribe*, betrayed and scared, headed for open sea at top speed with most of the Brigade's ammunition supply aboard. They had not signed on to fight, had been assured the invaders would control the air, and were without antiaircraft weapons for defense. Two of their sister ships were sunk, one exploding in their sight and its crew members possibly killed. The Yankee task force had only sat out there without the air support the men thought they had been promised. They had no idea what game the Americans were playing, but they were not going to wait around to find out.[97]

CIA officials in Washington were now scrambling to keep the invasion together. They knew the men on the beaches had only a one-day supply of ammunition. When the *Caribe* and *Atlantico* refused to answer radio calls, disappeared off the monitoring radar, and Washington deduced they were not coming back, jets were dispatched from the *Essex* to monitor their course.[98] The destroyer USS *Eaton*, after taking aboard a marine colonel with a briefcase full of money, was sent racing on an intercept course. By the time the two boats were rounded up and persuaded to return (the *Caribe*, the faster of the two, was intercepted 218 miles south of Cuba), it became late Tuesday afternoon before they arrived back at the "Point Zulu" rendezvous off the Cuban coast.[99]

Under fire, the remaining boats pulled back 50 miles into international waters. Rip and Gray, the CIA men, assured the Brigade they would return to complete the unloading, but with the communications van at the bottom of the ocean, there was no communication to the beaches during the rest of the day (or, as it turned out, on Monday night).

Back on the island, Brigade transport planes (five C-46s, one C-54) dropped 177 paratroopers at dawn to block the three roads. On the eastern front the operation worked well. But on the western front the equipment for one group landed in the swamp, Castro's swift response caught another group of "blocking" paratroopers behind enemy lines, and other men came down amidst heavy fire and were driven back.[100] By 10:00 A.M., then, two of the three roads to the beaches were open, the attackers had their supply lines cut, their back was to the sea, they had a one-day supply of ammunition, they were without effective radio communications, and they lacked the aviation fuel and munitions that would allow the Brigade B-26s to arrive from Nicaragua and provide sustained tactical air support from the beachhead.

But it did not seem desperate at that point. They expected resupply. They "knew" the Americans were offshore, in force, if they got into serious trouble, and air support did appear from Nicaragua. Two Brigade B-26s passed over the battlefield and headed toward a concentration of 900 or so Castro forces. They let loose with full loads of napalm and fragmentation bombs: within minutes the road was a wall of flame. *"No quedo ni el gato,"* said the local Brigade commander with pride, "Not even the cat was alive." "How beautiful it was," a Brigade soldier remembered.[101] In less than three minutes, 800 men had been incinerated or blown apart. That was how Bissell's "shooting gallery" defense along the three roads — and throughout Cuba — was supposed to work, and would, just as soon as the early snarls were worked out.

But the next few minutes illustrated a harsher reality for the invaders. The slow Brigade B-26s flew without tail guns to increase their payloads on seven-hour round trips from Nicaragua.[102] As the bombing runs finished and the planes pulled up, a T-33 jet trainer and a Sea Fury appeared — Castro's — and used their machine guns to shoot down both Brigade planes.

The men expected their resupply on Monday night. They did not know the problems with the *Atlantico* and the *Caribe*. Nor did they know that munitions aboard the American task force, by presidential order, were not available.[103]

For Tuesday morning, with approval of the president, Richard Bissell now ordered the D-Day strike (twenty-four hours later than originally planned), a dawn strike of six B-26s against Castro's key airfield to eliminate his remaining planes.[104] Luck was on Castro's side that morning: Heavy haze and low-lying clouds made it impossible for the B-26s to attack. The long distance to be flown on a return flight to Nicaragua did not leave sufficient fuel to wait for the sky to clear.[105]

By midmorning Tuesday, the Brigade was able to rig a radio hookup with the fleet offshore. They cursed the CIA but were reassured there was only a temporary delay in supply. Air drops of ammunition occurred during the day. They were promised their main supply that night.

In Washington, the communication snarl kept decision makers five to seven hours behind events. By Monday afternoon Kennedy knew there was serious trouble, and he was under increasing pressure to act with American forces. He did approve the Tuesday morning attempt to eliminate Castro's remaining planes. But it was not clear to him that the American navy could save the operation if it went in. And Kennedy was adamant that his guideline against American involvement stood — much to the surprise of his advisers, all of whom seemed to expect him to abandon his restriction rather than accept failure.[106]

The Brigade survived on Tuesday because Castro's forces did not press their advantage. Two captured paratroopers told conflicting stories. One said he was part of a group of 1,000 defending a position ahead. The second told the truth: only nineteen men defended the road. Castro's commanders anticipated an invasion force of 3,000 to 10,000. The Cuban officer thought the second man was lying to lead him into a trap — the Americans would never have put only nineteen men there — and spent hours waiting for artillery to be brought up to pound the position before sending his troops forward.[107]

Probably the second reason the Cuban advance delayed was that Castro himself had rushed north, to the west of Havana, after receiving reports at about 1:15 A.M. Tuesday that led him temporarily to believe the Bay of Pigs itself was a feint and that the main landing was now beginning in Pinar del Rio province on the west coast. This was the Pinar del Rio diversion (the planned companion to Saturday's aborted Mocambo diversion 1,000 miles away on the eastern coast), featuring what the CIA agents termed their "dog and pony" show. It was designed with the aid of the former employees of the Walt Disney studios who had designed the special effects for Guatemala. Eight boats, thirty-five to forty feet long, each towing several smaller boats, had sailed secretly from Miami to stations off the western coast. They were crammed with electronic gear. No CIA agents landed but, strung out along the coast, the boats created a spectacular array of lights, sound effects, and electronic signals to simulate a major invasion and battle. It worked to draw Castro to the west and to keep him from being physically present to press his commanders at the Bay of Pigs. But he judged he had enough troops in the Havana area and did not deplete his 20,000 man force encircling the Bay of Pigs.[108]

When the *Caribe* and the *Atlantico* reappeared Tuesday afternoon and evening, the CIA men offshore worked frantically to prepare the resupply for the beaches. Throughout the day they promised jet support, and many more plane drops than actually occurred, judging that they served the men — and the cause — best by keeping up morale. They expected that something would soon happen, that surely Washington would see the light. Then those jets would be authorized and cargo resupplies airlifted to Nicaragua would begin to be airdropped. They lied, but only in the sense of conveying facts they hoped would become true.[109] On the beaches, morale problems were beginning to occur, but the men believed the promises, by and large. They recalled early assurances that if they held the beach for a few days a new provisional government would land, be formally recognized, and then "all things are possible." With the airdrops that did arrive, and careful conservation of ammunition, they could hold out until the Tuesday night resupply.

But the crews of the *Caribe* and the *Atlantico* had other ideas than to face death while Americans cheered but stayed in international waters. They had learned about official promises. On their return — and perhaps wisely — they threatened mutiny if their skippers took them back to the combat zone on renewed promises alone and without visible, low jet cover from the American carrier. It was clear unloading could not be completed by dawn and without cover they would, once again, be vulnerable to Cuban air attack. Rip and

Gray, the two CIA commanders, sent additional urgent messages to Washington for approval of the jet cover and began a contingency plan to reload the *Caribe* and *Atlantico* supplies onto their own command boats, the *Blagar* and the *Barbara J*, and the small boats.[110]

Wednesday was the final day of the operation.

Late Tuesday night, President Kennedy had decided he would, as he put it to his brother, "rather be called an aggressor than a bum," at least to aid rescue of the men.[111] He authorized four navy jets to fly one hour of cover on Wednesday morning, from 6:30 to 7:30, interposing themselves between Brigade B-26s, which would attack Cuban ground troops, and Cuban planes. (The legalism involved was that, to shoot at the Brigade planes, Castro's planes would also need to shoot in the direction of the American planes.) American planes could not initiate fire, but they could return it. Kennedy's action reflected no long-term plan: Now he only sought to buy time and, perhaps, to make a minor concession to his advisers. It was as far as he was willing to go.

But by Tuesday night the Brigade air operation in Nicaragua was coming apart. There was no beachhead airstrip with aviation fuel.[112] The round trips were each seven hours and most pilots had been on continual duty for over two days, keeping awake with drugs. They were exhausted. They were also angry, scared, and disgusted. The Americans had inexplicably stopped their second, D-Day, strike just before launch. As a result, the Brigade's planes were being shot down (ten pilots were now dead) and without tail guns the pilots correctly judged that further flights were likely to be suicide missions.[113] Betrayal, fear, and fatigue were not easily overcome. No one believed American government promises that *this* time there would be air support.

Except Americans. On his own authority Richard Bissell authorized four American volunteer pilots to fly in these last desperate hours to try to turn the battle, or at least win a respite for a sea evacuation. He probably exceeded his authority in doing this (although it occurred at the same time Kennedy was allowing navy pilots into the battle zone).[114] But it was necessary to do it, or all was surely lost.

A timing snafu brought these Brigade planes over target an hour before their jet cover. They were shot down. The American pilots who believed the promises were killed.

The explanation of the timing error favored by earlier writers was that the Pentagon and the CIA, communicating to their separate forces through separate channels, had assumed different time zones (Washington versus Nicaragua time).[115] A more recent account by the chief executive officer on the *Essex* maintains that the carrier received its launch order at 6:30 A.M. (the order was for a 6:30 A.M. launch), and, even working at top speed, the crews could not be awakened, briefed, and airborne until well after 7:00. The reason for the confusion has never been resolved.[116]

At 2:00 A.M. President Kennedy's order came that the U.S. Navy was authorized to rescue the men from the beaches. Pepe San Roman was told, but he was not told the full story (which was not communicated, either, to the CIA commanders) that the invasion was over and would receive no American resupply. His Brigade, San Roman declared, would not retreat. He still expected the *Caribe* and the *Atlantico* at first light, and he would wait faithfully for the United States.[117]

In the early hours of Wednesday morning, instead of authorized air cover for the ships, the CIA men offshore had received only the cryptic message, "Hold where you are."[118] Their message reflected that there would be no further resupply. Bissell, Admiral Burke, and others had exhausted their arguments. They had proposed diverse options: naval air cover for the beaches, long-range gun support from the destroyers, the landing of a company of Marines.[119] But the president would allow only the one hour of "passive" air cover. (Judging it was out of the question, the CIA did not specifically request additional jet cover for arms resupply.) Just after midnight, early Wednesday morning, Kennedy had finally decided to scuttle the operation, concluding that "it was time to go guerrilla." And it was then, too, he had been shocked to learn that there was no guerrilla escape at this site: the impenetrable Zapata swamps, and three roads blocked by 20,000 Cuban troops, blocked any escape.[120]

Rip and Gray, the CIA commanders, thought "hold where you are" meant something would still happen.[121] They believed it could be turned around, that jets would come momentarily when clearances came through and that the leaders who wanted Castro eliminated understood the situation. Late Wednesday morning, their appeals to Washington inexplicably unanswered, the frustrated and angry CIA men unilaterally decided to violate orders and fight beside the men they had helped to train. They decided to take their resupply mission to shore and beach the boats rather than unload them. But as they set out, broadcasting the latest of their assurances, Pepe San Roman radioed that his ammunition was gone and Castro's troops were moving in. "Am taking to the woods. I can't wait for you." The battle was over.[122]

Among invading Cubans, 114 men died; among defending Cubans, about 1,200. Most of the invaders were captured by Castro's forces, and they were later ransomed by Kennedy.[123]

NOTES

1. Quoted in H. Parmet, *JFK: The Presidency of John F. Kennedy* (New York: Dial Press, 1983), p. 161. Note that Dulles did not tell the whole truth and mention explicitly the 20 percent chance of success he eventually held for Guatemala.
2. The actual invasion force was about 1,200. Altogether, 1,400 men were used in the invasion, the diversions, and the air strikes.
3. Walt Rostow, then an assistant to McGeorge Bundy. Quoted in P. Wyden, *Bay of Pigs: The Untold Story* (New York: Simon and Schuster, 1979), p. 325. Voicing

a common judgment at the time, another observer called it the most dramatically bungled operation "since the Light Brigade charged into oblivion at Balaklava." H. Johnson, *The Bay of Pigs: The Leaders' Story of Brigade 1506* (New York: Norton, 1964), p. 349.

4. For each of these cases I have attempted to render a consensus or standard account. Wyden in *Bay of Pigs* synthesized previous scholarship and then-declassified documents, cross-checking basic facts and interpretations by interviews with almost all of the American and Cuban principals still alive. All scholars are in his debt. I have interpreted events somewhat differently, with greater attention (for example) to the intellectual rationale provided by the Guatemala success and with greater weight to systemic factors and to a high dramatized and oddly wired sensibility of larger-than-life drama and the nature of power.

5. U.S. Senate. Committee on Foreign Relations. *Events in United States—Cuban Relations: A Chronology 1957–1963*. 88th Congress, 1st session. (Washington, DC: Government Printing Office, 1963), p. 1. R. Stebbins, *The U.S. in World Affairs, 1961*. (New York: Council on Foreign Relations, 1962) provides a similar semi-official view.

6. D. Wise and T. Ross, *The Invisible Government* (New York: Random House, 1964), p. 26 discuss Bissell's background. See also Wyden, *Bay of Pigs*, pp. 9–19; Parmet, *JFK*, p. 160.

7. On Dulles's character see L. Mosley, *Dulles: A Biography of Eleanor, Allen, and John Foster Dulles and Their Family Network* (New York: Dial, 1978); A. Schlesinger, *A Thousand Days: John F. Kennedy in the White House* (Boston: Houghton Mifflin, 1965), p. 241.

8. Wyden, *Bay of Pigs*, pp. 23–30, esp. p. 24. M. Halperin, P. Clapp, and A. Kanter, *Bureaucratic Behavior and Foreign Policy* (Washington, DC: Brookings Institution, 1974), pp. 196–218 discuss the strategy of involving the president.

9. Wyden, *Bay of Pigs*, pp. 24–25, 30.

10. Ibid., pp. 65–67. Nixon's advocacy of Castro's elimination had begun almost a year earlier. He announced his candidacy on January 9, 1960.

11. The *New York Times* ran Kennedy's statement on its front page. The conflicting accounts of duplicity are reviewed in Parmet, *JFK*, pp. 47–49; Wyden, *Bay of Pigs*, p. 67n. Nixon's presentation showed he understood the opposition argument well. For the key portion of Nixon's statement see S. Kraus, *The Great Debates* (Bloomington, Indiana: Indiana Univ. Press, 1962). In a slip of institutional memory, H. Kissinger, *White House Years* (Boston: Little, Brown, 1979), p. 633, misremembers Kennedy's consistent public pledge *not* to use American troops, reporting the opposite that Kennedy publicly advocated their use against Cuba.

12. It is doubtful the president felt bound by it, any more than any politician feels bound by what he says in public statements during an election.

13. Wyden, *Bay of Pigs*, p. 68 gives November 27. M. Taylor, *Operation ZAPATA: The Ultra-Sensitive Report and Testimony of the Board of Inquiry on the Bay of Pigs*. Introduction by L. Aguilar. (Frederick, MD: Aletheia Books, 1981), p. 8 gives November 18. (This is the Taylor Commission report, written in 1961, and is published (with the current title) from the "sanitized" version released under the Freedom of Information Act.)

14. Thus experience convinced the CIA that tight security could not be maintained by Cubans, who were too voluble and unprofessional. Later, they did not tell the Cuban underground of D-Day for this reason.

15. Quoted in Mosley, *Dulles*, p. 466.

16. H. Perloff, *Alliance for Progress: A Social Invention in the Making* (Baltimore, MD: Johns Hopkins Univ. Press, 1969), pp. 16–17.
17. The CIA's order to end guerrilla training and shift to conventional training for amphibious and airborne assault was sent to Guatemala on November 4, 1960. Taylor, *Operation ZAPATA*, p. 6.
18. The best reconstruction is that Eisenhower saw no specific plans. He did know an invasion force was being thought about. The record suggests that he did not carefully limit his remarks, and Kennedy may have mistaken the general's remarks to support the type of plan he shortly received. Ike was forceful, later, in noting that he had not seen or approved any specific plans while in office. As a military man he drew a sharp distinction between the process of "planning" and plans. There seems to be no good recollection about what exactly Eisenhower did endorse. Wyden, *Bay of Pigs*, pp. 87–88; C. Clifford (personal communication).
19. There were estimated to be 1,000 active guerrillas in the Trinidad area. U.S. Department of Defense. Joint Chiefs of Staff. Memoranda for the Secretary (JCSM 57-61, 166-61; 146-61: 1961). Appendix B to Annex A, p. 18. (Photocopy release under Freedom of Information Act.)
20. Castro and his commanders also knew these mountains well and became increasingly effective against the CIA's early guerrilla operations. Before the Trinidad invasion would have been launched, the Cuban government had eliminated the rebels, although the record is not clear that Kennedy's aides knew of Castro's antiguerrilla effectiveness.
21. Basic sources for the Guatemala case are R. Immerman, "Guatemala as Cold War History" *Political Science Quarterly* 95 (Winter, 1980–1981): 629–653; R. Immerman, *The CIA in Guatemala: The Foreign Policy of Intervention* (Austin: Univ. of Texas Press, 1982); S. Kinzer and S. Schlesinger, *Bitter Fruit: The Untold Story of the American Coup in Guatemala* (Garden City, NY: Doubleday, 1982). See also B. Cook, *The Declassified Eisenhower: A Divided Legacy* (Garden City, NY: Doubleday, 1981); S. Jonas, "Anatomy of an Intervention" in S. Jonas and D. Tobias, ed., *Guatemala* (Berkeley, CA: North American Congress on Latin America, 1974); S. Jonas, "Central America as a Theatre for Cold War Politics" *Latin America Perspectives* 9 (Summer 1982): 123–128.
22. The shipments were used as a pretext for American action. The government's planning for a covert operation began well before these public justifications of Communist "influence" via arms shipments. Treaties were signed with Nicaragua on April 23, 1954 and Honduras on May 20, 1954. See L. Etheredge, *American Defense Commitments* (Washington, CT: Center for Information on America, 1971). Airlifts of war material for "defensive purposes" were announced to both countries on May 24, 1954.
23. It is not clear if the McCarthy experience suggested the aspect of the 1954 plan.

    Ambassador Peurifoy lied and told a congressional committee that the January killings were to prepare the way for a full Communist takeover, were a standard Communist tactic, and the invasion alarm a callous fabrication of Arbenz acting under Soviet direction. See P. Taylor, "The Guatemala Affair: A Critique of United States Foreign Policy" *American Political Science Review* 50 (1956): 787–806.

    The killings and torture to break the back of the (nonexistent) internal resistance movement stepped up sharply after the clandestine radio began to broadcast in June. A lesson to foreign nationals is that these brutal murders and tortures were not included later, in the institutional memory of planners, when speaking of the low casualties of the Guatemala operation: The behavior reflects a sensibility about costs I discuss in chapter 6.

24. My account of the battle relies primarily on Immerman, *The CIA in Guatemala.* M. Alisky, reviewing T. Anderson's *Politics in Central America* in *American Political Science Review* 77 (1983): 482–483, asserts a substantially higher number for the invasion force (circa 1,000).

25. D. Phillips, *The Night Watch* (New York: Atheneum, 1977), pp. 55–56.

26. Castillo Armas survived for three years. He was assassinated in 1957.

27. Richard Bissell, Dwight Eisenhower oral history interview, Columbia University.

28. Cook, *Declassified Eisenhower*, p. 284, provides a contrasting view of a thoughtful, rational choice: "The survival of his country, the continuation of the revolution in the hands of his loyal military successors, and a belief that by his resignation the people of Guatemala might be spared further bombings, the possible use of napalm and the kind of bacteriological warfare that the Guatemalans believed the United States had used in Korea all contributed to [Arbenz's] decision."

29. The State Department hinted that, as a potential Communist state, Guatemala was ipso facto an aggressor, but the principal symbolic evidence of serious threat (a shipment of Communist arms) arrived in Guatemala well after the CIA began to plan its operation. See Taylor, "The Guatemala Affair" for a discussion of legal issues.

30. Ibid. See also C. Ronning, ed., *Intervention in Latin America* (New York: Knopf, 1970) for a discussion of law and intervention.

31. Officially the planes were sold to Nicaragua (the CIA supplied the money). D. Eisenhower, *The White House Years: Mandate for Change, 1953–1956* (Garden City, NY: Doubleday, 1963), pp. 420–427, discusses his decision.

32. After the failure, Kennedy said angrily America would not "be lectured on intervention by those whose character was stamped for all time on the bloody streets of Budapest!" "Address Before the American Society of Newspaper Editors" (April 20, 1961). In J. Kennedy, *Public Papers of John F. Kennedy, 1961* (Washington, DC: Government Printing Office, 1962), pp. 304–306.

33. Bissell told Robert Kennedy the odds were two-to-one in favor of the Bay of Pigs succeeding. A. Schlesinger, *Robert F. Kennedy and His Times* (Boston: Houghton Mifflin, 1978), p. 443. To understand these assassination plans in the context of the times it is well to recall that the key planners had served in World War II, in which millions died. They had not led sheltered lives. In the Cuban case of a "cold" war, given that a military invasion was planned, assassination was a pragmatic tactic to save American and Cuban lives. It had the same rationale as the World War II efforts to assassinate Hitler, with which Allen Dulles had been associated. Wyden, *Bay of Pigs*, p. 41.

34. U.S. Senate. Select Committee to Study Governmental Operations with Respect to Intelligence Activities. *Alleged Assassination Plots Involving Foreign Leaders.* Senate Report 94-465 (November 20, 1975). (Washington, DC: Government Printing Office, 1975) reviews assassination issues. See also T. Powers, *The Man Who Kept the Secrets: Richard Helms and the CIA* (New York: Pocket Books, 1979), pp. 184–200.

35. Wyden, *Bay of Pigs*, pp. 40–45; 109–110.

36. Rosselli and Giancana were both killed after they had been called to testify before the Church investigation but before they actually did so. Giancana was shot seven times in the throat and mouth as he was frying sausages in his kitchen. Rosselli was hacked to pieces and the pieces of his body stuffed into an oil drum and

dumped into the ocean off Miami. See A. Schlesinger, *Robert F. Kennedy*, p. 484. (The Church investigation resulted in the summary report, U.S. Senate, *Alleged Assassination Plots*).

37. Schlesinger, *Robert F. Kennedy*, pp. 483–484.
38. Ibid., p. 482.
39. Ibid., p. 484 discusses the timing.
40. U.S. Senate, *Alleged Assassination Plots*, p. 118; Powers, *The Man Who Kept the Secrets*, pp. 182, 193–198, 443.
41. Schlesinger, *Robert F. Kennedy*, pp. 488–498.
42. The alternative explanations, then, are: (a) their minds really worked this way; (b) this statement was part of a public cover-up story. "Embarrass": see U.S. Senate, *Alleged Assassination Attempts*, p. 121. Note, however, that Allen Dulles had socialized with the Kennedy family since Jack's school days. They were not strangers. See Parmet, *JFK*, p. 161.
43. Parmet, *JFK*, pp. 117–118, 120, 126–128.
44. Ibid., U.S. Senate, *Alleged Assassination Attempts*, p. 130; D. Martin, *Wilderness of Mirrors* (New York: Ballantine, 1981), p. 123, reports Campbell was also involved with Rosselli.
45. Whether Kennedy knew of the Giancana connection before Hoover's visit has not been established.
46. Robert Kennedy's involvement happened this way. Giancana said another of his girlfriends (the singer Phyllis McGuire) was two-timing him by having an affair with Dan Rowan (a comedian whose national television program was popular during the early 1960s). In return for Giancana's favors and to keep him in Miami working on assassination plans (instead of flying constantly to Las Vegas to check on McGuire), Maheu asked the CIA to wiretap Rowan's room in Las Vegas. The CIA refused to do this directly, but said they would pay a private investigator to do it. He did it, they paid, and Las Vegas police and the FBI became involved when the bug was discovered and the operative arrested. The CIA went to the Justice Department to stop the investigation: The memorandum from the inspector general of the CIA to Robert Kennedy discussed at least one earlier assassination attempt against Castro in which the CIA was involved. As Giancana could obviously afford his own bugging, it is a puzzle why the CIA went along with this. The Church committee heard conflicting stories. See U.S. Senate, *Alleged Assassination Attempts*, pp. 77–79. Martin, *Wilderness of Mirrors*, p. 122, reports Maheu suspected Giancana of bragging to McGuire, who might have gossiped to Rowan.
47. See also Powers, *The Man Who Kept the Secrets*, pp. 182, 193–198, 441. Senior officials who testified to Congress never showed the anger or deep alarm that would have been appropriate if CIA assassination efforts were truly unauthorized. And no one admitted to anything beyond what documentary evidence compelled.
48. U.S. Senate, *Alleged Assassination Attempts*, p. 121.
49. Ibid., p. 138.
50. It is also plausible, however, that McGeorge Bundy would have known.
51. The best discussion of strategic planning is E. Halperin, *The National Liberation Movement in Latin America* (Cambridge, MA: MIT Center for International Studies, 1959). Report No. A/69-6.
52. See also the discussion in chapter 5 of how Castro's success against Batista gave added reason to believe psychological collapse might be achieved easily. Allen Dulles's carefully worded statement was, "I know of no estimate that a spontaneous uprising of the unarmed population of Cuba would be touched off by the landing." Quoted in Wyden, *Bay of Pigs*, p. 139.

53. A summary of the president's favorable view is located in M. Bundy, "National Security Action Memorandum No. 31" (March 11, 1961) (Photocopy: Kennedy Library): "The President expects to authorize US support for an appropriate number of patriotic Cubans to return to their homeland. He believes that the best possible plan, from the point of view of combined military, political and psychological considerations has not yet been presented, and new proposals are to be concerted promptly." Meetings were large (15–20 people) and formal. In addition to the president they usually included McGeorge Bundy, Arthur Schlesinger, Jr., and (at times) Richard Goodwin from the White House; Dean Rusk, Thomas Mann, and A. A. Berle from the State Department; Robert McNamara, Paul Nitze, and Joint Chiefs of Staff representatives (General Lemnitzer, the chairman, and Admiral Burke, chief of naval operations, having principal roles, with General Gray present as an aide in charge of CIA liaison) from the Defense Department; Allen Dulles, Richard Bissell, and, at times, three to four other officials (Tracy Barnes, Gen. Charles Cabell, "Jake Engler" and Col. Hawkins) from the CIA.

54. Wyden, *Bay of Pigs*, pp. 100, 135.

55. Bundy's testimony in Taylor, *Operation ZAPATA*, p. 176.

56. This was the reason, as well, to use old, leased Cuban boats to conduct the landing rather than military vessels properly equipped for defense. The older, less capable equipment needed for the cover story was later criticized in Maxwell Taylor's postmortem (see chapter 3). But even without jets in Castro's hands, it was recognized by Pentagon analysts that destruction of Castro's air force was absolutely necessary. On March 10 the Joint Chiefs sent a report to the Secretary of Defense warning the landing would fail without absolute control of the air. They wrote that even one Cuban aircraft with a .50-caliber machine gun "could sink all or most of the invasion force." U.S. Department of Defense, "Memoranda for the Secretary." JCSM-146-61, enclosure A, pp. 8–9.

57. There was also an attempted army coup in Guatemala: The CIA used the expatriates to aid its suppression. But the preparations were well known and controversial in Guatemala and the government wanted the troops to leave. The November 13, 1960 attempt is discussed in Wise and Ross, *Invisible Government*, p. 33.

58. Schlesinger, *A Thousand Days*, p. 242; Wyden, *Bay of Pigs*, p. 100; Schlesinger, *Robert F. Kennedy*, pp. 453–454.

59. Note, especially, the expectation of a quiet landing.

60. Wyden, *Bay of Pigs*, p. 8.

61. See L. Etheredge, *A World of Men: The Private Sources of American Foreign Policy* (Cambridge, MA: MIT Press, 1978); Schlesinger, *A Thousand Days*, pp. 186–205.

62. For quantitative evidence that achievement and power motivation are part of a foreign policy syndrome that includes perception of challenges and threats, see L. Etheredge, *A World of Men*.

63. Fulbright's memo is reprinted in K. Meyer, ed., *Fulbright of Arkansas* (Washington, DC: Robert D. Luce, 1963). Robert Kennedy, in his Kennedy Library interview by Martin (vol. 1, p. 60) asserted that Fulbright received a later briefing, following which he indicated a modifying of his opposition. J. Fulbright (personal communication) has said this is untrue.

Kennedy returned from his trip more militant than before, according to Schlesinger, *A Thousand Days*, p. 251, Fulbright's memo notwithstanding. Kennedy was vacationing in Florida at the home of Earl Smith, Eisenhower's ambassador to Cuba under Batista and an old family friend. See H. Thomas, *The Cuban*

Revolution (New York: Harper & Row, 1977), p. 1309. Smith was passionately anti-Castro and alleged in his memoirs *The Fourth Floor: An Account of the Castro Communist Revolution* (New York: Random House, 1962), pp. 52–54 that Cuban communists had plotted to assassinate him and that the State Department had confirmed evidence of such a plan. Whether this was a contemporary belief and mentioned to Kennedy, or possibly fabricated and reported in Smith's memoirs as a later cover for the president should the administration's assassination plans become public, I have been unable to determine. An inquiry to the State Department using the Freedom of Information Act did not yield copies of any reports such as Smith implied he received, but this search was not definitive.

64. See H. Dinerstein, *The Making of a Missile Crisis, October, 1962* (Baltimore, MD: Johns Hopkins Univ. Press, 1976), pp. 80–87. Khrushchev was taken to be speaking figuratively when he initially said Soviet rockets would support Cuban independence.

65. Schlesinger, *A Thousand Days*, chapters 1–6; also Wyden, *Bay of Pigs*, p. 316, makes the case for such learning.

66. I discuss the risk reduction logic of this decision process further in chapter 6.

67. Rusk was equivocal, but Kennedy perceived him to be a supporter. See Wyden, *Bay of Pigs*, p. 305. For Berle's views, see A. Berle, "The Cuban Crisis: Failure of American Foreign Policy" *Foreign Affairs* 39 (October 1960): 40–55.

68. Note that Kennedy had received a long memorandum, via Schlesinger, from Harvard professors John Plank and Bill Barnes, also strongly arguing against the invasion. Plank's conclusion, "We had access to the top of power, and there was nothing we could do to stop it" is relevant to the discussion in chapters 5 and 6 that motivation, not failure to hear the available evidence and argument, was the central determinant. See Wyden, *Bay of Pigs*, p. 125.

69. Ibid. T. Sorenson, *Kennedy* (New York: Harper & Row, 1965) and other liberals have tended to see Kennedy as more reluctant.

70. In fact, he appears to have revealed himself differently, in these informal discussions, to men who shared the view he was expressing. This may have been politically astute, but I think he also instinctively surrounded himself with people who were, in effect, different aspects of himself. He then used them as sounding boards to express and integrate his different moods and reactions in decision making. Bundy himself was unsure of the president's true feelings. Recently he has said he thought, in 1961, that Kennedy did not like the invasion idea. Now, looking back, he believes Kennedy wanted the plan to succeed. Robert Kennedy's aggressive stance, and the role he played with the president's knowledge must count, I think, as expressing an aspect of the president's own personality. See Wyden, *Bay of Pigs*, p. 165 and Mosley, *Dulles*, pp. 464–474, passim. I will argue, in chapter 6, that the question is not either/or but that Kennedy was both confident and assertive *and* apprehensive and reluctant.

71. Wyden, *Bay of Pigs*, p. 318. There could be such deeper considerations at work. Freud would have said that deference and covert hostility toward older or more powerful male adults are commonplace. There are no accidents in mental life, the master said, and certainly some ordinarily very bright people "screwed up." There is no explicit evidence for or against the idea in this case.

72. Bissell's politics are discussed in Parmet, *JFK*, p. 160.

73. Wyden, *Bay of Pigs*, p. 120.

74. Ibid., p. 165. In fact, there is little evidence of this. At least by Schlesinger's account in *A Thousand Days* the manifest mood was belligerent. That Kennedy

thought otherwise might—but there is no additional evidence—suggest that he felt some of this instinct.

75. Quoted in Wyden, *Bay of Pigs*, p. 142.

76. A deeper sexual logic might mean, one step further, that if the president fully committed himself to the CIA's plans (America's power equals his power), they (these Eisenhower carry-overs) would have him by the balls . . . and he really did not like that idea. Whether Kennedy thought of power with these undertones is unclear: To leave the issue elusive, with a "fig leaf," seems to be what the evidence compels. A sexual analogy underlay Gray Lynch's postmortem schema for an operation which almost got him killed: "Superman was a fairy." Wyden, *Bay of Pigs*, p. 302.

77. These were all busy men, especially so at the beginning of a new administration. But there is no exonerating evidence that this was a hasty decision: No participants later complained they had lacked an opportunity to be briefed about the plan fully or to discuss it at length. Kennedy did not receive a full-dress military briefing, but he did not request it and felt he had ample time to take a Florida vacation. They apparently spent at least fifteen to twenty hours focusing on the problem in formal sessions with the president in the three months prior to the invasion. There were seven formal meetings involving the president: January 28, February 8, March 16, March 29, and April 4, 12, and 15 are listed by Bundy in "Memorandum to Lt. Col. Benjamin Tarwater," May 2, 1961. (Photocopy, Kennedy Library.) Wyden, *Bay of Pigs*, p. 99, adds a meeting on March 11. The most detailed discussion of the crucial April 4 meeting is Wyden, *Bay of Pigs*, pp. 146–150.

78. P. Blackstock, *The Strategy of Subversion: Manipulating the Policies of Other Nations* (Chicago: Quadrangle, 1964), p. 240. The president's decision was also conveyed in a memorandum on April 13 to Rusk, McNamara, and Dulles from McGeorge Bundy: "There will be no employment of U.S. armed forces against Cuba unless quite new circumstances develop." "Memorandum of April 13, 1961." (Declassified October 17, 1983). Photocopy, Kennedy Library.

79. Wise and Ross, *The Invisible Government*, pp. 13–14; Wyden, *Bay of Pigs*, pp. 175–176. Use of napalm was ruled out against the Havana area for fear of "concern and public outcry," but it was approved for the beachhead area. The restriction probably reduced the effectiveness of the D-2 strikes. See Taylor *Operation ZAPATA*, pp. 95, 346.

80. To retain security, the CIA (probably wisely) did not alert the indigenous Cuban underground. Earlier writers were unaware of the CIA's independent radio operator net, controlled separately from the Cuban underground, that was to be used. It is still unwise to reach a conclusion about how effectively Castro's sweep worked to disrupt operational plans, especially as the CIA believed 2,500 members of the Cuban military would aid the expatriate cause if it established momentum. Who these people were, where they were placed, what they were prepared to do, and whether they were vulnerable to the mass arrest counterplan Castro prepared is still classified.

81. Guantanamo was ruled off limits to the invaders; planes were forbidden to land there in the event of trouble.

82. See Taylor, *Operation ZAPATA*, pp. 96–97; Wyden, *Bay of Pigs*, pp. 170–172.

83. Wyden, *Bay of Pigs*, pp. 186–190; Stevenson declared the planes involved "to the best of our knowledge were Castro's own airforce planes." Wise and Ross, *Invisible Government*, pp. 15–17.

84. The *New York Times*, its lead story filed from Miami by Tad Szulc, was promi-

nent among the skeptics. But until several investigative reporters began to write skeptical stories, the major news services and many newspapers treated the CIA's defector cover story as authoritative fact. For example, AP's wire report from Havana on April 15 began with the lead, "Pilots of Prime Minister Fidel Castro's air force revolted today and attacked three of the Castro regime's key air bases with bombs and rockets." See Wise and Ross, *Invisible Government*, p. 18.

85. Wyden, *Bay of Pigs*, p. 189. Stevenson's cable arrived at the State Department at 7:33 P.M. The timing suggests it precipitated a call from Rusk to Kennedy.
86. Wise and Ross, *Invisible Government*, p. 45, add a fifth ship, the *Lake Charles*. Wyden, *Bay of Pigs*, p. 216, also records five ships; the *Lake Charles*, however, did not reach the beaches in time for the battle. Ibid., p. 292n.
87. The American naval vessels were also ordered to paint over their identification numbers, a maneuver that would presumably make them less "American" to reporters, if the ships should later be observed off shore, and also appear less "overt" to the Russians.
88. The carrier USS *Boxer* was also in the vicinity, equipped to use new helicopter assault ("vertical envelopment") tactics. See Blackstock, *The Strategy of Subversion*, p. 248. It was not officially part of the task force but its presence and capability were intentional.
89. Wyden, *Bay of Pigs*, pp. 217–220.
90. Ibid., p. 221.
91. Ibid.
92. The reason for the failure was never established, although it suggests sabotage by agents Castro would surely have attempted to place within the invasion force.
93. Equipment included tanks and other vehicles.
94. Wyden, *Bay of Pigs* is the principal English-language source for Castro's view of the operation, esp. pp. 248–262.
95. Ibid., p. 249; Taylor, *Operation ZAPATA*, p. 97 on Cuban troop coordination.
96. The reef misidentification is discussed in Wyden, *Bay of Pigs*, pp. 136–138. Cubans with the invasion force knew of the reef but the CIA officials relied on U-2 photographs and interpreters in Washington. Local CIA officials thought the Cubans who brought the problem to their attention were just nervous and responded with kindly reassurance that everything would turn out.
97. No Americans were aboard these boats because of Kennedy's orders to keep Americans out of the combat zone. This reduced American control at a crucial time.
98. The basic source on battle events is Wyden, *Bay of Pigs*, pp. 210–288, supplemented by Johnson, *The Bay of Pigs*. The Taylor commission testimony, taken before the imprisoned Brigade members were ransomed, is less reliable.
99. Distances are given in Taylor, *Operation ZAPATA*, p. 283. Without this crucial ammunition, the CIA tried to keep the invasion alive by airdrops and tactical air support for the beaches from Guatemala. The long distances, and the round trip required by the absence of a beachhead airstrip for refueling, gave planes only about 30 minutes over the beaches.
100. Castro's tactical grasp was excellent as, unknown to the CIA, the Bay of Pigs region was his favorite fishing spot. He urged great speed because he anticipated his greatest danger would come if a beachhead were established and America could "recognize" a liberation government to legitimate direct American involvement. See, for example, Wyden, *Bay of Pigs*, p. 258.
101. Johnson, *The Bay of Pigs*, provides eyewitness accounts.

102. Once on the ground it took one to two hours to turn around an expatriate plane for another run. See Taylor, *Operation ZAPATA*, pp. 119, 233. The absence of tail guns to increase payload was deliberate and reflected a consistent planning assumption between the CIA and JCS that either there would be air cover or complete destruction of Castro's air force. Castro's planes, of course, could be rearmed and turned around without seven-hour flying delays.
103. Communication snarls kept Washington from accurate knowledge of many issues, but the need for ammunition was clear to them. The *Lake Charles* was not due for several days.
104. R. Bissell (personal communication). Presidential approval reflected new consideration on Monday's situation and was not an automatic carry-over of the delay decision on Sunday.
105. Earlier efforts to obtain a closer launch point had not been successful, and the president had forbidden use of bases on the American mainland.
106. This is Walt Rostow's view. Rostow was present during these discussions. He later said, "It was inconceivable to them that the President would let it openly fail when he had all this American power." Wyden, *Bay of Pigs*, p. 270.
107. Wyden, *Bay of Pigs*, p. 180, on Castro's planning assumptions.
108. Ibid., pp. 258–259.
109. Some degree of delay can likely be attributed to Kennedy's cover-story insistence on going ahead with an apparently normal work (and weekend) schedule and to his reluctance to make any decisions until he had more facts. He insisted on making the key decisions but had not prepared himself to do so, lacked a good conception of the terrain, and did not take obvious steps, e.g., radio replacements from the naval task force, to get him the timely information he needed.
110. Wyden, *Bay of Pigs*, p. 281.
111. Quoted in Schlesinger, *Robert F. Kennedy*, p. 445.
112. It was used once to evacuate wounded.
113. Wyden, *Bay of Pigs*, pp. 235–236, suggests that Americans began to substitute on Tuesday.
114. President Kennedy was not informed of this violation. He only learned of it months later when the widow of one of the men — in the face of repeated official denials from the bureaucracy that it had no information about her husband — pursued the issue successfully through a member of Congress.
115. Wyden, *Bay of Pigs*, pp. 242–243; Wise and Ross, *Invisible Government*, pp. 68–71.
116. The navy destroyed all records of its operations, a standard procedure for covert work.
117. Wyden, *Bay of Pigs*, p. 227. Kennedy quoted the Brigade commander's refusal in a speech to a meeting of newspaper editors to illustrate the zeal of the men. J. Kennedy, "Address." It is unlikely he realized the CIA commander on the scene had unwittingly encouraged the men to wait for resupply, which the commander thought would be approved.
118. Wyden, *Bay of Pigs*, p. 218.
119. Wise and Ross, *Invisible Government*, pp. 67–68.
120. Wyden, *Bay of Pigs*, p. 271.
121. Ibid., pp. 281–282. Even twenty years later, the CIA commanders and naval commanders of the task force (who monitored the battle but continually had to refuse aid, by presidential order, to men being killed) were traumatized. Bissell likely judged astutely that, had he told the complete truth, the CIA commanders, loyal

to their men, would have disobeyed and effected a resupply early on Wednesday. Given Kennedy's views, and the hopelessness of further fighting, it likely seemed prudent, and perhaps an act of humanity, to cut off the Brigade's ammunition.

122. Ibid., p. 287.
123. Kennedy threatened an invasion to save the lives of the men, anticipating Castro might otherwise execute them.

Chapter 2 REALITY AND THE POLICY PROCESS: NINE STORIES

Many failures combined to produce the Bay of Pigs failure. This chapter reviews how, at nine points, erroneous beliefs substituted for a clear grasp of what, in retrospect, was reality. These beliefs were: (1) Kennedy held a wishful image of the Cubans. He considered them volunteer patriots motivated to attempt, on their own, to liberate their homeland.

About what would follow after the men hit the beaches, Kennedy was wrong in five assessments: (2) He reduced and eliminated air strikes without realizing these decisions meant military defeat; (3) he believed American involvement would remain secret; (4) he believed Castro would lose his nerve; (5) he believed the Cuban people would rise up to support the "liberation" of their homeland; (6) he believed he (and the men) had a costless guerrilla escape option.[1]

Others thought they grasped reality, but events proved they did not, on two additional issues: (7) Adlai Stevenson believed the CIA cover story for the defector pilot was true. And (8) almost all (and perhaps all) Kennedy's advisers, and the Cubans themselves, believed he would commit American military forces rather than allow an invasion to fail.

Finally, (9) there was a serious failure the invasion collapse obscured. Kennedy and his advisers did not consider the implications of a prolonged struggle that might have embroiled the United States had Kennedy not inadvertently scuttled his own operation at the beachhead.

1. *Kennedy imagined the Cubans to be volunteer patriots eager to liberate their homeland, on their own, to advance a "New Frontier" political agenda.*

Kennedy's problem — of both self-image and political symbolism — was how to commit an aggressive act without thinking of it as aggression, or how the United States could intervene in Cuba without violating the principle of nonintervention. He tried to find a way to reshape the CIA's original plan, and think about the operation, to achieve this objective.[2] His solution was to conceive this operation as American *support* of Cuban liberators. They were to be led by a liberation government whose "New Frontier" political program of liberal reform mirrored Kennedy's own progressive ideals.

Reality remained otherwise: the operation, from top to bottom, beginning to end, was American — American-conceived, American-inspired, American-financed, American-managed. The Cubans were stage props; the forced political coalition had no united program.

Lest the situation be misunderstood, it should be made clear that none of the soldiers were mercenaries. They were paid only a subsistence amount. They were, for the most part, younger, idealistic, passionate patriots who believed their ideals — and their country — were now betrayed by Castro. But the absolutely necessary ingredient in their participation was faith that the United States was behind them and would not let them fail. Castro had 250,000 regular troops and militia. You would have been crazy to join a band of 1,400 and invade Cuba on your own.

In March 1960 the CIA undertook to form a liberation government. They had difficulty doing so. There were over 100,000 Cuban expatriates and 600 different political groups in the Miami area. The first wave of expatriates came with the fall of Batista: They had strong incentives to return to former positions of power and wealth. They were also unacceptable: Having been liberated, the Cuban people would scarcely support the reinstatement of rightwing Batistianos. Only as Castro moved more explicitly in a Marxist direction, and began to purge the army and his governing coalition of his early leftist, but non-Communist, supporters and they began to arrive in Miami, could the CIA work seriously to form a credible "liberation" government. But to do so, they now had to deal with groups spanning most of the political spectrum, some of whom were anathema to others.[3]

To form a political coalition required consummate skill (especially in dealing with Cuban politicians whom even their supporters often considered prickly prima donnas). Bissell's ad hoc operation was forced to use some CIA agents who were not considered first-rate. In the Guatemala scenario the "liberators" were stage props, a low priority, so Bissell used his weakest people to handle that job. Gerry Droller, the Washington head of exile political contacts, spoke no Spanish and was openly condescending to Cubans. E. Howard Hunt was widely regarded in the agency as a charming man who seldom got anything done: He was designated to be head of political action, working in Miami and in touch with the politicians daily.[4]

Hunt was authorized to take off the kid gloves: "knock their heads together, kick them in the ass, anything at all."[5] But he could not produce a government. Finally, in mid-March 1961, with the invasion now tentatively approved, a D-Day in three to four weeks, and no liberation government formed, Bissell acted to get one. He fired Hunt and assigned a new man, "Jim Noble," former CIA station chief in Havana.[6] Noble's order was to produce the coalition government in a week. He assembled the expatriate leaders on March 18 at the Skyways Motel in Miami, and he issued an ultimatum cleared with Washington. He excoriated the Cuban politicians for pursuing "selfish little aims and petty differences. . . . If you don't come out of this meeting with a committee, you just forget the whole fuckin' business, because we're through!"[7]

Noble got a coerced alliance. It was a marriage of expedience, a vehicle for power. The "leaders" only exercised influence when they did what the American government wanted. Just after his selection to head the liberation government, Dr. Miro Cardona was requested to ratify the CIA's earlier selection of Manuel Artime as Brigade commander. Other political leaders objected, but Miro told them (rightly) that he had no choice.[8]

The CIA learned early that it must take charge: The Cuban politicians could not organize an operation that would bring a significant number of people into the streets to fight and die behind the banner of putting them into power. Early Radio SWAN broadcasts (from the CIA's propaganda radio on Swan Island in the Caribbean) were judged too candid about right-wing sentiments of some of the groups who proposed to return.[9] In New York, the Cuban leadership issued press statements — but thirty pages long and in Spanish. To mount a credible liberation the CIA hired a professional, the Lem Jones public relations firm on Madison Avenue (another of his clients had been Twentieth Century Fox). David Phillips, the CIA's propaganda chief, called the P.R. agency directly to dictate press statements on behalf of the Cubans. Even the invasion-day manifesto, explaining why their fellow countrymen should rise up to support them, was not written by the Cubans: E. Howard Hunt telephoned in the copy. The Cuban leaders were not told the day of "their" invasion. On a pretext they were put on a plane and then held incommunicado at a Florida military base ("kidnapped" some of them charged angrily), waiting for the CIA's decision to fly them to the beaches.[10]

Howard Hunt later discussed his impressions of the men involved (as the senior American official to know most of the key politicians firsthand, his perceptions bear on the realism of Kennedy's idealistic facade). Hunt had high regard for only a few. In the main, "they displayed most Latin faults and few Latin virtues. With one exception they were all professional politicians whose trade was public demagoguery and private intrigue. . . . I considered them shallow thinkers and opportunists."[11] Bissell was appalled by the original political manifesto the politicians drafted, which promised to undo many of Castro's progressive reforms; he instructed that (in his metaphor) a "sexier" set of proposals be drafted. Miro later met with Arthur Schlesinger to review a land reform package the White House was enthusiastic that his group adopt. He sighed; it could be put on paper, but almost any idea, including these bold reforms, was a matter of intense controversy among the politicians temporarily united under his leadership.[12]

Political conflicts, papered over in Miami, surfaced dramatically in Guatemala. In January 1961, half the 500 Cubans mutinied against the CIA when the agency — under pressure to expand the force quickly — began to recruit former members of Batista's army who were anathema to many Brigade members. The CIA reinstated control and stage-managed a conciliatory visit from preselected Cuban politicians. But about a dozen intransigent troublemakers were kidnapped, taken by seaplane and canoe to an almost inaccessible location in the northern mountain jungle of Guatemala, and held incommunicado by armed guards for three and a half months until the invasion attempt was completed.[13]

Nor did senior officials at the White House, under pressure to mount an invasion, have time to be well informed about everyone the United States was sponsoring as a "liberator." Jim Noble, recruited in March, briefed Bissell, A. A. Berle (an old-time New Dealer who was a Latin American specialist at the State Department), William Bundy from the Defense Department, and Richard Goodwin from the White House. Noble was shocked by the ignorance: "If I'd just thrown in Joe Blow's name and made up a fictitious background for him, he could have been named to the government, too."[14] His suggestion for a genuine political convention among Cubans in Miami was rejected because of a lack of time. No one had been concerned with it earlier.

It would seem reasonable, in retrospect, to doubt that Kennedy ever really believed the propaganda. But the evidence is that he cared about the reality and wanted it to be true. He developed a bottom-line test to assure himself that these Cubans genuinely wanted to go to the beaches for their own motives; he formally demanded the Cuban leaders accept the fact that there would be no American military involvement. (I will return to this episode, and why the message Kennedy received satisfied him—erroneously.) Kennedy used Arthur Schlesinger, Jr., in the White House, to develop an enraptured White Paper ("The Cuban people remain our brothers . . . ") to assure the world that the spirit of the "New Frontier" motivated the operation, that it would continue Castro's earlier programs: *Fidelismo sin Fidel.*[15] Kennedy ordered a leftist politician, Manuel Ray, included in the liberation government in order to shape its policies and (with his allegedly large underground network) increase the likelihood of a mass uprising. America would be Cuba's benefactor, not an "aggressor."[16]

Having tried to create a viable viewpoint from which to approve the plan, Kennedy apparently ended up believing it halfway, and probably more than halfway. About the realities and the gorier details of what they were doing, the CIA told him no lies, but they also told him few details. Nor did he ask.

So the CIA went ahead and substantially substituted image for reality. Its officials might have preferred the image to be the same as reality, but they had no time.

2. *Kennedy cut back and eliminated air strikes without realizing the disastrous consequences.*

> [T]here is unanimous agreement that at some stage the Castro Air Force must be removed. . . . [T]he revised landing plan depends strongly upon prompt action against Castro's air.
>
> —McGeorge Bundy,
> *Memorandum for the President,*
> March 15, 1961

There were two missions for the sixteen B-26s of the invader air force. On D-2 and D, the job was to eliminate Castro's air force. Afterward, from the beachhead landing strip, they were to fly tactical sorties against Castro's troops and destroy microwave and telephone systems so the (remaining) radio communications would be open to the manipulation that would multiply the apparent magnitude of the invasion and destroy the control and morale of the defenders.

Debate about how many planes to use, and when, continued throughout the planning meetings. Militarily, the CIA wanted "maximum" air power. The Department of State, concerned other countries not be implicated, wanted it "minimal."[17]

The CIA proposed full air power directed in one strike, on the morning of D-Day. The State Department argued this would be too spectacular, too large to appear to originate from indigenous defectors. The pretense of American innocence could be blown and the "international noise level" reach a crescendo if the Yankees of the north seemed back to their old tricks of invading and overthrowing Latin American governments and, to make matters worse, involving other Latin American governments in mutual military interference. The CIA compromised; they proposed the D-2 strike with the "defector" pilot who would fly to Miami to give it a plausible cover story.[18]

Initially, Kennedy agreed. But then Friday, April 14, James Reston, a senior *New York Times* reporter and columnist, angrily attacked the rumored Cuban operation in his column. Reston, outraged, claimed that it would reverse what he thought America's main historical purpose should be, "to put some kind of ethical base under the new world order." Later in the day, after reading the column, Kennedy called Bissell with the final "go" order for the D-2 air strikes the next morning. Kennedy gave his approval, but then, just before ringing off, he asked Bissell how many planes Bissell planned to use. Bissell said there would be sixteen.

"Well, I don't want it on that scale," said the president, "I want it minimal."[19] Bissell did not object, pleased, with over a year of his own work invested, that the president was willing for the plan to go ahead at all. He passed the word that only six planes would fly.

What happened in those few seconds was consequential for what followed on Sunday: Kennedy had pushed Bissell, and Bissell had readily accepted a fallback position. It showed political sophistication by both men. Kennedy likely expected that Bissell had padded his estimates to afford a safety margin and planned to use more aircraft than the number he needed. In fact, Kennedy phrased his order — to make the strikes "minimal" — to imply that the minimum should be what Bissell *really* needed to do the job; he did not instruct Bissell how many to use. Bissell's ready agreement could be interpreted as an implicit acknowledgment that he did pad and his plans could be cut back for political considerations without harm to military objectives.

In part, however, Kennedy and Bissell misread each other. The Kennedys were "personal conflict" learners. Kennedy was accustomed to the frank, even blunt, dealing of an inner circle of staff and family accorded the right of frankness in return for absolute personal loyalty. Earlier, when he was in the Senate, it had not been an awesome breach of protocol for staff to tell him he was wrong, or to argue with him. And if a staff member did not see eye to eye with him, or displeased him, he could always find another job with another senator.

But to a president, advisers became deferential. There was the aura of the office. His pleasure and displeasure now affected whether men, drawn to Washington to make an impact on history, could realize this central quest in their lives. Association with power in the White House was a "mountain top experience," one aide later put it.

When Kennedy gave a blunt order, "I want it minimal," his past style indicated he was not giving an absolute order, he was only saying what he wanted. He expected people to come back at him if it *shouldn't* be what he wanted. But since Kennedy's assessment was affected by the emotional intensity with which the argument was made, Bissell's quick deference confirmed, implicitly, that all the air strikes were not necessary.[20]

Bissell accepted because he *had* padded to give the plan a substantial safety margin. And he decreased the sorties, too, because he did not want to jeopardize a mission (with a final "go" signal needed from the president on Sunday) by unnecessary confrontation. A quick assent still left the D-Day strikes to finish the job.

U-2 photographic overflights of Cuba did not yield a certain count of how many planes were destroyed on D-2, but several planes clearly remained operational.[21] The D-Day strike was now considered crucial, and at full force: the men were unprepared for a contested landing, their boats were loaded with highly explosive fuel and ammunition, and they lacked antiaircraft weapons to defend themselves.

But throughout Sunday, Kennedy's doubts continued. He arranged to go to an estate in Virginia and to a racetrack, hit golf balls in a pasture, and appear to be on vacation (a cover story). But all who saw him that day said he looked gloomy, pressured, distracted. He had agreed to decide by noon. He did not call Bissell until 1:45 p.m. to say "go ahead."[22] (Bissell, again, had padded; the true "final" hour to abort the ship rendezvous was 4:00 — and the men would not, in fact, begin to hit the beaches until about midnight, so he actually had even longer.)

But after his approval, doubts continued to work on the president. He received no new factual information. But that morning the major newspapers had left the defector's cover story in shreds. Then, Stevenson learned he had been set up and his angry "Eyes Only" cable to Rusk arrived at the State Department.[23] Concern that the operation was becoming loud and public, and reaction to the "international noise level" in New York, prompted telephone conversations among Rusk, Bundy, and the president. Rusk initiated the calls, and Kennedy cancelled the D-Day air strike at the same time he ordered Mc-George Bundy to New York City, "to hold the hands of Ambassador Stevenson" (as Bundy expressed it) and give him an accurate briefing over breakfast the next morning.[24]

When Rusk spoke with the president, he urged the advisability of postponing any further air strikes until these could "plausibly originate" from within Cuba itself. To Rusk, this meant the air strip on the island should first be secured—which meant no dawn strikes. He found, to his surprise, the president did not remember any D-Day strikes were to originate from Nicaragua. "I'm not signed on to this," the president said, using navy parlance to indicate that he did not remember these details.[25]

On Sunday evening, General Cabell stopped by the CIA after a golf game to check on developments. It was there, about 9:30 P.M., that he received a call from Bundy; at the president's order the D-Day strikes were cancelled unless there were "over-riding considerations." If the cancellation created problems for Cabell, he should call Rusk; Bundy was leaving for New York.[26]

Cabell phoned Bissell and they went immediately to see Rusk at the State Department, arriving just after 10:15 P.M. Cabell and Bissell protested the cancellation very strongly to Rusk; Bissell, especially, was highly agitated. They told Rusk that if the president did not reverse himself, the landing was seriously endangered: Castro had operational aircraft, the Brigade lacked anti-aircraft capability; and men on the beaches would likely die under air attack. Rusk maintained that as the boats were expected to be unloaded and withdrawn by dawn, a delay would not be critical.

Rusk called Kennedy, reported to him that Cabell and Bissell were in his office, felt the cancellation would be "very serious," and briefed the president on their arguments. He concluded by restating his own original position, that in view of the problems in New York the cancellation stay and the CIA be allowed no further foreign-based air assaults. He listened for a moment, then turned to Cabell and said, "Well, the President agrees with me, but would you, General Cabell, like to speak to the President?"[27]

Cabell demurred. He had nothing to add and, as a good military officer—with his arguments heard and the case now overruled, twice, by the commander-in-chief—he decided there was no point to further protest. Bissell, too, judged Rusk had summarized the case fairly and further protest would be "hopeless" or its chance at best "negligible."[28] Returning to the CIA, Bissell, acting on his own authority, cancelled planned notifications to CIA agents within Cuba. He did not want to compromise them if the invasion should fail; it now seemed more likely that it would.[29]

At 4 A.M. General Cabell, still concerned about the error of the president's decision (and feeling intense pressure from his subordinates at the CIA), visited Dean Rusk at his apartment in the Sheraton-Park Hotel and awakened him to request American jet cover during unloading and withdrawal. Rusk called the president and put General Cabell on the line directly. At 4 A.M., it was too late for the slow Brigade B-26s to arrive from Nicaragua by dawn. The general's options used American planes and American pilots. The president did not comment, asked to talk to Rusk, and their conversation was very brief. Rusk hung up the phone, turned to Cabell, and told him all requests were disapproved.[30] Moreover, the president had ordered the carrier moved further out to sea and kept at least thirty miles away.[31]

Why did Kennedy cancel? The "international noise level" was the sort of political risk he had feared, and which he had whittled down the operation to prevent. The CIA-designed cover story for their defector was exposed. Stevenson was furious, and he could lead opposition from within the Democratic Party. Rusk also advised cancellation and, in his quiet professional way, spoke with the authority of the New York foreign policy establishment. Kennedy was upset and determined, whatever else, that his (America's) deniability would stay and he would not further risk a Soviet move against Berlin or elsewhere in the world.

But a cancellation was now irrational. It was too late. The only consequence was to affect the symbolic gesture (in an isolated area) that the sixteen planes first land at the secured beachhead strip before they could again take off and begin to bomb. One still needed to explain where they originated. It was now implausible they all could be portrayed as indigenous Cuban defectors, but the case was equally fanciful whether they arrived at dawn — to help secure the beachhead by eliminating Castro's air power — or in the afternoon. Moreover (it is unlikely Kennedy was attentive to this detail), the CIA's nose cone error was public: there was no credible way to convince reporters these Brigade B-26s belonged to Castro. Foreign correspondents in Havana would observe and report this; to expose the American government's lies had become the lead story in a competitive business.

Later Kennedy told his aide Ted Sorenson that he had not appreciated the consequences of his cancellation. Yet if he failed to understand the consequences, it was because he arranged it that way.

DeRivera, a psychologist, has written a shrewd discussion of decision making, commenting on how often we ask for advice from those we know will say what we want to hear.[32] Kennedy did this, too. Oddly, for a man who had followed such formal procedures until now, he spoke only with Rusk and Bundy before making the decision. Had he truly wanted informed military advice, he would have called Lemnitzer, Burke, Cabell, Hawkins, Bissell, Shoup (commandant of the Marine Corps) or many others who knew the military details. He spoke only with the two men who would agree that "international noise level" was the criterion he should use.

His D-Day cancellation itself, as we have seen, made no logical sense. Given

Kennedy's earlier moodiness, his distracted appearance, his delay in giving the "go" order, his last minute decision (again without consultation) to reduce the D-2 strike, his failure to request a military briefing — and his obviously poor memory of even those military details he had been told — the plausible inference is that Kennedy was ambivalent, conflicted about this plan.[33] Thus I think we have to conclude that "cutting out" his military advisers was a statement of what he did not want to hear.

One also surmises he was becoming very angry. As an astute politician, he surely knew what military advisers would tell him. Instinctively, he distanced them to dramatize his message. He was unwilling to hear from Cabell until after the decision; to appeal, he forced Cabell to go to Rusk. Then, by ruling against Cabell a second time *before* Cabell was asked whether he wanted to talk to him, he (surely, intentionally) put Cabell in a pressured and difficult situation. Kennedy leaned on the CIA hard, to make it work the way Kennedy wanted it, and within the badly fraying conditions of the secrecy they had promised. And, perhaps, Kennedy suspected that the CIA exaggerated the need for D-Day strikes, and they really did not need them (though their loss could make the job more difficult). They had accepted every cut to date; each of the earlier parts of the plan had included safety margins which could be trimmed to accommodate political realities.

Were Kennedy to hear forceful objections, these would come from senior advisers with the bureaucratic standing to call him directly. But that possibility was now hostage to chance and circumstance. A direct appeal could have come from Allen Dulles or the secretary of defense, Robert McNamara. But to effect a cover story, Dulles (tradecraft, again) had gone to Puerto Rico to give a speech. (*Tass* imaginatively charged he had gone to Puerto Rico to direct the invasion from a secret base.)[34] McNamara had remained peripheral to the earlier discussions and no member of the Joint Chiefs of Staff, who might have enlisted McNamara, did so.[35]

It is probably true Kennedy would have retained the D-Day strikes had he foreseen the immediate consequences. Under the circumstances, that required not only factual information but emotional force. But professional language and the deference of subordinates kept such emotional force from him.

The discussion with Rusk was professional, diplomatic, low key.The words used were "critical," "overriding considerations," "serious risk," "noise level."[36] Only outside of the presidential presence were men blunt. Back at the CIA, planners blasted Cabell without mercy. They were angry, shouting, red-faced; four-letter words filled the air, the pretense of rank and decorum gone. Marine Colonel Hawkins shouted at Cabell, a four-star general, "This is criminally negligent!" and at midnight, desperate and sobbing, he phoned Marine Commandant Shoup to tell him he was certain the invasion would now fail under dawn air attack. Shoup "damn near choked," agreed with Hawkins, but thought things had "gone too far" for him to help (nor did he have the bureaucratic standing to call the president).[37] General Gray, the liaison officer between the Pentagon and the CIA, was called at the Pentagon by CIA planners seeking allies: Gray quickly called General Wheeler (air force chief of staff) and together they made an emergency visit to awaken General Lemnitzer, chairman of the Joint Chiefs (at about 2 A.M.). Lemnitzer's reaction was that the president's decision was "absolutely reprehensible, almost criminal" in "pulling the rug" from under the Cuban soldiers. Lemnitzer agreed to Wheeler's and Gray's urging for immediate standby preparations for naval air cover in the morning in the event Kennedy reconsidered his order. These actions and contingency plans were the basis for General Cabell's visit to Secretary Rusk at 4 A.M.[38]

No such strong emotion and blunt talk, at the time, reached the president. Indeed, any subordinate who called a president "criminally irresponsible" to his face would surely have taken the step expecting to end his career. (And he would likely be ineffective: his own behavior would become the issue.) Presidents seldom hear messages with a strong emotional charge from subordinates, certainly not critical ones.

3. *Kennedy believed the American role would remain secret.*

To Kennedy, a secret or plausibly deniable American role was crucial. The Soviet Union would not be challenged by a success (nor would he or the United States lose moral standing). Too, the expatriates likely stood a better chance to spark a nationalist uprising if they publicly appeared to act on their own motives rather than to be mercenaries or surrogates for a Yankee invasion.[39]

Kennedy and his advisers relied on past experiences and faith in their own credibility. The CIA operations of the 1950s had remained secret. The press was part of the team. Never before had investigative journalists defected to score points by vigorously seeking and publishing information about covert operations: undoubtedly the McCarthy period, and the early cold war, had produced inhibitions that flowed from an elite consensus so marked there was no need to be overtly heavy-handed.

What changed? Soviet capture of a U-2 pilot in 1960, shot down during a spy flight over Russia, had trapped the Eisenhower administration into a public lie, admitted by Eisenhower. This probably made later intelligence exposés more acceptable (and newsmen and readers probably also learned they enjoyed such exposés).[40] Now, too, elite opinion was divided; many liberals in America supported Castro's overthrow of Batista; they were not sure America should oppose him now, especially without hard evidence that he was a Communist. Thus, this intervention was controversial, a story they would want to hear. Quite possibly a liberal president helped to make this a story; one could, in a sense, expose greater pretense.

A list of news stories that did appear (and an even longer list of those researched but withheld after White House pressure) prior to the invasion is a formidable indictment of Kennedy's odd, continuing hope. On October 30, 1960 the Guatemalan newspaper *La Hora* published a story by a well-known journalist disclosing construction of the CIA base. American newspapers did not monitor *La Hora*, but Professor Ronald Hilton, director of the Institute of Hispanic-American Studies at Stanford, learned the information while visiting Guatemala, and was told it was "common knowledge." He reported it in the scholarly *Hispanic American Review* and produced an editorial in the *Nation*, on November 19, condemning the operation and seeking to alert a larger national constituency. The editorial in the *Nation* called the planning "dangerous" and urged the reports be checked immediately by all U.S. news media with correspondents in Guatemala.[41] The planning was scarcely secret from the Soviet government: in November, *Pravda* and *Izvestia* began to run well-informed stories about the Guatemala training base and invasion preparations.[42]

The *Nation* dispatched copies of its editorial, by courier, to the *New York Times* and other major news media, and followed up with telephone calls. It produced no response, possibly because many editors were unsure this was a story they wanted the responsibility for pursuing. But a reader of both the *Nation* and the *Times* clipped the editorial and sent it, with a letter to the editor, to the *Times*, asking if such reports were true, and, if so, why was he not reading the truth in the *Times*? That seemed a good question, too, to the assistant managing editor on whose desk the letter landed — and the *Times* reporter in Mexico City was dispatched to investigate.[43]

His story ran, with a three-column headline, on the front page of the *New York Times* on January 10, 1961: "U.S. Helps Train an Anti-Castro Force at Secret Guatemalan Air-Ground Base." The *Times* included a map of the base. No one reacted, probably because Washington was between governments and there was no clear tie between the base and the new Kennedy administration.

But as the invasion drew closer, it was common knowledge, and easily learned, in the Miami Cuban community.[44] The Cubans were voluble and very enthusiastic, and American newsmen had easy access, at low cost, to news sources in Miami. A *U.S. News & World Report* newsman visited Arthur Schlesinger at the White House with the draft of an extensive, and accurate, story. The *New Republic* sent over galleys of what Schlesinger judged to be a "careful, accurate, and devastating" story. (Neither was published, because of White House influence.)[45]

The major erosion of security began by chance: Tad Szulc of the *Times* was on vacation from his assignment in Rio and stopped in Miami to visit friends.

Early for a meeting, and waiting in a bar, he spotted a man he had once met in Cuba. The man greeted him with enthusiasm, talked excitedly about the wonderful invasion and overthrow of Castro that would soon occur and which he assumed Szulc had come to Miami to report firsthand . . . and within a few days Szulc had the entire story, including an introduction to the CIA's chief contact man, "Eduardo" (E. Howard Hunt) at a party.[46]

Szulc opposed an invasion, and he thought the idea of a popular revolt sheer fantasy. He thought, and believed others shared, an uneasy feeling the United States was wrong to seek Castro's overthrow. It was a story, his superiors at the *Times* agreed, they had a duty to cover.

Szulc's story was whittled down to accommodate White House pressure. The editorial hierarchy of the *Times* eliminated specific reference to the CIA, to an invasion date, and toned down the headline when they ran it on Friday, April 7.[47] But the story did report an invasion "was near." Kennedy, livid, shouted at his aides, "I can't believe what I'm reading. . . . It's all laid out. . . ."[48]

Bissell's secrecy held so far as details were concerned. The date of D-Day, and the landing site, were not known in advance. Nor did Castro learn of the air strikes or the diversions in advance.

Why did Kennedy believe he would get away with it? The *New York Times* officially *defined* reality. Kennedy knew that several newspapers and magazines had the story. Those publications also knew, by implication, they might be set up and their professional credibility exploited by CIA cover stories. As a former journalist, Kennedy could have guessed (if he thought about it) how journalists would react to being manipulated. In a competitive business, who would parrot the official line when a competitor was likely to publish the true and more interesting story? Three factors probably led Kennedy to hope that secrecy could be retained. First, the *Times* — and other papers — had been willing, under White House pressure, to pull their punches: the CIA was not mentioned by name. Second, the invasion itself was supposed to be quiet, uncontested, at night, and in a remote area. By the time it hit the press there would only be Cubans ashore. Third, when the need to assess the situation arose, Richard Bissell was a gifted phrasemaker. He told the president the operation still had a "fig leaf." An apt and vivid metaphor — who could tell if it was right? — and it kept the policy on track.[49]

4. *American planners severely underestimated Castro's personal competence under fire.*

The key prediction of the Guatemala model was that Castro's government would disintegrate under pressure. In fairness to the CIA, we should recognize that Kennedy never gave psychological warfare its best chance. The daylight Trinidad landing, planned to be a dramatic catalyst, was abandoned when Kennedy wanted the introduction of troops via a quiet, remote night landing. Castro retained air power because Kennedy further changed the original plan. Technological tricks were never engaged in because no B-26s flew from the beaches to destroy microwave and telephone capabilities and leave radio communications vulnerable.

Still, Castro's record should have counted against the belief he would lose his nerve. With a handful of men he had launched (and won) a revolutionary challenge against Batista with an army of 40,000. On reflection, that scarcely looked to be a man who would collapse easily. Moreover, the Cuban charges to the United Nations, and in the press, specifically discussed Guatemala and it was doubtful psychological warfare would again be as effective against a leadership cadre prepared for it.[50]

American policymakers underestimated Castro partly because they saw no sane explanation for his increasingly passionate, and apparently self-destructive, anti-American course. They genuinely considered him mentally unbalanced. Schlesinger says people in Washington considered his vivid fears and fiery oratory "hysterical."[51] If so, it could be easier to produce nervous collapse than against Arbenz. Too, if Castro were mad, and messianically driven to spread revolution, there would be a clash of will and raw power sooner or later; it was prudent to act now, while he was still weak.

The CIA's intelligence branch put their judgment directly into psychological terms: Castro, they concluded, was "a psychotic personality." This judgment, made formally by the Board of National Estimates on February 21, 1961, and now declassified, is worth quoting directly.

The assessment addressed the question of why Cuba became allied with the USSR when Castro's 26th of July Movement was not originally Communist-inspired or directed. Deterioration of U.S.-Cuban relations, the report said, was "not a function of US policy and action, but of Castro's psychotic personality. It is evident, on the testimony of his supporters at the time, that Castro arrived in Havana in a high state of elation amounting to mental illness. . . . He became convinced that the US would never understand and accept his revolution, that he could expect only implacable hostility from Washington. This was the conclusion of his own disordered mind, unrelated to any fact of US policy or action."[52] The report's ultimate criteria: "no sane man undertaking to govern and reform Cuba would have chosen to pick a fight with the US."[53] After all, signing an *arms* pact with the Communist bloc? Ninety miles from *Florida*? And given the *Monroe Doctrine*? That was not a sane man.

On the surface Castro might appear psychotic: delusions of persecution (he thought capitalists, and especially the United States, were out to destroy him and his revolution), megalomania (being a revolutionary at all, the grandiosity to claim oneself as the vanguard and savior of Latin America, challenging the United States), aggressiveness (expelling or eliminating all competitors, having former Batistianos and alleged spies shot, establishing a police-state dictatorship, "picking a fight" with the United States). Certainly there *had* to be a strong, personal explanation. Betancourt of Venezuela, for example, was a liberal reformer whose contrasting style showed Castro's conduct was not culturally determined and who signed on to join the Alliance for Progress team. The apparently obvious diagnosis was that Castro was making up the whole world in which, in his "disordered mind," he was living.[54]

Unfortunately, the CIA's Board of National Estimates, which reflected and reinforced "informed" opinion, was independent of the "plans" division headed by Bissell. For security, these intelligence estimators were kept in the dark.[55] Castro better knew the reality of what others in the building were doing than they did. He knew there were plots to overthrow him or assassinate him and that the Guatemala base was a reality. Nor did he — with a network of active agents in Miami as well as Guatemala — hallucinate that the underground operations and airdropped supplies to terrorists who set fire to sugar cane fields and killed civilians with several bombs a week in 1960 were the sole work of private groups the United States simply had difficulty controlling (as the Department of State, itself misled, protested).

There probably was an added motive for believing that Castro was a mad, paranoid fanatic. American leaders could simply look at themselves and see decent, hard-working people trying to do good in the world. Many had liberal sympathies. To maintain vociferously that Americans were evil, Castro must have an overwrought and feverish imagination and be rather borderline in his grasp of reality.

Castro may have been an ambitious, driven man. But the report, reaching for sophistication, did not use the basic facts needed for prediction. Castro was a veteran guerrilla fighter who had fought against heavy odds before, not a fair-weather soldier in Guatemala reluctant to get a uniform dirty. He had courage and guts. And he knew the invasion was coming.

5. *Kennedy and most White House advisers incorrectly believed the troop landings would trigger widespread rebellion.*

The CIA provided two sorts of intelligence estimates: There were the official intelligence estimates, an example of which (from the Board of National Estimates) we have just seen. Bissell's group ran its own, independent intelligence operation. The first group of estimators knew nothing about the plan, and they made no uprising forecast. Bissell's group, with the Guatemala model, never expected a spontaneous uprising; at best, they expected it would take a week or more to establish momentum. They provided weapons with the invaders for 30,000 — but only for 30,000.[56]

Bissell's group gave the president modest numbers about what to expect: 2,500 hard-core supporters; another 20,000 would join once a movement began to build momentum; the majority of the Cuban people, they told the president, probably supported Castro; 25% of the population, they judged, would be favorably disposed to Castro's overthrow.[57] Their oral briefings were careful and professional: "Bissell said that you just couldn't tell whether this thing would ignite a real revolt. 'We have reports it will,' he said, 'but how can you possibly tell?' He was very cautious in his words. He promised nothing."[58]

After the defeat, "we were promised a mass uprising and it did not occur" became a self-serving White House line, partly a cover story to divert attention from Kennedy's disastrous D-Day cancellation by arguing that, well, it would never have worked anyway. And the CIA colluded: their radio network infiltrators were still in Cuba. To surface the *real* scenario would have put lives in jeopardy.[59]

Still, it seems certain that the White House and Joint Chiefs of Staff believed a mass uprising would be inspired to sweep the invaders to victory.[60] The specific efforts (detailed earlier) by Kennedy, Schlesinger, Goodwin, and others in the White House to create a political program to achieve mass support engaged mutual enthusiasm. In the end, they captured their own imaginations.[61]

The CIA did provide information on which their imaginations could work. There were, as we have seen, two CIA intelligence assessment tracks. The "unwitting" intelligence branch of the CIA painted an ambiguous picture, one from which people might conclude the Bissell group was too conservative. Their reports' contents were ambiguous and conflicting — but that was the nature of reality.[62]

For example, one agent on March 10, 1961, reported, "Many people in Camaguey believe that the Castro regime is tottering and that the situation can at any moment degenerate into bloody anarchy. . . . The opposition forces in the Escambray are enjoying great popularity."[63] (Castro's own mistrust clearly extended to at least 200,000 people whom he arrested after the D-2 warning.) Yet on the same day, another written assessment maintained "we see no signs that such developments portend any serious threat to a regime which by now has established a formidable structure of control."[64]

The conclusion that White House officials made up a cover story, tried to make it a reality, and then were carried along by their hopes, is strengthened by the numbers Bissell provided. Castro had 50,000 in his regular army and perhaps 200,000 militia: total, 250,000.[65] The CIA had no more than 2,500 hard-core supporters in the military. That means, Mr. President, that 99% of Cuba's military forces are not expected to support us.[66]

Or take the 25% figure. That means, Mr. President, that 75% of the Cuban people will not be favorably disposed to this liberation.

By the available evidence, then, Kennedy and his advisers made up the belief in a mass uprising because they wanted to believe it. Too, they felt Cubans would prefer the nationalistic, anti-Communist, and democratic liberal ideals they stood for to Castro's.

6. *A guerrilla escape was available if the invasion fell apart.*

Kennedy rightly understood that the Trinidad plan included a guerrilla-escape option. (He did not know the Cubans were never trained to use this guerrilla option; it was a CIA "selling point," not a seriously planned contingency.)[67] But the scramble for alternative sites after he rejected Trinidad eliminated the guerrilla option: the three roads and impenetrable swamp worked both ways and so it was impossible for 1,200 men to get out. In fact, a moment's thought would have shown a beachhead lock-in was a corollary of the site's advantages. But no one did think about it — or at least mention it.[68] If one assumes good faith, then the explanation is that Bissell, shifting from Trinidad to the Bay of Pigs, gave the president the better option he wanted by the criteria Kennedy specified publicly: A lost guerrilla escape was a minor change and so Bissell did not explicitly mention it. Possibly, if the "secure the beachhead and wait" scenario stalled, he assumed the naval task force in the area could be used. But he did not expect to fail, time was limited, and there were urgent and productive things to do rather than develop contingency plans to scuttle an operation which, if the president approved, and eliminating Castro now were a serious national objective, Kennedy would want to succeed.

The skeptical interpretation is simply that the CIA wanted the plan to go forward. The CIA never trained the men for guerrilla operations; thus, on the CIA's part, none of this talk was serious. They told the president that the Zapata swamp area had once been used by guerrillas, the truth but not "the whole truth" (the small pathways were unsuitable for more than a handful of men and Castro had helicopters that could hunt down men trying to escape). By such indirection they minimized the risk that a nervous president would bolt at the last minute.

This second interpretation now appears correct. According to the Taylor report, which I will review in the next chapter, officials had been encouraged to believe there was a viable guerrilla escape. If the president sensed, at some deeper level, that his CIA planners wanted his commitment but might not be entirely trustworthy in what they were telling him (and not telling him), his instincts were accurate. However, it is worth noting, for future reference, that Kennedy was not entirely candid with the CIA either. He placed great value on the guerrilla option, as did many of his own, non-Eisenhower appointees in the room. By not being forthright about his primary concern to be able readily to abandon their operation, the president was also stringing along the CIA, keeping up their morale: They got "the truth but not the whole truth" too.[69]

Also, there was a conflict between roles. Bissell was assigned to develop, present, and defend the plan. He made the best case, subject to the public instructions of the president. In such a situation, the president needed skeptical experts he did not provide for himself.

Even if the president had the staff to ask the questions that needed to be asked, the task would have been difficult. Almost nothing was in writing (for security reasons). There were no briefing books to read and ponder, no systematic checklists comparing invasion sites by all the criteria developed over earlier meetings.

Officials the president might have relied upon, the Joint Chiefs of Staff, failed him. They did not know what he expected of them. They had proposed in writing, in January, that they be included in development of the military plans. The memorandum was apparently lost during the change of administrations; they were excluded.[70] Now, asked to comment, their review was limited to the logistics and training and to agreement that the initial landing would likely be successful. They did warn that secrecy was almost impossible and estimated the probability Castro knew an invasion was coming to be at least 85 percent.[71] Kennedy did not specifically order them to review guerrilla or other escape options, and they did not do it. (The written account of the CIA plan they received at the last minute did not contain plans for a — nonexistent — guerrilla option.) As the invasion did fall apart, Kennedy's military adviser, General Lemnitzer (chairman of the Joint Chiefs), among others, still believed the men could escape "into the hills."[71a]

The gap between the images used by decision makers and the geography of the landing site illustrates a common source of difficulty in government policy, the tendency of bright men, new to a problem, to deal in "big think" abstractions, confidently, without their thought being grounded in a detailed appreciation of the situations in which plans will be implemented. The president "really didn't have a very good visual picture of the whole thing."[72] Kennedy probably relied on Bissell and Dulles to be responsible for details, and the Joint Chiefs to review the plan with more time and professional expertise than he could bring to second-guess them. Kennedy's ambivalence and growing inner doubts about the operation also probably kept him from internalizing all the details: he kept himself at a psychological distance. To his planners, the dictum of "no American involvement" was more personal than a public relations criterion: it was a metaphor of his own reservations.

7. *Adlai Stevenson believed (and gave an overly vigorous defense for) the cover story he delivered.*

> *Yes, Mr. Ambassador, yes, I'm sorry, but it's true. There is nothing more we can do. I'm afraid we've lost . . . No, we have nothing else to throw into it . . . Well, I'm sorry you're distressed. We all are . . . Yes, I'm sorry too that you weren't better informed . . . Well, good evening, Governor.*
> — Richard Bissell to
> Adlai Stevenson[73]

Stevenson's unrealistic belief is easily explained. They lied to him, and he did not expect he would be treated that way. Stevenson was misled, or explicitly lied to, three times. In early spring he suspected something was afoot; he came to Washington in March to express his alarm to Kennedy. Kennedy was evasive but assured him that whatever was being planned there would be no question of American involvement.

On Saturday, April 8, Kennedy sent two briefers (Tracy Barnes from the CIA and Arthur Schlesinger, Jr., from the White House) to New York to tell

Stevenson what would happen. Barnes did the briefing because Schlesinger missed his shuttle flight from National Airport and arrived an hour late. That he did so determined the character of what was said — and not said.

Barnes talked vaguely, in generalities: something would happen, it would "appear to be coming from the inside" of Cuba, there would be no American involvement, no one would leave from American soil. Essentially, Barnes gave a "broad brush" cover story. When pressed, Barnes lied and assured Stevenson there would be "nothing happening" while the General Assembly was in session.[74]

Kennedy thought he had ordered more than this. His order in the Cabinet Room was to brief Stevenson "fully." Adlai's credibility was a national asset and nothing he should say in New York should be "less than the truth," even if "it could not be the whole truth."[75]

That sounded good when Kennedy said it. But Barnes had to implement what were, in fact, contradictory orders. How could Stevenson provide a credible cover story without lying? Barnes had the privilege of working for a boss who wanted it both ways — and in Barnes's understanding, Barnes had to give it to him.

So Tracy Barnes mumbled. He gave the "broad brush," he talked around the point. Barnes gave Stevenson the model of what he *could* say sincerely and be credible: keep it a big picture, give general impressions, dance around. Just say there is no American involvement.

Why did Barnes lie to Stevenson about the invasion date? The likely reason is that Stevenson did not have a "need to know." (In national security parlance, this phrase meant Stevenson could perform his assigned role whether or not he knew the information.) Barnes may have made a mistake on the spur of the moment. He *might* have said, "Adlai, the president has not decided . . ." but that would imply it *might* occur within a week. And that was critical information no prudent CIA official would reveal, certainly not in a United Nations embassy in New York, to an outsider and known critic, without specific order. Barnes may have lied, too, because he knew Stevenson opposed the operation and, being politically sophisticated, recognized Stevenson had not asked an idle question. If Barnes had said yes, it *would* happen while the General Assembly was meeting, then Stevenson would have officially found his open door to ask for detail, and to fly to Washington and argue against the operation, especially when he learned it was far more offensive than the plan Barnes had described. By saying No, denying anything would happen during the United Nations session, Barnes kept Stevenson neutralized unless the president wanted him actively involved and invited him to Washington, as the president would have done if he seriously wanted Stevenson to be involved.[76] Stevenson's later anger came partly from specific lies in this briefing. But an implicit (and surely demeaning) message about his true place in foreign policy decisions would not have escaped Stevenson's notice:

he was an outsider, kept at arm's length in New York, and his "presidential" briefing gave him less truth than he would just have read in Szulc's article in the *Times*.[77]

The "need to know" bureaucratic code in national security affairs also led to the third incident of lying. When Stevenson called Washington to check the defector story, the State Department called the CIA—and the CIA lied to the assistant secretary of state who placed the call. In the CIA's view an assistant secretary of state had no right ("need") to know his part was a cover-up. A cover story was *better* if believed by its defenders: why uncautiously open the door to complication or entrust national security only to their acting ability? If the assistant secretary or Stevenson should have known, they would have been briefed by their bureaucratic superior (Rusk) who did know.

That last assumption, however, was inaccurate. Rusk was new, at least to this post in this administration. He had no expectation the CIA would lie to senior presidential appointees in his department. When the CIA said this defector was genuine, Rusk also believed it. (He thought *this* defector was genuine—he expected another defector might be the fake.)

The lie also was transmitted because Dean Rusk, in addition to being fooled, was in error about how the United Nations angle was to be handled. Ordinarily, the secretary of state would handle the U.N. issues. But the clear message to Rusk was that Stevenson was briefed and handled through special channels. Adlai Stevenson had been twice the Democratic Party's presidential nominee. Since Kennedy had said publicly that Stevenson was to have "cabinet rank" in this administration, it seemed this earlier promise was being activated and Adlai was not Rusk's subordinate in the operation. Kennedy, bypassing Rusk, had arranged that Stevenson be briefed through the CIA (Tracy Barnes) and his own White House staff (Arthur Schlesinger). There was no White House coordination, and everyone inferred someone else was taking care of it.[78]

8. *The Cubans, the CIA, and Kennedy's own advisers believed he would use American troops rather than accept failure.*

President Kennedy's guidance was firm and consistent: there would be *no* direct American military involvement in this Cuban operation. To be certain the Cubans understood it, he sent three personal emissaries, Arthur Schlesinger, Jr., A. A. Berle, and Harvard Professor John Plank, to New York to see Dr. Miro Cardona. Returning to Washington, Schlesinger told Kennedy he thought Miro was shaken by their message and did not believe it. Kennedy called Bissell immediately to say that Miro must understand—and agree—or the invasion was off. Bissell sent Tracy Barnes to New York the same day. Barnes returned to report he had "formal assent" from Miro—but Barnes added that he doubted Miro believed the prohibition.[79]

Taking considerable pains to be certain his message was received, the president acted with integrity to assure that the Cubans acted voluntarily and with-

out false hopes. In retrospect, integrity served him well: when the invasion
did fail he was able to retain the public support of the leaders, despite private
bitterness. But Kennedy was doing more. He wanted the Cubans to pass a
test: did they *really* want to do this (and accept the risks) on their own, for
their own ideals?[80]

But the test did not work. No one believed Kennedy. The CIA and Kennedy's own advisers did not think he meant it. Miro did not believe him. The
Cuban troops did not believe it.

The commonly accepted reason is that these men were too sophisticated.
They relied upon past experience: Presidents and other politicians often speak
for effect; later, as circumstances change, their pragmatic actions may differ from their earlier, verbal positions. They thought Kennedy talked tough
so the invasion planners and the Cubans would get their acts together and
accomplish the mission alone. But if American power and prestige were once
committed, and American planes or troops were *really* needed to complete
the job, then, they believed, he would act differently.

Of course this theory was also untestable. If you *asked* the president
whether he had just told you the truth or was trying to manipulate you, he
would have become angry and repeated himself. He would do that whether
it was *really* the truth or something he merely wanted you to believe.

But senior CIA officials did not merely imagine, without plausible corroborating evidence, that Kennedy might use American forces. He accepted the
U.S. naval escort task force they proposed: a task force which included seven
destroyers, an aircraft carrier with jets, and an augmented marine assault bat-
talion. In addition to this official task force, Kennedy was also aware another
carrier, the USS *Boxer*, was stationed nearby: it was newly equipped to use
"vertical envelopment" helicopter tactics. Not a great deal was made of the
formidable size of the task force at the time, but men of the sophistication
of Bissell and Dulles knew they provided the president with future options
should he wish to use them. It was a reasonable assumption that Kennedy
would have kept all American ships away from the island if he did not want
those resources nearby.

Again, however, the theory was untestable. Sophisticated men, who understood the difference between current verbal statements and future policy con-
tingencies, would recognize, almost subliminally, what was happening. It
would be poorly serving the president to ask, directly and publicly, whether
he wanted contingency resources. But for the president to say nothing allowed
the interpretation that he had a deeper, ultimate commitment to success, that
there were some scenarios where he might not rule out a later use for this
American force. In reading and honoring the subtleties of what men of sophistication leave unsaid, Dulles and Bissell apparently misread Kennedy's simple, and persistent, lack of attention to details and his desire not to be "drawn
in." Ostensibly, the ships were "escort," and Kennedy only said they should
stay in international waters.[81]

It is also true that the American "noninvolvement" formulation could easily appear, to the CIA, not a true limit. It was a public relations guideline. The money, the guns, the planes, the training, the ideas — everything was American except the men who would do the fighting. The plan called for formal recognition of the liberation government seventy-two hours after the beach-head was established and they were flown in. After *that* the plan anticipated open involvement: They would drop the fig leaf and logistical and other support could pour in.[82]

The message did not reach the Cuban soldiers in Guatemala for quite a different reason. CIA operatives lied, and they sent to Kennedy an ambiguous report at the last minute which falsely confirmed his belief that his conditions were understood and accepted.

The CIA men in Guatemala were caught in a bind by conflicting orders. They knew that to inform the Cubans of possible abandonment would destroy morale: the canopy of American power emboldened them. There have been later disputes about what the Cuban soldiers were told. It *may* be that no one ever *explicitly* lied to them. But it is well documented that the CIA produced atmospherics that were not the whole truth, a plethora of locker-room pep talk they knew people who were trusting, young, and innocent about the ways of the world would readily take as concrete commitments. "We're behind you all the way," was a typical assurance; "There will be a carrier offshore with blond-haired, blue-eyed Cuban pilots who don't speak Spanish . . . ;" "You're not alone. Others will be involved, too." "Pepe, when you hit the beaches, just keep walking, turn left, and you'll be in Havana," was said by an American commander to Pepe San Roman, and coming from an American he admired, he thought it meant America would be there to make it happen. In fact, most of the soldiers were under the impression they were part of a much larger invasion force, and many thought American troops would be fighting at other locations. But (security, of course) they did not ask to know details. It is absolutely clear that no one told the unvarnished truth: "If you get into trouble on the beaches, you're on your own. We're washing our hands of you."[83]

There may have been another motive for the bravura assurances; they would have been a sophisticated counterintelligence strategy. So experienced an intelligence operative as Allen Dulles would likely assume Castro's agents would effect at least low-level penetration of such a large operation, widely known in Miami and Guatemala. As ultimate success depended on Castro's erroneous belief the invasion was not a Guatemala-sized token but many times larger than 1,200–1,400 men, and that the United States was involved and committed to its success, it is reasonable to conjecture that some of this talk was intentional.

But Kennedy understood his message had gotten through to the Cubans. Especially he was misled by the enthusiastic report of Col. Jack Hawkins, the CIA's ex-marine military commander, who traveled to Guatemala for a last-minute inspection. Hawkins cabled that military readiness was high and the Brigade officers "enthusiastic . . . intelligent and motivated with a fanatical urge to begin battle. . . . The brigade officers do not expect help from the US armed forces."[84]

Robert Kennedy later said this cable from Hawkins, more than any other factor, finally persuaded the president to go ahead.[85] Bureaucratically astute, well-timed, and well-phrased, it appeared to say exactly what this president wanted to hear: the picture of men with a "fanatical urge to begin," without any American military help, confirmed the United States to be truly in the support role he desired. (And it confirmed to Kennedy that he had acted with integrity, could pull out, and the operation "go guerrilla" without any breach of promise. He was covered.) Yet Hawkins was *not* confirming what Kennedy thought he said. Kennedy's stipulation was absolute: no aid, even if this caused the operation to fail. Hawkins meant there was no expectation of American military involvement if things went according to plan.

In a sense, Kennedy abandoned the Cubans in good faith. But the consequences, the bitterness of betrayal and disillusion, have been paid for over twenty years by most of the Cubans who served and survived.[86] The orchestrated misunderstandings were consequential: had the Cubans decided to go ahead, and believed Kennedy's limits, they would have been less passive and would have worried about, and independently reviewed, their contingency plans. Kennedy might then have effected a timely naval rescue to prevent the costly appearance of dramatic defeat and long months of negotiations to ransom the prisoners. After the Joint Chiefs signed off on the CIA plan, Marine Commandant David Shoup lay awake at night worrying about the welfare of 1,200 men put ashore to face 20,000 with no escape route. Kennedy might have worried, too, if he realized how much they depended on him. Over the two and a half years he still had to live, his conscience might have been clearer.

9. *Kennedy and his advisers did not adequately consider what would happen after the beachhead was secure.*

The Bay of Pigs was not a mad scheme. It was bold, perhaps unlikely. But it had a rationale and was based on an established track record. If the president desired — and vital American national interest required — a low-cost way to overthrow Castro now, without having to use large numbers of American troops in hard-fought battles at a later time, the CIA's invasion plan, coupled with its assassination plan, was — in main outline — probably the best that could have been intelligently devised. Could it have worked?

The answer, I think, is that it could not have worked the way Kennedy hoped. There was not a realistic chance of secrecy for the American sponsorship. Not ninety miles from Florida, with the hottest news story of the year about to break and a public controversy to spur the competitive instincts of reporters. Szulc had been luckier, the *New York Times* bolder than other papers. But *New Republic, U.S. News & World Report*, and the Miami newspapers, among others, already knew the basic facts and were persuaded to delay publishing only by conditional arguments of the need to preserve secrecy before the invasion was launched. And there were enough knowledgeable people whose convictions were opposed to the operation and whose standing with personal constituencies was at stake—Bowles, Stevenson, Fulbright, Reston—to be sure the story got out and the president felt their outrage at the abuse he had done to their ideals for America.

The meetings with the president were filled with the pragmatic, easier, less contentious, and activist questions, "Could it work?" "How do we make it work?" Few people asked Senator Fulbright's question, "*Should* it be done?" Part of the answer to this question of "should" involves personal values and different conceptions of Latin American political development and international relations. But part of the answer to "should" rests on an appraisal of the probable scenarios to be encountered, not merely the desire that the operation succeed and Castro disappear.

The CIA's predicted scenario, Cuba equals Guatemala, was unlikely. Had there been one massive and fully successful air strike (no prior warning to trigger police roundups), and the B-26s been moved to the beachhead strip, the beaches probably could have been held indefinitely, given American logistical support and continuing shelling and bombing along the built-up causeways of the three access roads. It might have stuck there. What would Kennedy have done then, without a guerrilla escape?

Since Castro expected the Guatemala model, and assuming assassination plans failed, it is unlikely he would have surrendered. At best, even if others tried for a negotiated settlement to stop the B-26 bombing raids, he would likely have moved to the mountains to continue the type of guerrilla warfare he had practiced against Batista. (There is indirect evidence he had such contingency plans.)[87] Even if 10% of his military and armed militia were loyal, he would have 25,000 men with him, and aid from a significant portion of that 75% of the population the CIA thought would not support their "liberation," and at least some of whom deeply resented America's past interventions.[88] It could have been Vietnam five years early.

There would not have been a quick or antiseptic victory. Kennedy's expected mass uprising could have produced civil war. Castro would have been fighting for survival, as would his military commanders and local political leaders, who could not have expected to retain power. Castro had a militia of about 200,000, well armed:[89] unlike Arbenz, Castro had already widely distributed arms to the populace, and both the CIA and Joint Chiefs knew it. Hundreds or thousands of deaths, mounting day by day, were not implausible. By the CIA's best scenario it would have gone for a week, probably several weeks. And journalists could have hired boats from Florida to cover the war and shown the increasing carnage to the world, and to Americans, on dinner-hour television. Yet Kennedy did not stop to imagine—or apparently ask for estimates — during all of the sophisticated discussions, how many thousands might die, on both sides, if he said Yes.

But, deferring any plan for an end game to see, first, what developed, he likely would have faced serious consequences, the details of which he had not begun to imagine. His liberal constituents would surely have turned querulous. Even if he had won, the price of success would have been a specter of blood haunting his administration for the rest of its days.

In retrospect, then, one might say: Kennedy did not make a mistake after all. It turned out for the *best*. He could not have cancelled, he was trapped by the disposal problem. It would have been disastrous to press forward militarily from the beachhead. The best solution was the simple guerrilla "disappearance" of the Cubans Kennedy counted on. Without it, scuttling the operation on the beaches was the best thing he could have done.

Perhaps a revisionist historian, with new evidence, will someday argue that Kennedy shrewdly planned it this way. I think not, although he likely expected, when he said "go ahead," to use his guerrilla escape quickly and write off the operation unless a dramatic public uprising quickly followed. The best evidence against manipulative scheming is that Kennedy, had he thought through his options, probably could have gotten out, albeit with a short-term cost, more easily than it seemed.

The key was the Cuban politicians. Eisenhower's endorsement had always depended on the CIA's production of a credible government. "Boys," he said to Dulles and Bissell, "if you don't intend to go through with this, let's stop talking about it."[90] But until mid-March there was no liberation government. The exiled soldiers were mistrustful and suspicious of the politicians (the soldiers were there for ideals, and the usual variety of other motives that take people to war, but not from loyalty to the politicians who would return to power). Kennedy might have cancelled the operation and, if necessary, blamed the failure of the Cuban politicians to unite while an operation might still be conducted. He might have ordered background briefings to convey the message that the operation could not have succeeded without Hungarian-style carnage. That overt American invasion to change the balance of power precipitously in isolated Cuba could produce the danger of a tit-for-tat Soviet response in the growing Berlin crisis was a consideration responsible leaders of foreign policy opinion — in these years, a European-oriented New York network — would likely have accepted.

It would not have been an elegant solution. But if Kennedy wanted out, it had the sustaining virtue of being based on the truth. Yet the enduring reality, amidst all the questions that were not asked and his own ambivalences, was that Kennedy did not want to get out: he wanted to succeed, if possible at acceptable risk and certainly to try if the political cost of a failure could be minimal.

NOTES

1. I will not discuss separately the failure to estimate the domestic and international costs of failure because it was derivative: this mistake (6), plus the secrecy assumption (3), forestalled analysis of such costs. See the later discussion of political costs and the quality of decision making in chapter 6.
2. H. Morgenthau, "To Intervene or Not to Intervene" *Foreign Affairs* 45 (April 1967): 425–436, p. 431.
3. A. Schlesinger, *A Thousand Days: John F. Kennedy in the White House* (Boston: Houghton Mifflin, 1965) reviews Cuban issues, passim.
4. P. Wyden, *Bay of Pigs: The Untold Story* (New York: Simon and Schuster, 1979), pp. 31–32; E. Hunt, *Give Us This Day* (New Rochelle, NY: Arlington House, 1973) provides a personal account.
5. Wyden, *Bay of Pigs*, p. 114.
6. "Noble" is a pseudonym.
7. Wyden, *Bay of Pigs*, p. 116.
8. Schlesinger, *A Thousand Days*, p. 245.
9. Wyden, *Bay of Pigs*, p. 118.
10. Ibid., pp. 207–208.
11. Hunt, *Give Us This Day*, p. 81. An assessment which also concludes that the Cuban politicians were further to the right than White House propaganda chose to describe is R. Stebbins, *The U.S. in World Affairs, 1961* (New York: Council on Foreign Relations, 1962), p. 312: "Comparatively conservative elements that reflected the interests of the Cuban propertied classes and wanted to undo most of the Castro economic and social program would seem to have been favored. . . . "
12. L. Mosley, *Dulles: A Biography of Eleanor, Allen, and John Foster Dulles and Their Family Network* (New York: Dial, 1978), p. 467; Wyden, *Bay of Pigs*, p. 116.
13. Schlesinger euphemistically calls this an "arrest." CIA agents have no "arrest" powers. Schlesinger, *A Thousand Days*, p. 236.
14. Wyden, *Bay of Pigs*, p. 115.
15. Schlesinger, *A Thousand Days*, p. 245.
16. Ibid., pp. 229–231, 243–244.
17. State Department pressure also eliminated plans for massive leaflet drops to distribute pro-liberation propaganda over Cuba. Their opposition was on the same grounds, reducing "noise level."
18. Wyden, *Bay of Pigs*, chapter 4. Note that these calculations interacted primarily with the self-image decision makers wished to maintain and their estimates of how the press might "play" the story. Castro and the Soviet Union already knew America was behind the operation.
19. Wyden, *Bay of Pigs*, p. 170. Note that $N = 16$ was the entire force. This suggests Dulles and Bissell only respected the State Department's concern for a "low visibility" first strike rhetorically and, as the controlled operational details, privately decided to make no change to the original plan. Bissell's actual plan was to hit Castro's air force twice, with everything he had, rather than once. Wyden, *Bay of Pigs*, overlooks this deception.
20. Kennedy had also sent word, indirectly, that he planned to make Bissell CIA director after Dulles's retirement. The implication was that if Bissell made good on the Bay of Pigs, there would be a reward for serving the president well.
21. Wyden, *Bay of Pigs*, pp. 193–194.
22. Ibid., pp. 194–195.

23. K. Meyer and T. Szulc, *The Cuban Invasion: The Chronicle of a Disaster* (New York: Praeger, 1962), p. 124, describe Kennedy as "shaken" by the force of Stevenson's anger. Stevenson was a proud man, and his standing among Democratic Party liberals would have given added weight to his reaction if he had resigned over the abuse of his credibility. Later, during the Cuban missile crisis, Stevenson was to be "set up" for the public by White House leaks scornful of his "soft" line. The virulence against Stevenson may have reflected strong feelings about his earlier last-minute influence on a decision many thought gutted the Bay of Pigs operation.

24. Wyden, *Bay of Pigs*, p. 197.

25. Ibid., p. 199.

26. Ibid., pp. 196–197, correctly reports CIA subordinates blamed Cabell for initiating a phone call to double-check his final authorization, thereby allowing discussion and a last-minute cancellation decision. (They observed only that he entered his office after stating this intention.) In fact, Cabell received the call from Bundy at that time, the result of earlier consultations among Rusk, Kennedy, and Bundy that were probably triggered by Stevenson's cable. The fury directed at Cabell later that night apparently stemmed in part from the belief he had caused the cancellation when he should have kept his mouth shut.

27. Ibid., pp. 199–200.

28. Ibid., p. 200.

29. Likely the CIA's own operatives were the radio specialists who would use Guatemala-style tricks against Castro's military communications. There was no plan to alert the Cuban underground of the invasion; past experience showed it was penetrated and unable to keep secrets.

30. Wyden, *Bay of Pigs*, pp. 205–206.

31. Presumably to dramatize the point.

32. J. DeRivera, *The Psychological Dimension of Foreign Policy* (Chicago, IL: Charles E. Merrill, 1968).

33. See also the discussion of liberal activism and larger-than-life drama in L. Etheredge, "Strong Imaginative Systems: The Liberal Activist Case" (Photocopy, 1983).

34. Wyden, *Bay of Pigs*, p. 190.

35. It is unlikely McNamara would have acted aggressively so early in a new administration when his department was not a "principal" in the operation and he had been cut out of the decision.

36. Wyden, *Bay of Pigs*, pp. 199–200.

37. Ibid., pp. 204–206.

38. Ibid.

39. One of the puzzles is this assessment of Soviet conduct. Were they so easily fooled or manipulated? American policymakers, for example, had no inhibition against forceful challenges to Latin American governments (Guatemala, Cuba) even without the provocation of Soviet military action. Nor did the Czech coup in 1948, or the crushing of Hungarian resistance in 1956 in the name of the Soviet's "liberation" puppet government, deter American policymakers. The Soviets might only play tit for tat (no "overt" invasion of Berlin if there was no "overt" American invasion of Cuba) but there would surely be effects. What Kennedy imagined these would be is unclear.

40. So far as Castro's information was concerned, the president need not have been concerned about leaks. Castro was well informed about American preparations, as indeed he had every incentive to be. Miami was an open community, and his agents there kept him abreast of the recruitment drive. He knew of the Guate-

mala base, and protest against American-planned invasion was the reason Dr. Roa, the Cuban Foreign Minister, was in New York at the United Nations. Assuming high CIA officials were correct in their assessment of a high-level KGB "mole" in the agency during these years, Castro may also have learned details through this route. The "hunt for the mole," and the chains of logical inference by which his presence was deduced, make a fascinating story, not least because it shows how increasing levels of sophistication by actors and analysts can make reality indeterminant and produce paralysis. The issue is a digression here; the CIA specialist at the *Newsweek* Washington bureau has produced a well-informed account. See Martin, *Wilderness of Mirrors*.

41. W. Hinckle and W. Turner, *The Fish is Red: The Story of the Secret War Against Castro* (New York: Harper & Row, 1981) review the conduct of the press. The *Nation* mailed (and hand delivered) many copies of its original story before the *New York Times*, via the route described by Wyden, picked up the story. See also R. Hilton, "Commentary: The Press and the Bay of Pigs" *World Affairs Report* 12 (1982): 151–152.

42. H. Dinerstein, *The Making of a Missile Crisis: October, 1962* (Baltimore, MD: Johns Hopkins Univ. Press, 1976), p. 114.

43. See Hinckle and Turner, *The Fish is Red*, p. 68. The *New York Times* reporter had earlier visited Guatemala but only filed a routine denial provided by its president. He was now instructed explicitly to "get out into the field" to check the story, a slap on the wrist from the head office which produced the map he included with his story.

44. There is a partial defense for other papers; expatriate communities are well known to be alive with rumors of plots and plans to return.

45. Wyden, *Bay of Pigs*, pp. 142–146.

46. Ibid., p. 143.

47. Wyden, *Bay of Pigs*, pp. 153–155; Hinckle and Turner, *The Fish is Red*.

48. Wyden, *Bay of Pigs*, p. 155.

49. Ibid., p. 142.

50. See, for example, R. Roa, "Charges Delivered Against the United States Before the U.N. Security Council" *New York Times* (January 5, 1961), p. 5.

51. Schlesinger, *A Thousand Days*, p. 293.

52. U.S. Central Intelligence Agency. Board of National Estimates. Sherman Kent, Chairman. "Memorandum for the Director: Why the Cuban Revolution of 1958 Led to Cuba's Alignment with the USSR" (February 21, 1961) (Photocopy).

53. Ibid.

54. This theory of Castro's emotional imbalance is where the idea to "push him over the edge," via chemicals to make his beard fall out mysteriously, originated.

It would have been a heroic act of political "sophistication" for Castro to understand this as an expression of how deeply the United States cared about, and wanted, good relations with him, one way or another. At a high enough level, of course, that is what it was: a desire, with a vengeance, for good relations.

55. This also, as a general principle, may serve to keep intelligence estimation more independent.

56. Recall, however, that the plan was never to attempt a military victory.

57. M. Taylor, *Operation ZAPATA: The Ultra-Sensitive Report and Testimony of the Board of Inquiry on the Bay of Pigs*. (Introduction by L. Aguilar.) (Frederick, MD: Aletheia Books, 1981). Prepared from the sanitized and declassified original report of 1961. See p. 20. U.S. Senate, Committee on Foreign Relations, *Executive Sessions: Historical Series* 13(1) (Washington, DC: Government Printing Office,

1984). The hearings were originally held in 1961.

58. L. Mosley, *Dulles*, p. 469, quoting William Bundy.

59. Note that the Schlesinger and Sorensen accounts omit the Guatemala strategy and thus make the operation appear less intelligent than it was.

60. JCS documents made a routine distinction between initial success (the beachhead) and ultimate success (political). See U.S. Department of Defense. Joint Chiefs of Staff. Memoranda for the Secretary of Defense: JCSM 57-61, JCSM-146-61, JCSM-166-61. (Photocopies)

61. Their belief that such rhetoric had been crucial in the presidential election likely encouraged this enthusiasm.

62. This is important to emphasize. There were about 5,000 active guerrillas and a badly performing economy. No one could be sure what might develop: Wyden, *Bay of Pigs* excoriates the CIA for "waffling" and, I believe, misses the point that a decided judgment probably was impossible. "How," as Richard Bissell asked, "could you possibly tell?"

63. Wyden, *Bay of Pigs*, p. 99.

64. Ibid.

65. The question, however, was primarily of *will*: whether these forces would surrender readily, especially if the United States was perceived to be the sponsor of the invasion.

66. If one takes the highest number mentioned, about 25,000 active supporters, and even if one assumed them all to be within the military forces, 90% of the military would not be active supporters.

67. Such training ended in November; although it is not clear how crucial specific guerrilla training might have been, there would be major tactical and logistical implications requiring pre-planning to effect an escape. Intense tactical air support, for example, might have opened the eastern road, and additional vehicles would have made escape to the mountains possible quickly.

68. Reportedly there were small footpaths, but the men were not equipped with maps and the route was unusable by large numbers of men, especially if they were hunted by the 20,000 Castro troops the CIA also estimated would be deployed along the three roads.

69. In sexual imagery: if he could cut his losses and abandon the operation at any time via a guerrilla escape, Kennedy had the CIA "by the balls," and the CIA may not have liked that idea.

70. Taylor, *Operation ZAPATA*, p. 8.

71. Ibid., p. 10.

72. Wyden, *Bay of Pigs*, p. 271.

73. Telephone conversation reported in J. Smith, *Portrait of a Cold Warrior: Second Thoughts of a Top CIA Agent* (New York: Ballantine, 1981), p. 340.

74. Wyden, *Bay of Pigs*, pp. 155–158 details the Stevenson briefing story.

75. Wyden, *Bay of Pigs*, p. 156.

76. Likely this was a crucial signal to Barnes that Stevenson was to be briefed as a bit player, not as a decision maker.

77. Also, he had genuine reason to be concerned, as the General Assembly was scheduled to debate Cuban charges on what turned out to be D-Day. The *New York Times* stories were making it increasingly difficult for him to mount a credible defense in the forthcoming debate.

78. It may also have seemed impolitic to Rusk to assert his formal authority to supplant the White House channel he knew the president had ordered.

79. He said so in the Cabinet Room, many times. After the major meeting on April

4 he met privately with Rusk, Dulles, and McNamara to stress this ruling; it was likely from this meeting that the detailed rules of engagement issued to the naval task force also originated. After Miro's "formal" assent, the matter apparently rested there, with nothing further done. Wyden, *Bay of Pigs*, pp. 166–168; Schlesinger, *A Thousand Days*, p. 265.

80. Kennedy may also have been probing to see if he could scuttle the mission by making such a hard line demand.

81. They also provided the communication to Washington.

82. To the CIA, if noninvolvement were *too* convincing, the invasion was lost: If Kennedy grasped the logic of their plan, he had to recognize that 1,200 men could never defeat 250,000 unless, along with the other aspects of the psychological warfare, Castro and the Cubans believed absolutely that the United States was sponsoring this and would not let it fail.

83. These conversations are discussed in H. Johnson, *The Bay of Pigs: The Leaders' Story of Brigade 1506* (New York: Norton, 1964), p. 68, et passim, and by Wyden, *Bay of Pigs*, pp. 190–193 et passim. Later, the American in charge of training was also asked by the Taylor Commission why the men had received no further training in guerrilla warfare, since this was the fallback contingency. He felt the men would have mutinied as they believed a frontal assault was essential.

84. One suspects Dulles's "tradecraft" in the timely arrival of a cable that could be distributed to the White House. Hawkins was scheduled to fly back to Washington and would normally have dictated a report there. See Wyden, *Bay of Pigs*, p. 169.

85. Ibid.

86. The Cubans have also been further used, rather cynically, for mere harassments never seriously designed for the liberation they were willing to risk their lives to achieve.

87. Wyden, *Bay of Pigs*, pp. 103–108, 179.

88. American policymakers seemed obsessed by the belief that such past experiences made no difference and America would be welcomed as a benefactor. When American policymakers speak of "foreign" interference in Latin America they mean "not United States'."

89. In Guatemala the military was centralized and arms not widely distributed among the populace.

90. Quoted in Wyden, *Bay of Pigs*, p. 31.

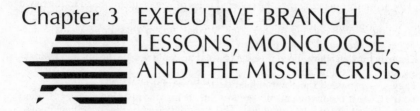

Chapter 3 EXECUTIVE BRANCH LESSONS, MONGOOSE, AND THE MISSILE CRISIS

To learn from failure, President Kennedy asked Maxwell Taylor (a retired general) to conduct a top-secret inquiry. The President appointed his brother, Robert Kennedy (the attorney general) to serve on the commission together with Allen Dulles and Admiral Arleigh Burke.[1] In this chapter I define a conception of government learning and, in this light, analyze the commission's findings. I then describe the pressures in Laos and Berlin the president faced in these months, and contrast his decision to begin Operation MONGOOSE with his decisions during the October 1962 Cuban Missile Crisis.

DEFINING GOVERNMENT LEARNING

I will define government learning as changes in *intelligence* and *effectiveness*. I will be concerned primarily with identifying individual learning by the president and senior policy officers.

To assess the growth of intelligence, I will use three criteria: (1) growth of *realism*, recognizing the different elements and processes actually operating in the world; (2) growth of *intellectual integration* in which these different elements and processes are integrated with one another in thought; (3) growth of reflective *perspective* about the conduct of the first two processes, the conception of the problem, and the results which the decision maker desires to achieve.[2]

An example of this conception of the growth of intelligence is the evolution of thinking about the physical universe. By an early view, the physical universe was composed of only four elements (earth, air, fire, and water); this has been replaced by the modern periodic table recognizing over 100 different elements, arrayed according to shared properties. The development of the intelligence embodied in this achievement was aided by the self-reflective creation and use of the scientific method.[3]

Effectiveness can be measured by the achievement of different values. In this book I will take the decision makers' own professed values as criteria.

Thus, this chapter poses two general questions: Following the Bay of Pigs, did the president and the executive branch become more intelligent? As a result, did they become more effective? As a first step, I will review the Taylor

Commission's report: originally classified "Top Secret," "Ultra-Sensitive," and "Eyes Only," it was substantially declassified several years ago and has been published, together with extensive minutes of evidence.[4]

EXECUTIVE BRANCH LEARNING
The Taylor Commission Report

There is a time when you can't advise by innuendoes and suggestions. You have to look him in the eye and say, "I think it's a lousy idea Mr. President." And nobody said that.

— General Maxwell Taylor[5]

The Taylor Commission was asked to diagnose the causes of failure and draw lessons for future paramilitary operations. It interrogated fifty-four witnesses and drew the following conclusions:

1. The operation had grown too large to sustain the disclaimer of American involvement. By November 1960, "this should have been recognized and the operation formally reviewed by the Eisenhower Administration."[6] If the decision was made to continue, the amphibious operation should have been transferred to the Department of Defense.
2. Efforts to retain plausible denial for American involvement should have been introduced or maintained "only if they did not impair the chance of [military] success."[7]
3. Kennedy's advisers did not always present their case "with sufficient force and clarity to the senior officials of the government" so the latter would "appreciate the consequences of some of their decisions. This remark applies in particular to the circumstances surrounding the cancellation of the D-Day strikes."[8]
4. Military capabilities were too marginal to sustain the operation in the face of its operational problems.[9]
5. The effectiveness of Castro's military was underestimated, and the short life of the beachhead was insufficient to trigger a popular response. Popular reaction was also made impossible by Castro's effective use of his police, which was underestimated.[10]
6. The president and other senior officials were told on many occasions "that the Zapata area was guerrilla territory, and that the entire force, in an emergency, could operate as guerrillas." "Greatly influenced" by their belief that this alternative was available, they believed "a sudden or disastrous defeat was most improbable."[11]
7. Communication problems created time delays too great for the operation to be run adequately from Washington; especially on the night of D + 1 a better understanding of the ammunition shortages would have strengthened the case for U.S. air cover and better ammunition resupply plans.[12]
8. The Joint Chiefs of Staff gave the impression of approving the plan, but

in their own view they had only acquiesced to it. Absence of written documents inhibited their review and left them with major differences in their perception of the plan.[13]

9. Intelligence failures did not contribute significantly to the defeat. Formal CIA estimates of 2,500 committed supporters in the military, 20,000 active supporters in the population, and a favorable attitude by 25% of the Cuban people appeared reliable and responsibly made.[14]

10. A formal decision process should replace the ad hoc and poorly coordinated Bay of Pigs process.[15]

The commission then declared America to be in a life-or-death struggle, to need more capability for paramilitary operations (perhaps, again, against Castro) and recommended:

11. Reorganization of the executive branch, and possibly a declaration of national emergency, to make the fight against Communism a major national priority.

12. A new official under the president be designated to give full time and attention to these operations and be delegated broad operational authority to conduct them subject to overall approval and guidance by the president.[16]

The Taylor report was factually accurate but weak in causal diagnosis. Its character reflected one cause of self-limited government learning: *The president's selection of advisers limited what he learned.*

Maxwell Taylor, a retired military officer, subscribed to a simple theory of organizational success. Commanders should forthrightly decide the objectives to be achieved. Staff should produce competent and forthright analyses. Subordinates should know their jobs, be assigned the resources needed for success, and do their duty. The report's diagnoses were a list of deviations from such an authoritative ideal.

Taylor's simple theory ignored the fundamental problem of improving the deliberation process required before a policy decision. This president and his advisers were not experienced military commanders with simple objectives and making familiar decisions. They were beginners, making complex judgments about novel problems in unfamiliar situations. Before becoming authoritative, they needed a process of learning, deliberations to allow them to assess reality, to grasp the rationales of proposals, to identify the new information and further advice they needed, to consider the values at stake, the trade-offs among objectives, and what choices they were willing to live with. The president needed to decide, after viewing the options and trade-offs, what he wanted.

For example, although the Taylor Commission concluded it "should have been recognized" in the fall of 1960 that this operation was too large to maintain the secret of its American sponsorship (a responsibility artfully delegated to the Eisenhower administration), it did not press beyond this disembodied, surface observation that "someone" should have recognized it. Taylor's approach to improvement could be applied to simple, known-answer jobs ("Tell them to push the 'stop' button when the red light comes on."). But this failure was not the type to be corrected by authoritative injunction: it occurred when smart, experienced men did not have a process which allowed them to see a red light. Neither Nixon, who monitored the operation in the Eisenhower administration and wanted to implement it, nor President-elect Kennedy, saw "what should have been recognized."[17] Taylor's authoritative solution — put someone in charge — evaded the problem of what a new decision maker should do differently.

The report was also limited because it respected authority too conventionally and thereby glossed over crucial facts; especially, it did not adequately and candidly criticize the president. Highly classified, with only one copy prepared, it might have ventured such criticism. It was written after a press conference at which Kennedy accepted responsibility for the failure. There was no external reason, only a cautious, deferential courtier attitude (which the Taylor report enjoined Kennedy's subordinates to overcome, yet itself repeated) to refrain from advising the president what his personal mistakes had been. Criticism of the president was not put into writing.[18]

Yet the report, an official truth all members of the panel and the government could live with, implied the president to be free of responsibility. The king can do (and would have done) no wrong — if only properly advised. Staff had not been sufficiently forthcoming: the failure was on their heads alone. The report was silent about the president's failure to recognize the disposal problem he created for himself in November, when he assented to an expanded force. It was silent about the apprehension formal large-group settings produced in his advisers. It was silent about his failure to give clear instructions to the Joint Chiefs to effect a critical review. It was silent about his failure to review the CIA's past record to see the sources of success and failure. It was silent about his own complicity in the defeat by cutting out and distancing people with military expertise when he cancelled a second air strike: it said only that Cabell and Bissell declined Rusk's offer to speak to the president, which misportrayed what happened in those moments.[19]

Such deference kept from the president a clear and forceful statement of how his own system worked and how, wittingly and unwittingly, he had acted, and failed to act, as a cause of the failure he wanted to understand. The Joint Chiefs and CIA had strong, sharp, and even realistic views about how the president himself had "screwed up." The president heard these only indirectly, via leaks to the press, not from his top secret committee.[20]

A third block to intelligence was failure, after recommending strong authoritative norms, to say how to implement such a prescription. To the extent stronger authoritative norms were needed, they ought to have been strengthened. But it was farfetched to believe that only by writing a "Top Secret," "Eyes Only" report, stating norms to make the world work better, one could accomplish this objective. Placing authoritative injunctions atop a malfunctioning system does not correct its behavior, either in people or organizations. The world has not been lacking in virtuous, plausible, authoritative prescriptions: the Ten Commandments and the Golden Rule are examples; even God has had implementation problems. A useful analysis of Kennedy's implementation problem was needed.

The fourth limit to learning reflected in the report was the questions it did not raise. The four men self-limited their sense of responsibility.

Among its formal charges, the group was instructed to develop general lessons for future paramilitary operations. It overlooked evidence before it and endorsed the preconceptions of its members.

Consider the finding that Castro's preparations and effective response blocked any incipient uprising. This implied, against future opponents who also learned from history and prepared for a Guatemala-style operation, that regular American troops would be required. Realistically, "paramilitary" warfare had become a dubious idea.

The commission also overlooked the complications past CIA operations produced for the American government's ability to interpret reality. Had the commission reviewed Cuba's detailed charges submitted to the Organization of American States in late 1960, to the United Nations in 1961, or *Pravda* and *Izvestia*, it would have concluded that Castro's alleged paranoia and hostility had been a response, at least in part, to realistic information.[21] This implied—and I will return to the issue in chapter 5—that the earlier diplomatic tests of the Eisenhower administration to explore the possibilities for a modus vivendi were inconclusive. The American government had not yet conducted a credible test of whether Castro was a dedicated Marxist whose primary commitment was to become an ally of the USSR and spread anti-American revolution. Before embarking upon Operation MONGOOSE (described below), an increase of American-sponsored violence certain to increase the Soviet role, the commission needed to ask whether this was the only alternative. Was it not time to accept, even if begrudgingly, a stalemate? Could not Cuba now become a partial advantage—Castro's threat providing political motivation to secure momentum for the Alliance for Progress, and Cuba's survival now become a prime bargaining chip for Soviet sobriety in Berlin and Laos? The questions were not asked.

The Taylor Commission's fervent recommendation to strengthen paramilitary activism also ignored the issue of foreign public opinion. America's adversary was a charismatic guerrilla leader with a strong nationalist and socialist-communist appeal. The White House hope that his people would join to overthrow him also imagined, against the background of America's past associations with Batista, that America was a benevolent rescuer. Now, there was no evidence to believe such ethnocentric premises—and good reason, too, for thought about why they had been believed. The Taylor report had no comment on the problem.

Too, American public opinion was divided, and important sectors of opinion were angry about official deception. Domestic support for foreign policy requires, in part, that crucial American ideals (or at least symbolisms) be honored, and liberals were ambivalent about counterrevolutionary interventions in Central America. It is easier to recognize this lesson (and the one above) in the light of later experience in Vietnam. But the public outcry was so consequential (it led Kennedy to stop the D-Day strikes) and news media disaffection so badly miscalculated that the failure of the Taylor Commission to consider the issue (and boldly recommend a declaration of national emergency to override criticism) was a stark omission.

That such issues would be overlooked was predictable. Kennedy appointed a chairman with a military view of organization, and all appointees shared similar political outlooks and agreed that paramilitary operations were necessary. He excluded plausible appointees who might have wanted to re-argue old questions or cast doubts on the future of paramilitary operations: When Stevenson , Bowles, Fulbright, Schlesinger, other liberals, and politicians, were excluded he had already determined the issues he did not want debated. Kennedy pre-selected the advice he would receive and excluded what he did not want to hear. That he got what he wanted, and liked its spirit, is suggested by his next assignment for Taylor: That fall Taylor and Walt Rostow from the White House staff were sent to Vietnam where, predictably, they found a situation in which they imagined greater American counterinsurgency involvement could be successful and America a benefactor welcomed by the people.

These aspects of reality that (primarily as a result of preselection of advisers) were either not recognized or not integrated into the report are summarized in table 3.1.[22]

Table 3.1. Learning and the Taylor Commission Report:
Important Elements of Reality Not Recognized or Integrated

I. *Cuba and Future Paramilitary Operations*
   A. Against intelligent and prepared opponents, past CIA successes were unlikely to be repeatable. The issue was not addressed.
   B. Long-term consequences for American and foreign public opinion were not assessed.
   C. New alternatives for Cuban policy were not assessed, especially the risks of failure to find a modus vivendi and of increased hostilities.

II. *The Policymaking Process*
   A. Design of a deliberation process for learning by beginners facing novel, complex problems and unwelcome trade-offs.
   B. Methods for safeguarding presidents from their own hasty actions that are uninformed or demand results that are unrealistic.
   C. Design of bureaucratic "trip wires" to sound alarms when earlier crucial assumptions need reevaluation or growing constraints jeopardize success.
   D. Ways to induce people to tell the complete truth to the president.
   E. Ways to overcome intellectual deference and the muted force of critical arguments made by subordinates.

Kennedy's Lessons

After he appointed a review board, Kennedy's next decision was political: Dulles, Cabell, and Bissell would have to go. He kept Dulles in office for several months to work with the Taylor Commission and likely because, as he was a Republican tied to the Eisenhower administration, Dulles inhibited criticism of the failure.[23] Kennedy named another Republican, John McCone, to replace Dulles.

Kennedy thought about administration in terms of people, not organizational design. His basic theory was that he needed new people who would be straight with him and look out for his interests. He appointed a tough, experienced Washington lawyer, Clark Clifford, to a new board to monitor foreign intelligence. He included men with strong personal loyalty to himself to be in the room during future foreign policy crises, especially Robert Kennedy and Ted Sorenson. He supported an expanded role for McGeorge Bundy and his NSC staff in the White House. He appointed Maxwell Taylor to "watchdog" the CIA's execution of Operation MONGOOSE (discussed below) and later appointed Taylor his new chairman of the Joint Chiefs of Staff.[24] He changed the CIA's leadership, appointed in the Eisenhower administration, for this reason as well.

To those who had entered the administration with him, Kennedy provided leadership to help them recover from the experience and use it constructively. He took full public responsibility and put out the word that he meant it; he did not want faultfinding in press leaks. There was more than enough blame to go around, he said. He told them to keep the failure in perspective, that it would pass—"We'll be kicked in the can for a few days"—and maybe it was better that, if it had to happen, it occurred at the beginning. He was not openly vindictive, treated the departures of the top CIA men as a political necessity, and was personally gracious to them.[25]

Yet support for his staff had a limit and, ironically, Chester Bowles became the scapegoat. After the failure, Bowles angered the president and other advisors by a long-winded, poorly organized discussion of future, nonviolent alternatives for eliminating or blocking Castro.[26] His fate was also sealed when he appeared to leak stories to his friends about his personal opposition to the entire Bay of Pigs scheme.[27]

Unconsciously, Bowles was likely set up: He was given little time to prepare a plan and the task—a nonviolent way to eliminate Castro—was not realistic. The key decision makers were not in the mood to be chastised, particularly not by a man who appeared egregiously soft-headed. The brief byplay and execution of a liberal dissenter (on the alleged grounds he was a weak administrator, which appears not to have been the case) can probably be interpreted as reflecting Kennedy's inner process of dealing with his own liberal instincts and their fate in the decision for MONGOOSE.[28]

Kennedy accepted the proposal to run his large-scale "irregular" operations through the Defense Department, ordered its capabilities expanded, and gave special emphasis to the Green Berets corps (designing their uniform personally). He did not officially declare a state of limited national emergency, but did speak fervently in public about America's need to compete against guerrilla insurgencies he feared would increase, worldwide, in the 1960s.

The White House staff loyally created a public relations image to assure liberals (and the world) that Kennedy had been misled by the CIA. Leaks suggested he was outraged, would now "get control," that he was forewarned and would resist any further paramilitary schemes. In fact, this intelligent and effective learning to maneuver public opinion obscured a movement of policy in the opposite direction: Kennedy implemented Maxwell Taylor's recommendation to place a single man in charge of paramilitary operations (it was Taylor, to review operational details), and assigned him to get rid of Castro without press-generated constraints and damage. Rejecting the ineffective half-measures from Bowles and State Department liberals, Kennedy acted in concert with the Taylor Commission's emotional consensus which, although not based on a thoughtful study, did reflect his own feelings: "We feel we are losing today on many fronts . . ." and "There can be no long-term living with Castro as a neighbor."[29]

AT CENTER STAGE: LAOS AND BERLIN

To understand the subsequent MONGOOSE phase of America's Cuban policy it is necessary to discuss the simultaneous, grave pressure Kennedy felt on a world stage. Conflicts were not merely local; they were battles, too, in this larger war: tests of resolve for oneself, public demonstrations of resolve to deter other anti-American initiatives.

America faced, by Kennedy's perception, new and dangerous Soviet assertions of power. Before he assumed office, the USSR had begun to deploy newly developed intercontinental ballistic missiles capable of delivering nuclear warheads throughout much of the United States. Kennedy's earlier belief that Soviet missiles outnumbered America's changed by February 1961, when McNamara reviewed top secret U-2 spy plane evidence the new administration had not previously known to exist (and which Bissell had made possible), but the fact remained that Soviet Premier Khrushchev increasingly boasted of his new rockets in warnings to the West.[30] His country also advanced to a dramatic lead, both psychological and technical, in outer space: The Soviet Union orbited the first earth satellite, Sputnik, in 1957; the first man placed into earth orbit was Yuri Gagarin, a Soviet cosmonaut — and his success (April 12, 1961) occurred the week before Kennedy's Bay of Pigs debacle.[31] Anticolonial movements in Africa and Asia adopted Marxist rhetoric and threatened to expand the territory friendly to, or neutral toward, the so-called Sino-Soviet bloc. Just prior to Kennedy's inauguration, on January 6, 1961, Khrushchev had proclaimed Marxism-Leninism preeminent in the world, at the forefront of history. (Earlier, he had boldly applauded Castro's victory, declaring the Monroe Doctrine dead and recommending it be interred as "a stinking corpse.") Now, he declared Soviet support for expanding the revolutionary movement around the world.[32]

Khrushchev also began to act on such bold movements. By March 1961, a massive Soviet airlift began to supply advancing pro-Communist Pathet Lao forces in Laos. A dangerous, and possibly nuclear, confrontation appeared likely in Europe. Kennedy's assertiveness (and caution) in dealing with Cuba reacted to these global conditions.

Laos

The situation in Laos presented a tangled history of indigenous factions and personalities drawn into cold war politics even though the categories Washington applied — "freedom" versus "Communism" — had only modest ability to provide clear analysis of the motives of the contenders. The Eisenhower administration had desired to make Laos a "bastion of freedom" in Southeast Asia. It made strenuous efforts to prevent a coalition government which included Communists or which might otherwise become neutral in the cold war. By 1960, more American aid per capita had been provided Laos than any other country; almost none served the cause of economic development, but did pay the full cost of the Royal Laotian Army. Widespread graft and corruption, and spreading Western influence, gave those excluded two additional issues, virtue and nationalism, to unite a competing movement and, with Marxist rhetoric, to solicit aid from the Soviet Union. With massive Soviet aid, pro-Communist Pathet Lao forces made steady military advances and Kennedy's advisers judged they would win without American intervention. As he decided what to do about Cuba, Kennedy devoted even more time to Laos.[33]

As Kennedy saw it, the problem was that past American policy had been wrong and neutralization was the proper answer. But such a viable long-term policy was now out of the question: American prestige had been publicly committed. This, then, made Laos important in the cold war, and he could "not accept any visible humiliation."[34] However, the Lao proved, for the most part, to be a people without zeal for warfare ("not believing in getting killed like the civilized races," remarked John Kenneth Galbraith, then on leave from Harvard as Kennedy's ambassador to India), and the fierce nationalist determination of the numerically smaller Pathet Lao seemed likely to prevail if America only supplied arms to the defenders.[35]

In March, President Kennedy had made diplomatic and military preparations to intervene with American troops, not for the purpose of combat but to demonstrate resolve and serve as a dramatic warning and bargaining chip, their removal to be part of a hoped-for neutrality agreement with the Soviet Union. He also moved elements of America's Seventh Fleet to the South China Sea, had helicopters and 500 marines relocated to Thailand across the Mekong River from Laos, and placed combat troops on alert at American bases in Okinawa.

Initially, the demonstration of toughness seemed to work: Khrushchev signed a neutralization agreement on April 1. However, agreement on a cease-fire was not forthcoming, and Kennedy's advisers again feared the Pathet Lao could overrun the country while the Soviets strung Kennedy along by a paper agreement. On Thursday, April 20, the day after the Bay of Pigs defeat, the president decided to send a renewed message of toughness in Laos, ordering American military advisers there to wear uniforms (rather than the civilian clothes they had previously been instructed to wear) and giving them official designation as a Military Assistance and Advisory Group. But the gesture failed; within the week, on April 26, 1961, the Pathet Lao launched a new, major offensive.

A turbulent meeting of the National Security Council found the government in disarray. A month earlier, the Joint Chiefs had recommended Kennedy deploy 60,000 troops, although they declined to guarantee success. Chastened by the Bay of Pigs defeat, and consistently opposed to land wars in Asia ("Even the Marines don't want to go in" Robert Kennedy noted), they now wanted 140,000 men and authorization to use tactical nuclear weapons before they would tell the president they could guarantee victory if an all-out war ensued.

Burned badly by problems at the Bay of Pigs landing site, Kennedy now critically probed the new military plans for Laos. Focusing—this time—on detail, he found the two airstrips in Pathet Lao territory, proposed for use, could accept 1,000 troops a day but were surrounded by 5,000 Pathet Lao; airborne resupply to the disembarking troops would be restricted to daylight hours; and in the event of prompt and vigorous Pathet Lao counterattack— akin to Castro's—it would be more than a week before land reinforcements could reach the outnumbered defenders. He was not impressed by this military planning (perhaps especially because he discovered such problems himself), and he also gave the impression of being frustrated and angry with the Joint Chiefs for insufficient enthusiasm, for resisting a limited intervention, and for wanting nuclear and massive manpower commitments from him before they would guarantee success.[36]

From the Bay of Pigs failure Kennedy learned skepticism toward the government's top experts, and his earlier failure likely prevented immediate intervention in Laos.[37] But Kennedy still prepared to do it and ordered 10,000 marines on Okinawa to stand ready. That dramatic escalation apparently made the difference at the negotiating table. By May 1 a cease-fire was signed, and its effectiveness confirmed soon thereafter.[38] Khrushchev, apparently observing his locally advantageous position and expressing his new confidence, later said Laos had not been worth going to war for, especially as it would, in the course of events "fall into our laps like a ripe apple." (In 1962 Kennedy began another covert war in the country to forestall this possibility, an effort that was eventually to recruit 30,000 Meo tribesmen and cost $300 million.)[39] On May 11, 1961, the president moved boldly to block a Cuban- or Laotian-style deterioration in neighboring South Vietnam, declared (in his National Security Action Memorandum #52) a U.S. national objective "to prevent Communist domination of South Vietnam," and ordered 400 Special Forces advisers to that country to begin to train the army of its central government: 3,200 American adviser-soldiers were there by the end of the year.[40] Throughout the rest of 1961 and 1962, the question remained unanswered whether the Laos cease-fire would hold, whether American firmness would be called as a bluff. Whether Kennedy *was* bluffing is not clear. Probably he was not, although likely he was undecided and postponing a decision he hoped, ultimately, not to make.

Berlin

The new Berlin confrontation, which Kennedy faced simultaneously with these other crises, was a legacy of World War II. At the end of the war the Allies shared occupation of different sectors of the German capital, Berlin, located 120 miles within the new East Germany (the Soviet sphere); France, Great Britain, and the United States held rights of air and land access to their sectors of Berlin along a corridor from West Germany. The arrangements were considered temporary, but a final settlement was never achieved. Stalin had once attempted to choke off Berlin in 1948, resulting in a Berlin airlift by the Allies to sustain the Western sector until the Soviets backed down.

In 1958, Khrushchev boldly raised the Berlin issue again and demanded a German peace treaty to legitimate the division of Germany and end Allied occupation rights within East Germany's sovereign territory (i.e., Berlin). His demands were to be discussed at a 1960 Paris summit with President Eisenhower, but Khrushchev walked out of the conference. (He linked his action to America's arrogantly insulting and intrusive U-2 spy plane operations over Russia, publicly revealed after the shooting down of a U-2 plane in May 1960, the capture of the pilot, Francis Gary Powers, and Eisenhower's admission he had authorized such overflights).[41]

Khrushchev presented new demands forcefully at a meeting with Kennedy in Vienna in June 1961. He bluntly announced that there would be a negotiated treaty to end Allied occupation by the end of 1961 or, unilaterally, he would sign such a treaty with East Germany. After he did so, he said, if the West then sought to violate East Germany's territorial sovereignty by asserting occupation and access rights to Berlin, the Soviet Union would be forced to defend that sovereignty. If the United States wanted war, so be it. "No force in the world," Khrushchev declared, would prevent the USSR from signing a treaty.[42]

This heavy-handed ultimatum threatened a nuclear confrontation. If Khrushchev made good his threat, Soviet conventional superiority in East Germany would compel NATO to use nuclear weapons in an all-out military contest if it were to avoid defeat.

Kennedy, shaken, interpreted Khrushchev's ultimatum to mean he had sent a dangerous message of weakness by his Bay of Pigs equivocation. Khrushchev had acted decisively and brutally to suppress the 1956 Hungarian uprising. If Kennedy was not tough enough to use violence to see through an effort to eliminate Castro, ninety miles from American shores, would he not surely back down over remote Berlin when faced with the threat of direct nuclear reprisal against America?[43]

Kennedy responded to the Berlin deadline crisis with public firmness, called former Secretary of State Acheson from retirement to develop contingency plans, requested Congress grant standby authority to call up reserves, augmented American forces in July, consulted allies, and adopted other open preparations, convinced Khrushchev must be dramatically deterred else he miscalculate.[44] During the summer of 1961, while he debated what to do about Cuba and Laos, Kennedy's greatest concern was how to manage his Berlin deadline crisis.

Accepting, at least temporarily, the neutralization of Laos, Khrushchev now appeared to increase his pressure on Berlin. On August 13, 1961, Soviet troops built the Berlin Wall to seal boarders between East and West Berlin by a high wall, barbed wire, a mined "no-man's land" and guard posts. Those seeking to escape were shot. The wall was designed to end a westward exodus of East Germans which, by that summer, totaled 3.5 million and, because economic prosperity in West German contrasted sharply with the poor performance of the East German economy, had increased to over 10,000 a week. The outpouring depleted East Germany, in a public and humiliating way, of able and ambitious workers. Arguably, Khrushchev's actions were forced upon him, but given the climate of the time and the belligerence of Kremlin rhetoric, the wall was judged a maneuver to demoralize West Berlin and an ominous sign of the dangerous turn in Soviet-American relations.[45]

OPERATION MONGOOSE

"You could sack a town and enjoy it!"

— Maxwell Taylor to Robert F. Kennedy (commenting on RKF's browbeating of CIA officials).[46]

Operation MONGOOSE was ordered by Kennedy in the early fall of 1961.[47] His order was to do everything that could be done—secretly and without using American troops—to destroy Castro. The logic of the enterprise was to strike against the economic well-being of everyone on the island, and MONGOOSE planners developed a steadily escalating campaign of commando raids and sabotage to destroy crops and every major plant and factory on the island. Worldwide operations coordinated from Frankfurt were intended to block, delay, or sabotage all Cuban international trade, especially imports of machinery and repair parts. Every CIA station and embassy was directed by Washington to assign a "Cuba" officer, develop plans, and be effective.[48] "No time, effort or manpower be spared," Robert Kennedy ordered, with the authority of the White House behind him.[49] The orchestrated campaign of espionage and worldwide economic warfare would exact punishment; if it destroyed Castro it would do so because the Cuban people would suffer such grievous economic hardship that, believing Castro to be the cause, they would rise against him.

MONGOOSE did not emerge from a systematic and thoughtful policy process; after Chester Bowles was unable to suggest nonviolent measures that would eliminate Castro, meetings of the National Security Council quickly consolidated an emotional consensus that made prolonged thought unnecessary. The discussion of Cuban policy was highly emotional, "almost savage," "the emotional reaction of people unaccustomed to defeat whose pride . . . had been deeply wounded." Their sessions were filled with "fire and fury," recalled one participant, and a large majority urged the president to invade Cuba immediately with American troops.[50]

Although Kennedy did not accept the majority's advice for an immediate invasion, he was determined that Castro be eliminated. He restricted further policy debates to a small group of like-minded men. (Arthur Schlesinger, Jr., his attitudes known from his earlier dissenting memoranda, was excluded. So were other liberals.) He appointed the CI (Counter-Insurgency) Group, chaired by Taylor, pushed by his brother, to get control of the CIA, review every detail (down to "the gradients on the beach and the composition of the sand") and produce results.[51] Kennedy judged (accurately) that large, dramatic operations attracted the press.[52] These were forbidden. He redoubled both his pressure for results *and* his initial restrictions that all vital trade-offs be honored: eliminate Castro, absolute secrecy for American complicity, and no regular troops.[53]

MONGOOSE remained secret (from Americans) for almost a decade and, because it never appeared dramatically on the front page of the *Times*, the impression has remained that MONGOOSE was inconsequential. In fact, the operation was several times larger and more destructive than its Bay of Pigs predecessor. Under White House pressure the CIA quickly expanded its station in Miami to become the largest in the world, with 600 full-time agents.

A larger expatriate force, now 3,000 Cubans, was recruited and commando raids were launched almost weekly. Almost 100 "safe houses" were purchased or rented, dozens of small "front" businesses (travel agents, boat repair, etc.) were bought or begun. A large paramilitary fleet was acquired: "mother boats," attack craft.[54]

Robert Kennedy's approach to management did not depend on organization charts but on a combination of leadership, drama, and tyranny: he fiercely demanded results, "the elimination of Castro." The rude way Bobby Kennedy treated the CIA—"chewing my ass out" Richard Bissell described it—was not designed to produce gestures or be kindly of excuses.[55] QJ/WIN, a foreign-born contract assassin, was used; William Harvey, one of the CIA's gun-toting stars was brought in, and—with tradecraft to forge documents and make it appear the work of a Soviet-bloc agent—the CIA tried six more times during the next year to assassinate Cuba's self-advertised "Maximum Leader."[56]

The president was consistently informed the CIA could see no way to overthrow Castro by clandestine means.[57] And the CIA's forecast of improbable success was realistic, albeit unacceptable to the Kennedys and a source of their anger. They hadn't "a god-damn asset in the place," and Castro was even more of a national hero.[58] Assassination was an intelligently integrated policy tool prior to an invasion: now Castro, if it succeeded, would be a martyr and Ché Guevara, Raoul Castro, or other hard-liners would just take over. His Board of National Estimates warned the president, in the fall of 1961, that "it is improbable that an extensive popular uprising could be fomented . . . [Castro's death] would almost certainly not prove fatal to the regime."[59] There was no end game.

The American planners, of course, spoke of the American-sponsored violence as "economic sabotage"—or sometimes "boom and bang"—rather than as "terrorism." And perhaps, judged with definitional rigor, it was not terrorism: that term implies a coherent policy to effect terror in a population. Bombs exploded every few days in Havana, but there was no well-conceived plan to achieve specific objectives, only determination that (in the phrase of Robert Kennedy's partisan, Arthur Schlesinger) "the terrors of the earth" should be directed against the collective entity "Cuba" and its personification, "Castro."[60]

Why did the president order MONGOOSE? Along with the strong (and probably competitive) emotions stirred by Castro, Communist challenges in Laos, Berlin, and elsewhere likely made it seem prudent to act toughly, yet without the use of regular American troops.[61] It was the wrong time both to acquiesce passively to a new, revolution-espousing Soviet state in the Caribbean and to provoke the Soviet Union to a tit-for-tat response in Berlin or Laos. And these major pressures from other arenas probably contributed to stress and the difficulty of thoughtfully designing a patient, complex diplomatic effort.[62] MONGOOSE was likely a case, too, of simply redoubling

commitment and effort after initial failure rather than rethinking basic motives.[63] That was consistent with a Kennedy theory of political causation; the
missing ingredient in success was the will and vigor to make it happen.

The record suggests MONGOOSE was an emotionally driven policy, not
a thoughtful one: "We were hysterical about Castro at the time of the Bay
of Pigs and thereafter," Robert McNamara acknowledged in retrospect (and
he was not a man easily given to hysteria).[64] Robert Kennedy was militant
and zealous: he warned that America's defeat now made Castro truly dangerous, and, with the president's knowledge, made the elimination of Castro
a personal obsession.[65] He spoke of an insult to America, Castro "thumb-
ing his nose" at the United States, of Castro "crowing."[66] Over many months
he was on the telephone constantly to CIA officials at all levels prodding,
pushing, demanding to know why there were no results, attending weekly
review meetings which often extended to seven hours of tough questioning
and detailed review.[67] (And Castro, passionately denouncing the "imperialist
worms" who attempted to conquer his country and destroy his revolution,
opened schools in Cuba to train guerrilla cadres for anti-imperialist revolutions throughout Latin America.)

Robert Kennedy, writing in his private journal, confessed "not to know
whether it will work" but he saw "nothing to lose in my estimate" by trying.[68]
"Nothing" included, in reality, the economic welfare of the Cuban people,
dozens and perhaps hundreds of people killed in the first year of MONGOOSE,
and some degree of his own reputation. It was a judgment reflecting a sensibility about power that, I will argue, in chapter 6, underlies such policies.
But he was proud of the activity he was generating: "[By August, 1961, it]
was better organized than it had been before and was having quite an effect.
I mean, there were 10 to 20 thousand tons of sugar cane that was [sic] being
burned every week."[69]

Was MONGOOSE More Intelligent?

Was MONGOOSE more intelligent than the Bay of Pigs? In some respects,
yes. The learning to avoid trouble in the press was rapid: only small raids were
used and the source of previous leaks (liberals) appeared correctly diagnosed.
And the chance of undoing the Cuban revolution appeared, technically, to
be realistically estimated, although the estimate was rejected as a basis for
policy.

But if technical aspects of the operation reflected tactical learning, the rationale for the operation itself became less intelligent. Its principal result —
an unanticipated nuclear confrontation — made it, in reality, a menace.

Setting aside momentarily the Missile Crisis, was it worth the cost? To decision makers, the Bay of Pigs had a positive "expected value": a "no cost"
guerrilla dissipation and a positive chance for success. Now, a national securi-

ty rationale for MONGOOSE — given it could not eliminate Castro — was that it "increased the cost to Castro" of pursuing his revolutionary objectives. Yet the Soviet Union could increase aid to offset the severity of the punishment — and it did so. The net economic cost to the Cuban people would not topple Castro. While the data are still classified, several hundred expatriate commandos and Cuban defense forces probably were killed. No questions were raised about the benefit/cost ratio to America, the waste involved, nor about a better use, elsewhere, for the money and lives.

Beyond harassment, there would have been two reasons to "raise the cost" via MONGOOSE. The primary purpose was to deter Soviet expansion by conveying a message of American toughness; but, as I will discuss momentarily, Khrushchev began secretly to introduce nuclear missiles into Cuba in the summer of 1962. Obviously, then, no credible deterrent message of tough resolve was conveyed; planners had become too self-absorbed by the tough militancy of their own mood.

A second justification would have been "message sending" to other potential revolutionaries. The logic of this justification is complicated. If MONGOOSE was *truly* secret, no one (Soviets or otherwise) would believe it to be American policy, infer they faced similar punishment, and be deterred. It had to be recognized as U.S. policy *elsewhere* in the world yet *not* in the American press. If this is unlikely footwork could have been achieved, MONGOOSE might have had a deterrent effect.

However, what messages *were* sent is obscure. MONGOOSE *might* have sent deterrent messages to other revolutionaries. Or it might have taught them Kennedy would not use America's regular troops (even ninety miles from America's shores) and thus would be an ineffective opponent. Or it might have taught idealistic youth in Latin America to see the United States in a Marxist light, as reactionary (as it did in the case of the founders of the Sandinista movement in Nicaragua, as I will discuss in chapter 7). Or it might, in the later unfolding of history, have had all these effects or none at all. MONGOOSE ended too quickly for us to know what the long-term results might have been. (Among these results, the willingness of many of Kennedy's advisers to send hundreds of thousands of American troops to Vietnam several years later, to an area of the world of far less geopolitical significance than the Caribbean, suggests an invasion might have been launched if a modest, indigenous anti-Castro movement could have been created.)

The intellectual integrity of Operation MONGOOSE was lower than that achieved for the Bay of Pigs plan. The president split off and abandoned his liberal ideals and human instincts; thus he reached, and probably crossed over, the edge of hypocrisy. Earlier, he had said he wanted to be a benefactor of the Cuban people. Now, they and their welfare ceased to exist; there was no Cuban benefit from devastation that had "no evidence" for success and no end game. Robert Kennedy's "nothing to lose" phrase echoes across the decades as a lesson of the limits of technical rationality when applied only within a self-absorbed world.

Without an end game, the use of Cuban expatriates also became cynical. Again, they were motivated by American handlers with the fantasy that America supported their success. (The CIA could not motivate people to risk their lives merely to "increase the cost.") But the Bay of Pigs had been judged to have a realistic chance. With greater perspective than Robert Kennedy, Maxwell Taylor later admitted, "in a strategic sense [the commando raids] weren't anything more than just pin pricks," and there was no American commitment to ultimate success.[70] The patriotic illusions rallied by the CIA among its 3,000 surrogate troops must count as a cruel and hypocritical maneuver that men of conscience could design or be involved with only by a massive and systematic disregard of conscience, reality, or both.

Table 3.2 reviews government learning from the Bay of Pigs to MONGOOSE.[71] The Kennedy administration ended MONGOOSE abruptly, in fear, when the U-2 photographic reconnaissance overflight on October 14, 1962, showed the Soviet Union had introduced nuclear missiles into Cuba. Analysis of this next encounter is the final concern of this chapter.

THE CUBAN MISSILE CRISIS

> *JFK: Now why does he put these in there though? [W]hat is the advantage of that? It's just as if we suddenly began to put a major number of MRBMs in Turkey. Now that'd be goddam dangerous, I would think.*
> *Bundy: Well, we did, Mr. President.*
> — White House Tapes, October
> 16, 1962, 6:30–7:55 P.M.[72]

Why did American leaders not anticipate Khrushchev might place nuclear missiles into Cuba? On its face, such a move had precedent: American had placed its own nuclear missiles in Western Europe in the territory of its allies and — early in the Kennedy administration — had placed them directly on Russia's borders in Turkey. There had been no American expectation Russia would risk nuclear war to prevent or reverse such actions (and, while angrily denouncing the danger of such moves, it did not).[73]

Apart from the international norms America had created, there were at least three other reasons to expect a Soviet move. First, Khrushchev was perceived to become bolder, even reckless, in other areas (e.g., Laos, Berlin). Second, an inner group of advisers knew of Operation MONGOOSE and its aggressive message that theatened an invasion, which neither Russia nor Castro could reliably forestall by conventional arms. If Kennedy would face the nuclear brink to secure America's Berlin outpost, would it be farfetched to believe Khrushchev might not take a similar risk to secure, dramatically, Russia's own Cuban outpost? And third, could not Khrushchev expect major symbolic ad-

Table 3.2. Changes in Executive Branch Intelligence and Effectiveness:
The Bay of Pigs to MONGOOSE

I. *Intelligence*
   A. *Realism of Assessments*
   + 1. Assessments of Cuban reality were apparently accurate: MONGOOSE judged unlikley to succeed.
   + 2. Bureaucratic redesign to effect control of the CIA well thought out (assuming the MONGOOSE assassination plans were intended by the president.)
   + 3. "Trip wire" for American press covereage correctly learned and incorporated into the new design.
   − 4. Major costs ignored as "nothing."
   − 5. Deterrent message to the Soviet Union incorrectly calibrated.
   − 6. Cuban and Soviet fear of an imminent second invasion underestimated.

   B. *Integration of Thought*
   − 1. No end game or integrated negotiation strategy.
   − 2. Conflicting messages to Latin America and other potential revolutionaries not assessed.

   C. *Perspective and Value Integration*
   − 1. "Forgetting" and original purpose to contribute to the welfare of the Cuban people.
   − 2. Dishonest recruitment and use of expatriates for an operation expected only to "increase costs."
   − 3. Personalized revenge motives as a basis for national policy.
   − 4. Overlooking Castro's vital contributions as a potential hostage to effect Soviet forebearance in Berlin and Laos and to spur Alliance for Progress momentum.

II. *Effectiveness*
   + 1. Modest increased economic cost to USSR and to Cuba.
   − 2. "Expense to America"/"damage to Cuba" ratio probably was quite high.
   − 3. Long-term demoralization and bitterness of Cuban expatriate forces and some CIA case officers.
   − 4. Modest loss of domestic and international credibility and legitimacy as assassination plot was revealed in next decade.
   − 5. Deterrent v. arousal effects on Soviet Union, Castro and others in other arenas unclear.
   − 6. Undeterred (and partially created) confrontation crisis threatens nuclear war.

Note: + = increase; − = decrease.

vantages from placing his missiles in the Western hemisphere, underscoring his message to the underdeveloped countries of the region that the Monroe Doctrine was dead and Soviet power on the march?

The American government's position in the crisis was that the Soviet missile introduction was so unthinkable, no senior administration official or Soviet expert had predicted a move so alarming and dangerous to world peace.[74] Given the available record, that appears to be true, *strictly* defined as an assertion that no one has come forward who predicted the emplacements to be *likely*.[75] But beneath the confident conviction, which stemmed in part from the fact that the Soviets were thought to be extraordinarily cautious and had made no forward emplacements in Eastern Europe, ran a deep undercurrent of worry that a missile emplacement *was* conceivable. John McCone, director of the CIA, was aggressive and serious about monitoring the possibility of offensive missiles.[76] By the end of the summer of 1962, the apprehensions of Kennedy's advisers were sufficiently great to cause him to issue public warnings against Soviet offensive weapons in Cuba or use of Cuba as a Soviet base.[77] The U-2 reconnaissance overflight of Cuba which detected the missiles had been specifically ordered to test an offensive-missile hypothesis. The shock when missiles were finally discovered was oddly disconnected from the uneasy anticipation which motivated the search. (I return to this disconnection in chapter 6.)

Perhaps no one could have known a missile emplacement was likely, and we do not know why Khrushchev acted as he did. But several analysts have concluded, probably correctly, that Khrushchev simply failed to anticipate that the American response would be to declare a crisis and to move to a nuclear confrontation and the brink of nuclear war.[78] In retrospect, Kennedy failed to estimate what was required to deter any emplacement and probably failed to anticipate one of the grave threats—a visibly humiliating destruction of his Cuban ally—that Khrushchev wished to prevent in a theatre with massive American conventional superiority.

As we have seen, MONGOOSE obviously did not convey messages that deterred Khrushchev. "Pin-prick" raids were scarcely the sign one faced a tough competitor. Kennedy did communicate several warning messages directly to the Soviet Union, and in public statements, but—as best we can determine—these came in the summer of 1962 after Khrushchev's decision had been made, the Soviet government committed, and the missiles on their way.[79] Moreover, in retrospect, it is difficult to read the messages without wondering whether they contained loopholes, especially in what was not said. "Offensive" weapons were ruled out, but there was no certain, definitive statement that *any* such weapons would be destroyed promptly. The statement that an act may be intolerable, or dangerous, could be variously interpreted as angry rhetoric, a bluff, or—as it turned out—a serious warning.[80]

In retrospect, it would have been more intelligent had Kennedy used consistent methods to communicate deterrent resolve to the Russians (i.e., acting as he had done to dramatize serious resolve elsewhere, in Laos and Berlin, by mobilizing troops and conducting massive war game exercises in the waters around Cuba), eschewing ambiguity and spelling out directly (and privately) the consequences of immediate invasion and destruction of any missiles. There was something unconnected, almost dreamlike, in his thinking about Cuba and Russia. (I will want to consider this problem further in chapter 6.)

While, as far as we know, Kennedy had no intention to invade Cuba, the restraint of MONGOOSE apparently did not communicate that fact.[81] In his memoirs, Khrushchev wrote that when he observed MONGOOSE, he thought it an obvious preparation for a serious, larger invasion with regular American troops. It was a prelude while the next round was being prepared—and he did not expect Kennedy to fail the second time.[82] The Soviet and Cuban fear was probably a fear anyone in their circumstances would reasonably share.[83]

The American press, public, and most members of Congress, unaware of MONGOOSE's ferocity, faced a mystery and were led to believe the nuclear missiles were unjustified, solely introduced by Khrushchev to threaten America and change the global balance of power. To be sure, there were more missiles introduced than would be needed "rationally" to deter America, and Khrushchev would receive major symbolic, geopolitical advantages to counter America's own forward deployments. But in retrospect, it seems likely that nuclear missiles were the only reliable means open to Khrushchev to deter his own "visible humiliation" in Cuba, and Castro's sole (albeit risky) means to secure his own survival. And, for those purposes, both men calculated correctly:[84] Kennedy settled the crisis with a "no invasion" pledge for Castro and removal of American missiles from Turkey.[85] He also stopped Operation MONGOOSE.[86]

In retrospect, MONGOOSE was a bizarre and badly designed geopolitical plan. It was sufficiently fierce to arouse fear of a second invasion, too ineffectual to succeed, and too weak, indecisive, and covert to communicate that its author would boldly risk a nuclear war over conduct which had been deemed acceptable for America.

There is a further, albeit elusive, issue raised by the failure to recognize the fear which American actions — taken for self-perceived defensive purposes — could engender. American national security managers may have had an inner conviction of virtue and innocence — and great difficulty recognizing that use of their viewpoint to define reality could be a presumption lost on other nations, and American policies experienced by others as inherently hostile. We now know the brief exchange during the missile crisis deliberations, captured on White House tapes quoted at the beginning of this section: It suggests Kennedy had not previously stopped to consider that America's "deterrent" missiles in Turkey, placed there during his administration (the decision had been made earlier, by President Eisenhower), would engender Soviet fear or motivate Soviet counterassertion. Soviet assertiveness was attributed to something about Khrushchev, not to American actions. The evidence is inconclusive, but it does suggest that American leaders imagined too readily that their minds were read — almost telepathically — by the other side, and that their own understanding of the character of American policy — the expression of a nation that was tough, determined to avoid visible defeats, but not aggressive — would be the understanding to which others, even those with a Marxist perception, would respond.[87]

Learning and the Policy Process

From the Bay of Pigs defeat, the important lesson for Kennedy's advisers was the experience itself and the knowledge, their personal abilities and past success notwithstanding, that they could be disastrously wrong. Their pride was hurt. Perhaps naturally, each searched his conscience but concluded the major fault had been elsewhere. (The White House thought the CIA to blame, and the Joint Chiefs who failed to watchdog the CIA; the Joint Chiefs believed the president and the CIA had made a botch of it; the CIA's view was that the president scuttled his own operation.) But the civilians did become more of a genuine deliberative group after the departure of Dulles and Bissell, less an assemblage of individuals unsure of their standing. Schlesinger reports they became more assertive, more openly skeptical, more given to irreverent remarks. Chastened, now they seemed to want honest discussions, were able to convey that to one another, sense it within one another, and make it work.[88]

The missile crisis deliberations showed that a marked improvement in the policy process *could* occur. In doubt, the president wanted genuine discussions, not presentation of agency positions staged for his benefit. Aware that his own presence had created inhibition before, he excluded himself from many deliberations of the NSC executive committee and brought in former Secretary of State Dean Acheson, who would not be deferential to him nor awed by the titles of the men seated around the table. He used his brother to monitor discussions, give voice to arguments he felt should be heard, and to produce closure when he, himself, had decided. He added informal discussions with individual members of his staff away from the formality of official meetings.[89]

But there is an important caveat. Decision makers did eschew a first instinct to use violence, debated intensely for over a week, and their resulting policy of measured firmness (a naval "quarantine" to force a Soviet missile withdrawal without direct violence) produced an acceptable outcome.[90] Thus the new crisis could be resolved without violence, and they adopted a lengthy deliberative procedure which allowed them to see possibilities they had not originally imagined. They had the capability for creative and productive discussion, and they used it. The question is: why thoughtful deliberations, measured use of coercive diplomacy, and negotiation now – but not in the earlier MONGOOSE decision?

The record is persuasive that the *invocation* of this capability for collective thought was a function of political power: specifically, the Soviet nuclear threat caused a more thoughtful and systematic policy process. During the first week of debate, almost all advisers favored immediate air strikes and American invasion *even* considering the Soviet military personnel on the island. What stopped the immediate and devastating resort to violence – and made them think further – was the presence of nuclear missiles which might be launched against the United States.[91] Nuclear deterrence worked, it sobered decision makers, engaged their individual and collective capacities to think, and produced a measured reaction.

We may observe, in the contrast of MONGOOSE with other policy processes (Berlin, Laos, and the Cuban Missile Crisis), an important conclusion: the learning rate, how much people thought and to what effect, was a function of motivation, itself an effect of the issues of power at stake. Against powerful opponents, when the potential damage to America was great, or American troops might be required, latent capacities for extensive, searching analyses of alternatives and reflective discussion were used. But the capacities were not engaged when — as in MONGOOSE — a challenger was perceived weak in power to retaliate.[92]

NOTES

1. The CIA's inspector general conducted his own investigation. It was tough, even brutal, and produced a rebuttal ("reclama") by Bissell's group. Neither document has been declassified but they are knowledgeably discussed by L. Kirkpatrick, "Paramilitary Case Study: Bay of Pigs" *Naval War College Review* (November–December, 1972), P. Wyden, *Bay of Pigs: The Untold Story* (New York: Simon and Schuster, 1979), pp. 322–324, and T. Powers, *The Man Who Kept the Secrets: Richard Helms and the CIA* (New York: Pocket Books, 1979), pp. 132–147.

2. For discussions of aspects of integrated complexity see L. Etheredge and J. Short, "Thinking About Government Learning" *Journal of Management Studies* 20 (1983): 41–58, which includes a more technical discussion of measuring learning and intelligence as systemic properties; P. Tetlock, "Integrative Complexity as a Variable in Political Decision-Making" Paper delivered at the annual meeting of the International Studies Association. (Photocopy: March, 1980); P. Tetlock, "Accountability and Complexity of Thought" *Journal of Personality and Social Psychology* 45 (1983): 74–83, which has special relevance to effects of national security secrecy on policy formation; J. Loevinger with A. Blasi, *Ego Development* (San Francisco: Jossey-Bass, 1977); E. Jaques, ed., *Levels of Abstraction in Human Thought and Action* (New York: Heinemann, 1978); E. Jaques, *A General Theory of Bureaucracy* (New York: Heinemann, 1981); R. Axelrod, "Schema Theory: An Information Processing Model of Perception and Cognition" *American Political Science Review* 67 (1974): 1248–1266; R. Axelrod, ed., *Structure of Decision: The Cognitive Maps of Political Elites* (Princeton, NJ: Princeton Univ. press, 1976); D. Campbell and W. Gruen, "Progression from Simple to Complex as a Molar Law of Learning" *Journal of General Psychology* 59 (1958): 237–244; A. Miller and P. Wilson, "Cognitive Differentiation and Integration: A Conceptual Analysis" *Genetic Psychology Monographs* 99 (1979): 3–40. Earlier discussions include J. Langer, "Werner's Comparative Organismic Theory" in P. Mussen, ed., *Carmichael's Manual of Child Psychology*, 3rd ed. (New York: Wiley, 1970), H. Werner, *Comparative Psychology of Mental Development* (New York: International Universities Press, 1948), H. Werner, "The Concept of Development from a Comparative and Organismic Point of View" in D. Harris, ed., *The Concept of Development* (Minneapolis, MN: Univ. of Minnesota Press, 1956) and H. Werner and B. Kaplan, *Symbol Formation* (New York: Wiley, 1948). See also the references cited earlier, in the introduction.

3. By using the concept of integrated complexity I rule out a general conception of learning as *any* change produced by experience. The reason to emphasize the criteria of effectiveness will become clearer in chapters 6 and 7: complex and highly

integrated thought may lack external validity, or otherwise reflect an interpretive system which blocks efficacy.

4. M. Taylor, *Operation ZAPATA: The Ultra-Sensitive Report and Testimony of the Board of Inquiry on the Bay of Pigs.* (Frederick, MD: Aletheia Books, 1981 (1961). The inquiry was extensive and serious. It also appears factually accurate. However, the subject of assassination is not discussed in the report.
5. Quoted in Wyden, *Bay of Pigs*, p. 317.
6. Taylor, *Operation ZAPATA*, p. 40.
7. Ibid.
8. Ibid., p. 41.
9. Ibid.
10. Ibid.
11. Ibid., pp. 41–42.
12. Ibid, p. 42
13. Ibid.
14. Ibid, pp. 20, 42.
15. Ibid., pp. 41–42.
16. Recommendations 11 and 12: Ibid., pp. 44–53.
17. Nor (to take another example) was it adequate analysis to say only that requirements imposed for secrecy should not have affected the chance of military success; the president was decisive about the constraints he wanted to honor. If he had to chose "all or nothing," it would have been "nothing." He wanted to do better than that.
18. There is no evidence such criticisms were made orally. The taboo against criticizing the president in writing would likely have been so well understood that it was not an option considered. As I will discuss in chapter 4, such automatic deference appears a more consequential inhibition than the small group dynamics of a "groupthink" syndrome. See also Dexter (1977).
19. Taylor, *Operation ZAPATA*, p. 21.
20. Kirkpatrick's analysis paralleled Taylor's, although it was more critical of the CIA. It directed its most severe criticisms at the effort to mount a large covert military operation in which the requirement for deniability stifled the operation itself. It was too big to hide, too small to succeed. Kirkpatrick was harsh on his professional associates at the CIA for promoting it. He characterized their Guatemala precedent as succeeding only by unusual good luck, and he believed its use to guide the Cuban mission uninformed and overconfident. His judgment was that, below the top, people assigned to Bissell's team were of C-quality; the operation did not fail because of them, but it was slipshod. He criticized both the lack of contingency planning and the failure to stand firm against political pressures that weakened the operation. Robert Amory's interview in the Kennedy Library contains a good discussion of the report and some of the personality issues involved. See also Kirkpatrick, "Paramilitary Case Study," Wyden, *Bay of Pigs*, pp. 322–324, Powers, *The Man Who Kept the Secrets*, pp. 131–148.
21. R. Roa, "Charges Delivered Against the United States Before the U.N. Security Council" *New York Times* (January 5, 1961) discusses his country's formal charges. See also H. Dinerstein, *The Making of a Missile Crisis, October, 1962* (Baltimore, MD: John Hopkins Univ. Press, 1976), passim.
22. "Preselection" is an interim diagnosis. I will reconceptualize the problem in chapter 6 and there will discuss it as a symptom rather than a cause.
23. A. Schlesinger, *A Thousand Days: John F. Kennedy in the White House* (Boston: Houghton Mifflin, 1965), p. 290.

24. Powers, *The Man Who Kept the Secrets*, p. 169 et passim discusses Taylor's role. See also R. Schlesinger, *Robert F. Kennedy and His Times* (Boston: Houghton Mifflin, 1978), pp. 443–498 passim.
25. Schlesinger, *A Thousand Days*, pp. 295–297 discusses these actions. Cabell's dismissal is noted in Martin, *Wilderness of Mirrors*, p. 119.
26. Schlesinger, *A Thousand Days*, p. 472.
27. It may be less likely lessons are learned if they require recognition of unpleasant truths, and especially if they imply a decreased sense of efficacy. See A. Bandura, "Self-Efficacy: Toward a Unifying Theory of Behavioral Change" *Psychological Review* 84 (1977): 191–215; D. Campbell, "Blind Variation and Selective Retention in Creative Thought as in Other Knowledge Processes," *Psychological Review* 67 (1960): 380–400; D. Campbell, "Evolutionary Epistemology" in P. Schilp, ed., *The Philosophy of Karl Popper*, vol. 14-I (LaSalle, Illinois: Open Court Publishing, 1974).
28. Kennedy may not have known that Bowles was angry because he had wanted to present his opposition but had been put off by Rusk. Whether Rusk was forthcoming with the President about the incident, or remained silent and allowed the departure of an unwanted subordinate, is not clear. Schlesinger's *A Thousand Days* account of the departure must be treated skeptically: As a liberal, he appears to have been manuevered by the President to accept the more broadly stated rationale of Bowles's "managerial ineffectiveness." Bowles clearly felt deeply hurt and, a decade later, in his memoirs, provided a long rejoinder to this charge and to the allegation that he had leaked his views to the press: C. Bowles, *Promises to Keep: My Years in Public Life, 1941–1969* (New York: Harper and Row, 1971), p. 453 et passim. A common theory, advanced by W. Bundy, "The National Security Process: Plus Ça Change . . . ?" *International Security* 7 (Winter 1982/1983): p. 99, is that opponents — especially those who are excluded from the policy process — are the most likely to leak. It is possible that Stevenson or Reston, seeking to promote Bowles' career, were the source of the stories.
29. Taylor, *Operation ZAPATA*, p. 52. G. Wills, *The Kennedy Imprisonment: A Meditation on Power* (New York: Pocket Books, 1983 (1981), chapter 20 puts these events into correct perspective.
30. Schlesinger, *A Thousand Days*, p. 302. Dinerstein, *Making of a Missile Crisis* reviews Soviet statements during this period. For a review of the missile estimates issue, see J. Prados, *The Soviet Estimate: U.S. Intelligence Analysis and Russian Military Strength* (New York: Dial Press, 1982).
31. Quickly following his Bay of Pigs defeat, Kennedy publicly committed the United States to beat the Russians to the moon. See H. Young, B. Silcock, and P. Dunn, "Why We Went to the Moon" *Washington Monthly* 2 (April, 1970): 29–58, who discuss the political connections.
32. Kennedy regarded the speech as an authoritative statement: Schlesinger, *A Thousand Days*, pp. 302–304.
33. Schlesinger, *A Thousand Days*, pp. 329 et passim. C. Stevenson, *The End of Nowhere: American Policy Toward Laos Since 1954* (Boston, MA: Beacon Press, 1972) discusses the background and evolution of Laotian policy.
34. Schlesinger, *A Thousand Days*, p. 332.
35. Ibid.
36. These details of Kennedy's policy are drawn from Schlesinger, *A Thousand Days*, pp. 323–334; H. Parmet, *JFK: The Presidency of John F. Kennedy* (New York: Dial Press, 1983), pp. 131–155.
37. Robert Kennedy oral history interview (JFK Library), vol. 1, p. 72.

38. However it proved temporary: D. Hall, "The Laotian War of 1962 and the Indo-Pakistan War of 1971" in B. Blechman and S. Kaplan, ed., *Force Without War: The U.S. Armed Forces as a Political Instrument* (Washington, DC: Brookings Institution, 1978), pp. 135–221 discusses the next round.

39. T. Fain, K. Plant, and R. Milloy, ed., *The Intelligence Community: History, Organization, and Issues* (New York: R. R. Bowker, 1977), p. 702.

40. L. Gelb and R. Betts, *The Irony of Vietnam: The System Worked* (Washington, DC: Brookings Institution, 1979), p. 80.

41. D. Wise and T. Ross, *The U-2 Affair* (New York: Random House, 1962). The Soviets had possessed the military capability to bring down the planes for several months. That they had not done so previously was grounds to speculate Khrushchev designed the sequence of events to dramatize his new assertiveness. Likely there were other causes, especially nationalistic pressures within the Soviet government to use the improved missiles. There could have been no assurance the pilot would survive to give proof of American sponsorship and thus force Eisenhower to retract the CIA cover story of an off-course weather plane: thus, it is unlikely Khrushchev's scenario was planned in advance.

42. Schlesinger, *A Thousand Days*, p. 366–374, reviews the meeting with Khrushchev.

43. N. Lebow, "The Cuban Missile Crisis: Reading the Lessons Correctly" *Political Science Quarterly* 98 (1983): 431–458, reviews the sources of this story and discusses the validity of the interpretation.

44. For detailed reviews see S. Walker, "Bargaining Over Berlin: A Re-Analysis of the First and Second Berlin Crises" *Journal of Politics* 44 (1982): 152–171; R. Slusser, *The Berlin Crisis of 1961* (Baltimore, MD: Johns Hopkins Univ. Press, 1973); A. George, D. Hall, and W. Simons, *The Limits of Coercive Diplomacy* (Boston: Little, Brown, 1971). For general reviews of the problems of lesson drawing in coercive diplomacy and deterrence see A. George and R. Smoke, *Deterrence in American Foreign Policy: Theory and Practice* (New York: Columbia Univ. Press, 1974).

45. See N. Khrushchev, *Khrushchev Remembers* (translated by S. Talbott) (Boston: Little, Brown, 1970), p. 454 and Talbott's editorial note, ibid.

46. Quoted in Martin, *Wilderness of Mirrors*, p. 135.

47. The name was intentional: A mongoose is a small, ferret-like animal noted for its ferocity in attacking and killing poisonous snakes.

48. General reviews include T. Branch and G. Crile, "The Kennedy Vendetta: An Account of the CIA's Entanglement in the Secret War Against Castro" *Harper's* 251 (1975): 49–63; Martin, *Wilderness of Mirrors*, pp. 130–137 et passim, Powers, *The Man Who Kept the Secrets*, pp. 171–181 et passim. U.S. Senate, Select Committee to Study Governmental Operations with Respect to Intelligence Activities. *Alleged Assassination Plots Involving Foreign Leaders*. Senate Report 97-465. November 20, 1975. (Washington, DC: Government Printing Office, 1975), pp. 134–179 et passim reviews assassination planning. Schlesinger, *Robert F. Kennedy*, pp. 452–498, 533–534 is based upon access to still-restricted documents (e.g., Robert Kennedy's private journal). W. Hinckle and W. Turner, *The Fish is Red: The Story of the Secret War Against Castro* (New York: Harper and Row, 1981) introduce a wide range of issues, including the post-1962 period.

49. Quoted in Powers, *The Man Who Kept the Secrets*, p. 174.

50. These characterizations are drawn from Bowles, *Promises*, pp. 330–331, 450. (I will return to this characterization in chapter 6). Schlesinger, *Robert F. Kennedy*, p. 473, reports that the early emotional consensus for invasion faded by early May.

51. Martin, *Wilderness of Mirrors*, p. 135. There were overlapping groups with varying members, including the SG/A (Special Group Augmented).

52. Branch and Crile, "Kennedy Vendetta" imply widespread press collusion to maintain secrecy during this period.
53. Powers, *The Man Who Kept the Secrets*, p. 178 et passim.
54. See Branch and Crile, "Kennedy Vendetta" for a general review.
55. Martin, *Wilderness of Mirrors*, pp. 123–124; U.S. Senate, *Assassination Plots*, pp. 139–170.
56. The count varies slightly depending on sources and definitions.
57. Martin, *Wilderness of Mirrors*, pp. 140–141.
58. Ibid., p. 128.
59. Ibid., p. 127.
60. "Every few days a bomb explodes in Havana, sometimes in a park, sometimes in a show window, sometimes in a hotel washroom." E. Halperin, "Cuba on the Kremlin Path" *Die Zeit* (December, 1961), p. 51. See also Martin, *Wilderness of Mirrors*, p. 480.
61. L. Etheredge, *A World of Men: The Private Sources of American Foreign Policy* (Cambridge, MA: MIT Press, 1978), chapter 1 et passim provides a more detailed review and discussion of President Kennedy's personal orientation.
62. See M. Hermann, "Indicators of Stress in Policymakers During Foreign Policy Crises" *Political Psychology* 1 (1979): 27–46 for a review of such effects.
63. L. Festinger, H. Riecken, and S. Schachter, *When Prophecy Fails* (Minneapolis, MN: Univ. of Minnesota Press, 1956) discuss this phenomenon; see also R. Jervis, *Perception and Misperception in International Relations* (Princeton, NJ: Princeton Univ. Press, 1976), pp. 404–406.
64. Quoted in Schlesinger, *Robert F. Kennedy*, p. 472.
65. Castro was seen as a charismatic foe who taught Communist revolutionaries they could challenge even the United States and win.
66. For example: Lansdale remarked, "[RFK] felt his brother had been insulted . . . He felt the insult needed to be redressed rather quickly." Quoted in Branch and Crile, "Kennedy Vendetta," p. 50. Ray Cline, the Deputy Director for Intelligence at the CIA: "Both Jack and Bobby were deeply ashamed . . . and they became obsessed with the problem of Cuba. . . . [T]hey vented their wrath on Castro . . . in all ways that they could. . . . "[RFK] was as emotional as he could be." Ibid., pp. 50, 60. The existence of a parliamentary system, in which a government would fall after the Bay of Pigs failure, would have prevented this intrusion of personal pride and perhaps increased intelligence.
67. Quoted in Schlesinger, *Robert F. Kennedy*, p. 472.
68. Quoted in Schlesinger, *Robert F. Kennedy*, p. 476.
69. RFK oral history interview, Kennedy Library, vol. 3, p. 411.
70. Taylor spoke of MONGOOSE awkwardly as "a neighbor who is kicking you in the shins" and America showing it could "retaliate a bit and remind him that we're still around—an oddly casual metaphor for the hoped-for devastation of an economy and the resulting suffering of people the president has been so enthusiastic to aid. Quoted in Branch and Crile, "Kennedy Vendetta," p. 60.
71. After the Bay of Pigs, and to his credit, Robert McNamara ordered the Weapons Systems Evaluation Group (WSEG) studies to monitor the behavior of government decision makers during foreign policy crises and draw cumulative lessons for improved crisis management. The 14 reports, based on studies conducted automatically during the remaining major foreign policy crises of the 1960s, typically run to 600 pages or more and were based, in part, on wiretaps of senior government officals during these crises (without the knowledge of many). When eventually declassified, these reports may prove the most important contribution to government learning from the Bay of Pigs fiasco. They were highly classified,

and their original circulation restricted, to preserve the integrity of the unobtrusive measures. Reportedly, the Defense Department has retained possesion of the original, still-classified tapes.

There may have been other lessons drawn, possibly involving government employees. Four groups had motives to engage in a conspiracy to kill the president: Castro, in retaliation for efforts to assassinate him; the Mafia, which was being threatened and hard-pressed by Robert Kennedy; lower-level CIA operatives bitter at Kennedy's indecisiveness that had resulted in unnecessary deaths of personal friends; and Cuban expatriates, their private supporters, and CIA operatives who could combine revenge with Oswald's pro-Castro link to induce Lyndon Johnson to retaliate against Castro and finish the job. These issues are extraneous here: in evaluating the evidence it is useful to keep in mind that, via standard "tradecraft," agents may be misled about who, in reality, they are working for, i.e., if Oswald displayed pro-Cuban sympathies, this does not necessarily mean that it would be pro-Cuban groups who might have hired or supported him. A useful introduction to the complex problems of inference in counterintelligence is Martin's *Wilderness of Mirrors* account of the "search for the mole" in the CIA.

72. Transcript, John F. Kennedy Library, p. 26.
73. Parmet, *JFK*, p. 295; Eisenhower had decided to install the missiles in 1959, but they were put in place during the Kennedy administration. Their removal (prior to the crisis) had *not* been ordered by Kennedy, contrary to the cloud of dust kicked up to sell the missile crisis settlement to the public. See B. Bernstein, "The Cuban Missile Crisis: Trading the Jupiters in Turkey?" *Political Science Quarterly* 94 (Spring, 1980): 97–125.
74. I will return, later, to the fact that Kennedy, McNamara, Marine Commandant Shoup, and others felt it "made no real difference" to American security that the missiles were in Cuba, although they felt they could not act upon that interpretation.
75. See R. Wohlstetter, "Cuba and Pearl Harbor: Hindsight and Foresight" *Foreign Affairs* 43 (1965): 691–707; Parmet, *JFK*, pp. 282–284. The CIA's Board of National Estimates concluded an evaluation on September 18, 1962 that the Soviet Union would not install offensive missiles: Martin, *Wilderness of Mirrors*, p. 142. General discussions of the problem of deception and surprise, with relevance to analyzing lessons, include K. Knorr, "Failure in National Intelligence Estimates: The Case of the Cuban Missiles" *World Politics* 16 (April, 1964); R. Betts, "Analysis, War, and Decision: Why Intelligence Failures are Inevitable" *World Politics* 31 (1979): 31–89; R. Betts, "Surprise Despite Warning: Why Sudden Attacks Succeed" *Political Science Quarterly* 95 (1981): 551–572; and R. Heuer, "Strategic Deception and Counterdeception: A Cognitive Process Approach" *International Studies Quarterly* 25 (1981): 294–327.
76. Martin, *Wilderness of Mirrors*, p. 142; Powers, *The Man Who Kept the Secrets*, pp. 203–205; Parmet, *JFK*, pp. 282–284.
77. The Soviet government also lied to Kennedy about the missile emplacement, but Kennedy's warnings may have come after the emplacement decision had been made and the missiles were en route. See Lebow, "The Cuban Missile Crisis."
78. Lebow, "The Cuban Missile Crisis," reviews these issues. See also Dinerstein, *Making of a Missile Crisis*, pp. 150–183 et passim; the Soviet press expressed continuing anxiety concerning a new invasion.
79. Schlesinger, *A Thousand Days*, pp. 795–801. Kennedy also asked for standby authority to call up reserves but linked this with publicly calming statements that "defensive" weapons were acceptable, leaving ambiguous where he would draw the line. See also the review by Lebow, "The Cuban Missile Crisis."

80. A. George, ed., *Managing U.S.-Soviet Rivalry: Problems of Crisis Prevention* (Boulder, CO: Westview Press, 1983) reviews efforts to standardize Soviet-American communication.
81. A Soviet tendency to misperceive American improvisations and ambivalences as a rational coherent policy is discussed in L. Bloomfield and A. Leiss, *Controlling Small Wars: A Strategy for the 1970's* (New York: Knopf, 1969), p. 404. See also O. Holsti, *The 'Operational Code' as an Approach to the Analysis of Belief Systems*. Final Report to the National Science Foundation. Mimeo, (1977) and Jervis, *Perception and Misperception*, chapter 8, for related discussions of this phenomenon.
82. Khrushchev, *Khrushchev Remembers*, pp. 494–495: "I said it would be foolish to expect the inevitable second invasion to be as badly planned and as badly executed as the first. I warned that Fidel Castro would be crushed if another invasion were launched against Cuba . . . "
83. Further corroborating evidence for a defensive motive is that the missile emplacement was part of a broader defense buildup. By the end of August 1962, Soviet ground-to-air missiles had been supplied to Cuba and were operational. After the discovery of the Soviet MRBMs (October 14) and the president's national speech (October 22), low-level aerial reconnaissance revealed 5,000 well-armed Soviet combat troops, equipped with battlefield rockets, at four sites on the island apart from the missiles.
84. Whether Soviet actions deterred a second invasion that might have been launched eventually is unknown, but it is worth recalling that within a few years the American government – with most of the same senior decision makers – was dispatching hundreds of thousands of American troops to South Vietnam, an area of the world with far less geopolitical importance to the United States, and with far less rationale for doing so, than in the Caribbean area.
85. G. Allison's classic book, *Essence of Decision: Explaining the Cuban Missile Crisis* (Boston: Little, Brown, 1971) was written before knowledge of MONGOOSE came to light. Now I think we can see more clearly why Kennedy felt a no-invasion pledge, and removal of Jupiters from Turkey, would be an acceptable *quid pro quo* to settle the crisis. National security secrecy surrounding MONGOOSE did make it more difficult for Kennedy to operate with "outsiders" (e.g., Congress) who did not know that an American invasion of Cuba would have seemed imminent. See also M. Halperin, "Covert Operations: Effects of Secrecy on Decision Making" in R. Borosage and J. Marks, ed., *The CIA File* (New York: Grossman, 1976), pp. 159–177.

Commentators may have under-estimated Khrushchev's dramatic threat to West Berlin as a policy to deter American aggression against Cuba, a deterrent which appears to have worked. See R. Slusser, "The Berlin Crises of 1958–59 and 1961" in Blechman and Kaplan, ed., *Force Without War*, pp. 343–439 for a partial reconstruction of reciprocal lessons and interpretations in the early 1960s.
86. Parmet, *JFK*, p. 297. "Low level" sabotage was resumed in early 1963. Ibid., p. 299.
87. For example, when Kennedy ransomed the Bay of Pigs prisoners he declared publicly, in an emotional speech: "This [Brigade] flag will be returned to this Brigade in a free Havana!" Kennedy did not intend this to be a promise he would assure the overthrow of Castro, but it was one of a series of statements, in addition to MONGOOSE, that could be interpreted as ominous. Quoted in Powers, *The Man Who Kept the Secrets*, p. 168.
88. Schlesinger, *A Thousand Days*, pp. 296–297.
89. Ibid.

90. See Parmet, *JFK*, p. 297. We now know Kennedy did promise Khrushchev the removal of the Turkish missiles although he felt he had to do it secretly and could not tell the American people at the time. In fact, Adlai Stevenson was publicly trashed in the press for suggesting such a move of "weakness": in retrospect, one has the impression Stevenson and Bowles often gave good counsel but took substantial damage as a result. Thus, Schlesinger's perception of the personal dangers of this route probably were accurate. An extraordinarily critical view, characterizing the decision as succeeding by "plain dumb luck," is by former Secretary of State Acheson, whose criticisms have suffered the fate—to be ignored—that Rusk (in the case material) and Cleveland predict for critics of policies which succeed: Dean Acheson, "Dean Acheson's Version of Robert Kennedy's Version of the Cuban Missile Crisis" *Esquire* (February, 1969); H. Cleveland, "Crisis Diplomacy" 41 *Foreign Affairs* (July 1963): 638–649.

91. See Schlesinger, *A Thousand Days*, pp. 794–819; Parmet, *JFK*, pp. 277–300; Allison, *Structure of Decision* passim.

92. Longer-term lessons are reviewed in G. Duffy, "Crisis Prevention in Cuba" in A. George, ed., *Managing U.S.-Soviet Rivalry*, pp. 285–318.

Chapter 4 BLOCKED LEARNING IN THE EXECUTIVE BRANCH

In this chapter, I begin to restructure the case material to diagnose the barriers to government learning. As a first step, I draw from the historical record evidence of seven common, self-blocking patterns of behavior within the executive branch. Next, I will evaluate current theories that learning is blocked by inadvertent failures of rational analysis, i.e., that in major foreign policy decisions there are arguments (unheard) or facts (known but not made available) that would result in major improvements in intelligence and effectiveness if organizational changes made them available.

Earlier appointments determined later outcomes. President Kennedy determined whom to include in policy debates and whom to exclude. As when he appointed the Taylor Commission, he selected people who favored directions other plausible appointees would have opposed. Sensing what was wanted, others in the administration acted in the same spirit, producing a weight of advice favorable to presidential instincts that later experience proved too hasty and unrefined.

Originally, during the Bay of Pigs deliberations, people with personal ties to Kennedy (who might have been candid and alert to his political stakes) were excluded, especially his longtime counsel and speech writer, Ted Sorenson, and his brother Robert. Apparently, these exclusions resulted from the new president's formal decision-making process; those included were there by virtue of their formal bureaucratic positions. Others with more experience in foreign policy (like Dean Acheson or Washington lawyer Clark Clifford) were not brought in, presumably because of this formal criterion.[1] (There was only one exception: An outsider, Senator Fulbright, a Democrat and chairman of the Senate Foreign Relations Committee was invited to the decisive meeting on April 4, apparently at the last moment.)[2]

Kennedy's preference in appointments can be read as a metaphor expressing different aspects of himself. He placed a premium on "quick, tough, laconic, decided people."[3] He honored liberal idealism but in a secondary role, especially in foreign policy: Schlesinger and Goodwin were junior aides, Bowles was in the cabinet but as the number two man under Rusk, Stevenson was kept at a distance in New York.

Kennedy also weighted, by personal instinct, the advice he received. Like many men in public life, he tended to consider the adviser and his advice jointly and to discount advice if he was uneasy with the personal style of the adviser. He was inwardly impatient with moral objections from the idealistic liberals of his party. They (he said privately, never in their presence) "lacked balls."[4] Later he was to explain to Ted Sorenson that doubters were fundamentally scared—they were "grabbing their nuts."[5] Adlai Stevenson, Chester Bowles, Fulbright, and Arthur Schlesinger, Jr., were treated with public graciousness and inner suspicion by Kennedy—and kept on the periphery.

Dean Rusk excluded two people. His top intelligence analyst, Roger Hilsman, learned of the plan from Allen Dulles and Richard Helms. Dulles casually mentioned the operation to Hilsman but gave few details; apparently he intended to keep a bureaucratic colleague on friendly terms while excluding him.[6] Helms mentioned the Bay of Pigs scheme to Hilsman at the end of a meeting officially on another matter. Helms left Hilsman with an unstated message that the president would be seriously mistaken if he believed there would be an uprising.[7] Hilsman, as Helms probably expected, went to Rusk and asked to have his Cuban staff evaluate the operation. Rusk said no, it was being too closely held.[8]

Under Secretary of State Chester Bowles first heard of the Bay of Pigs plan in late March when he attended a White House meeting in Rusk's absence. He sent Rusk a memo saying he was appalled, and he asked to see the president if the plan was approved. Rusk put him off.[9]

Rusk's personal style probably explains both exclusions. He did not lack an instinct for power: A man does not become secretary of state without one. But he was a diplomat, kept his own counsel, and believed in quiet diplomacy. (Once, asked if he intended to solve the Berlin problem, his eyes twinkled and he said no, he wasn't that vain, he simply hoped to pass it along to his successor.) He was not a man to do public battle and cross-examine people with acerbic intelligence as Acheson had done for Truman.[10] Apparently, in the early deliberations he also misjudged, believing the folly would be obvious and the president would drop the plan, and he was too cautious to gear up for a major battle when there was no compelling need. Later, he believed that changing the dramatic Trinidad assault to a quiet night landing at an isolated site had solved the international noise-level problem and made further policy battle unnecessary.[11] He probably also judged that Bowles's passionate moralism—Bowles thought Allen Dulles should have been "thrown out of Kennedy's office" for even suggesting the plan—would be an embarrassment and ineffective, and he perhaps knew that Bowles's long-winded, idealistic arguments got on Kennedy's nerves.[12]

Finally, one of America's top experts on guerrilla warfare, Col. Edwin Lansdale, a man who would have been certain to spot the missing guerrilla fallback option, and who was deeply skeptical that peasants anywhere jumped into mass uprisings, especially against a national hero, was cut out, but apparently by circumstances. He was being sent on an advisory mission to Vietnam.[13]

Among those cut out there is a common pattern: in national security affairs idealistic liberals were kept at the periphery. And that was not an accident. The kind of advice Kennedy had confidence in, he arranged to represent prominently in the inner circle.[14]

Neither bureaucratically nor personally did anyone accept complete responsibility.[15] How a man defined his personal responsibility (typically, by his formal role) established — and limited — what he thought about, what he argued for, what he remained silent about, and his judgment of the plan.

"Defeat," Kennedy said at a press conference afterward, "is an orphan." The CIA certainly thought so. A collective government operation? No. General Gray, the Joint Chiefs liaison, told them after the D-Day cancellation, "There goes *your* invasion."[16] Kennedy said, publicly, that he was responsible. Privately he thought about it differently and asked, "How could I have been so stupid to let *them* go ahead?"[17]

Such reactions were more than post-failure buck passing. If the "rational analysis problem" (or "national interest") was to overthrow Castro within the constraints of secrecy and no American involvement, it was bureaucratically "owned" by no one. The CIA wanted to overthrow Castro and was willing to sacrifice both secrecy and American noninvolvement. The State Department wanted secrecy and no American involvement and was willing to reduce the chance of military success to preserve both limits. The policy issue Kennedy defined was what to do with this holdover Eisenhower plan, how to reduce risk to himself — and, in a wider world, to America. When he gave the final order, the only objective he took responsibility to achieve was, as he put it: "If we have to get rid of these 800 (*sic*) men, it is much better to dump them in Cuba than in the United States, especially if that is where they want to go."[18]

Policy meetings were highly ritualized. Sophisticated participants judged no one would learn or rethink views in the light of arguments and evidence that could be presented.

Within the group of advisers, the way men dealt with one another, and what they expected from one another, reinforced the tendencies for a collective decision process to produce a policy which lacked intellectual integrity.

If we view the new Kennedy administration when all its members first heard of the plan — late January 1961 — and then observe them again on the eve of the invasion, in mid-April, there was no fundamental change in anyone's thinking. The CIA people were still strong advocates. Kennedy was favorable on the surface, still instinctively seeking to adjust the plan so that he faced minimal risk, holding it at a distance, with ambivalence. Rusk still counseled quiet and moderation. The Joint Chiefs appeared favorable, addressing only the limited technical question of whether the beachhead could be initially secured, given CIA assumptions. (And privately, of course, they felt this was *not* the way *they* would do the job.) Schlesinger, still silent in meetings, still wrote private memos to the president articulating his doubts.

Expectations of collective nonlearning in their meetings seemed widely shared. Participants thought about the "positions" other people were taking. They did not think of hypotheses or theories, but of "viewpoints" whose standing in the universe derived, in Schlesinger's terms, from the "weight" of the institutions they "represented."[19] It was not a group of fifteen experienced men trying to make sense of a complicated world.

The Cabinet Room was a stage set; everyone's role was written, the forms of interaction were rituals. The arguments were not mutual dialogue, but a presentation for an audience of one, the president. The CIA and the State Department replayed the same roles from 1954: The CIA urged approval, the State Department criticized each move for its "noise level," the issues of legality and morality never elicited much inner-circle interest, the junior men kept their mouths shut. The military, as it was often to do, was willing to sign, privately grumbled that insufficient manpower and excessive political constraints made military victory uncertain, but so long as the president understood this, they had done their job and would go along.[20]

Bureaucratically specialized viewpoints are not inappropriate, and a president whose diplomats become enthusiasts for war, or whose military officials are habitually uninterested to guarantee their own battlefield superiority, is a president who had best find new diplomats and new military commanders. However, when such agency viewpoints organized the analytical work at senior levels in the Cabinet Room, they also transformed this formal division of labor into a fragmented sense of personal responsibility.[21]

This awareness of their own sociology, and perhaps their personality assessments of others in the room, led men to doubt there was much interest in rethinking views of the world or learning. Given the known facts, could anyone really have expected to change Rusk's mind, or Bissell's, or Fulbright's, or Schlesinger's? These men were probably sophisticated enough to doubt that anyone would be persuaded to change from what he really wanted to do anyway. Attempting to affect such fundamental mind-sets by discussion was, one man later recalled, "like talking to a wall."[22]

Viewpoint lock-ins, produced within a system, are not uncommon. But they are odd: on grounds of intellectual integrity, untried proposals and ambiguous realities should produce shifting positions, congealing to formulas only if the facts are clear. But that is not what these worldly men expected, and not how they played it with one another.

Thus, beneath the surface of the policy, there was no sense of a common enterprise, not even a common theory about how the operation was to succeed. The personal sophistication of individuals was high, but by any reasonable definition of collective learning, no process ever came together. Collectively, there was no intellectual integrity.

Lying within the executive branch, and deceptive, politically sophisticated behavior produced a system that moved incrementally further from reality. Politically sophisticated men often, as we have seen, "precalculated" likely responses and then obscured candid communication, to elicit a desired effect. But the entire system — which actually relied, in the long run, on realistic behavior by the people involved — slowly began to lose touch with reality.

In Table 4.1 I have drawn from the case material a list of major lies, and the intentional dissembling of "the truth but not the whole truth" (which was more typical).

Decision processes designed to affect choices rather than to clarify them inhibited learning. Kennedy did not use systematic procedures to assure the most thorough evaluations the executive branch could produce. He seems to have known in advance the nature of advice he would judge constructive and to have understood the decision process to be a *political* process as much as an intellectual one. Thus Stevenson's exclusion was not simply intellectual (i.e, because his assumed arguments were prejudged, found wanting, and he would

Table 4.1. Lying and Dissembling That Reduced the Intelligence
and Effectiveness of Collective Action

1. The "fake-out," by national security secrecy, of most public officials about the realism of Castro's perceptions and actions, with consequent suggestion he was mad, thus unstoppable by rational means, and an easy pushover for clever psychological warfare.

2. Colonel Hawkins's "bonsai" message erroneously portraying the state of mind of the Cuban troops.

3. CIA failures to communicate upward their nonimplementation of Kennedy's strictures and orders (possibly in the belief he did not want to hear the truth).

4. Lying to Stevenson about the nature of the Cuban operation, the date, and the defector cover story.

5. Messages from headquarters to CIA operatives that failed to include the context of the message as a means of avoiding "upsetting" people: messages to Rip and Gray that did not tell of the D-Day cancellation, the veto of final appeals for jet support, the reason naval evacuation was being offered.

6. Incomplete briefing of the Pinar del Rio diversion commander.

7. Probable dissembling about the importance of the guerrilla escape option to retain the CIA's impression Kennedy's group was behind them.

8. CIA's "failure to be completely candid" to the president and his other advisers that there was no viable guerrilla option at the Bay of Pigs. And that there had been no training or planning for this fallback contingency.

9. CIA operatives misinforming the Cuban soldiers, during the Bay of Pigs and MONGOOSE, to keep up their morale and (some would say) serve them.

merely repeat them) but because inclusion would have placed a prestigious Democrat *on record* opposing a scheme Kennedy was already (according to a National Security Memorandum circulated in March by McGeorge Bundy) "expecting to approve" once a proper plan was developed.[23] If allowed expression, Stevenson's formal opposition would then be overridden and later "place him in a difficult position," a polite way to predict that, when the plan was approved and Stevenson's opposition eventually leaked, it might create political problems for the president as well as undermine Stevenson as a credible U.N. spokesman for American policy.

Similarly, we may infer that the president did not want to be placed in the position of canceling the D-Day strikes *after* senior military advisers had formally opposed the cancellation (as would be expected). Thus, they were not given the opportunity to be consulted. In both cases Kennedy appears instinctively to have designed a decision process, with political sophistication, thinking two steps ahead.

In MONGOOSE, the circle of advisers was even further restricted. Even critics who earlier had raised valid objections (e.g., Schlesinger) were excluded. The most likely reason was that Kennedy suspected that critics, losing in the inner council, would take their case secretly to like-minded members of the press. And so, appreciating the broader political processes and allegiances of various men in his administration, Kennedy excluded from debate, and knowledge, all who might be critical. He lost no Cuban expertise, but did lose the emotional force a determined critic could have brought.

We may then observe political artistry in Kennedy's decision process (but note, too, the long-term costs he paid).[24] Kennedy was not a neutral courtroom judge but was engaged in a different occupation. No doubt he believed that such precalculation was prudent, dealing with decided men in a contentious world, if he were to produce, politically, the policies he wanted.

Collective learning was inhibited because subordinates were at personal risk if they told the truth. If the inhibited critical analysis and muted emotional force observed by the Taylor Commission came partly from a perception Kennedy wanted "doers," not "doubters" or "worriers," this perception was not merely a fantasy. The Kennedy activist style was to lean on people to get the job done the way the Kennedys wanted it done. If you did not produce, they looked for someone else. Subordinates, "risk averse," attended to these risks. The consequences were self-created and predictable, not accidental.

Dovish advisers were intimidated and hid out in meetings. Schlesinger, who attended, wrote memos to the president rather than speak in open meetings. He said (later) he was intimidated because of his low official rank; he lacked the standing, as an assistant White House aide, to be a principal discussant. And as an idealistic liberal in these settings, he felt uneasy and vulnerable to criticism. Hard-liners had the rhetorical advantage in foreign policy: "they could strike virile poses and talk of tangible things like fire power, air strikes, landing craft, and so on. I could not help feeling," he wrote, "that the desire to prove to the CIA and the Joint Chiefs that they were not soft-headed idealists but were really tough guys, too, influenced the State Department's representatives at the Cabinet table."[25]

To keep his job, another man excluded himself voluntarily. Richard Helms, then Bissell's deputy (chief of operations) at the CIA, would ordinarily have played a key role. But he did not like the plan. He thought American involvement could not remain secret. He considered both the mass uprising and Guatemala scenarios unrealistic. He thought the planning was sloppy. Yet he was also a realistic judge of his bureaucratic position. Dulles and his own boss, Bissell, wanted this plan to succeed. Thus, they did not want doubters, they wanted people to put it together, to make it work. Helms judged the plan would be approved and, after it failed, their involvement would end the careers of the senior CIA planners associated with it. But he could not oppose the plan successfully: he would be ineffective and it would cost him his career. He maneuvered privately to alert Hilsman to make the case from within the State Department, but he personally stayed out.[26]

In retrospect, Helms was right in each assessment, although even an optimal strategy almost cost him his job. Predictably, Bissell certainly did want a deputy who did more than stay out, and he went to Dulles to suggest that Dick Helms might find a job abroad — London, for example — more compatible. (Dulles did not approve. Firing Helms would raise questions. Too much visibility.) In the course of events, the plan was approved, secrecy came apart, the invasion failed, Dulles and Bissell did lose their jobs. And Richard Helms, the survivor, became director of the CIA (in 1966). A man used his intelligence to assess (realistically) the personal constraints imposed by his bureaucratic situation, and the system became less intelligent as a result.[27]

The Joint Chiefs of Staff restrained themselves because deference was expected from the military profession concerning issues outside its formal area of expertise and bureaucratic responsibility. (Thus JCS Chief General Lemnitzer later argued, "You couldn't expect us to say this plan was no damn good, you ought to call it off. . . . That's not the way you do things in government . . . The responsibility was not ours.")[28]

Kennedy's formality also intimidated mere expressions of nervous uneasiness. The deliberations were large, full-dress meetings chaired by the president. Dulles and Bissell, superbly prepared, briefed the participants, Bissell often with a pointer in hand. With an agenda structured primarily by Bissell, the meetings shifted quickly to practical detail. Bissell's own gifts probably contributed both to the tendency to trust him and to uneasiness about challenging him by people not sure of their ground. He was a man who seemed to have an answer to every question. He was candid about uncertainties and never estimated more than a two-to-one chance for success. Walt Rostow called him "the most articulate man that has ever been." Even men of substantial ability and intellectual accomplishment admired him, and they continued to respect him after the failure.[29]

Personal effectiveness in large, formal meetings chaired by the president typically requires hard questioning or boldly made arguments. Astute men who value their reputations seldom will become advocates in such settings without a well-informed view to defend, certainly not outside their areas of "official" expertise. And their expertise *was* dubious, given the nature of the problem: Bissell and Dulles were the recognized experts on covert operations. They put their double signature on the check to the president. No other adviser had overthrown a government, judged the likelihood of a mass uprising, or been part of an inner group that discussed such matters. What most of them knew of Cuba came from the *New York Times* and what the CIA told them. Robert McNamara stayed out for this reason: had the topic been the defense budget, he would have intellectually dominated any discussion. But this was not his field. The same was true to a lesser degree of the president. He too initially deferred to his best experts in a field in which he was an amateur. As he put it: "If someone comes in and tells me this or that about the Minimum Wage Bill I have no hesitation about over-ruling them. But you always assume that the military has some secret skill not available to ordinary mortals."[30]

As a consequence of their position in the executive branch, subordinates felt inhibited from delivering critical messages, with emotional force, upward. Admiral Arleigh "Thirty Knot" Burke, a forceful man (downward), later fumed about the second air strike, "What the Chiefs could have done is pound the desk and insisted. . . . We should have been tough but we weren't."[31] (But his open assertiveness was retrospective, in retirement: deference and fear of the consequences of talking straight to a new, and still unknown, commander in chief, made it unthinkable at the time.) Kennedy heard direct moral criticism, face to face, only from Senator Fulbright, a man with an independent power base.

Richard Bissell too acceded deferentially, against his better judgment, to decisions by the president that increased the chances for Kennedy's approval but reduced the project's chances for success: from the bold psychological impact of a daylight assault at Trinidad to a covert, nighttime landing at the Bay of Pigs, from a massive D-Day strike to two strikes to reduce the noise level (but allow Castro to arrest 100,000–200,000 suspected traitors), from sixteen airplanes to six on the first strike, dropping the second strike. Indirectly promised the directorship of the CIA after Dulles retired, Bissell never drew the line and said: "If you do that, Mr. President, we can't guarantee success. You should drop it." A subordinate does not easily give such ultimatums which imply he cannot do the job, because the boss (and this was quite probably true of Kennedy) could attribute the problem to lack of ability or commitment, or to coercive manipulation or just plain willfulness on the part of the subordinate — and not, as the subordinate saw it, to the nature of the problem or the lack of crucial resources.[32]

Thus, as a consequence of locations within bureaucratic systems, people kept reservations to themselves. If they were lower down — such as Bissell's subordinates at the CIA — they swore about it, perhaps talked about resigning (as several of Bissell's key aides did after the D-minus-two reduction), they said (to each other) the president was "criminally irresponsible" (General Lemnitzer), but they did not tell him this, and as "good soldiers" they tried to make the best of it.[33]

Were these men unrealistic — individually — to size it up this way? Later, after the trauma of defeat had jarred them to recognition of the need for candor and the mutual support of one another's best efforts — in the Missile Crisis — I think they would have been. Here, in this situation, I think each was right about the personal risks of being a lone protagonist, especially when lacking expertise. If one were successful, there would be resentments and a suspicion of inadequate courage (strange, given the courage needed to take a bold stand for "intangibles" in such a situation); the disposal problem and soft-on-communism issues would hurt the president and his programs; people would remember — and leak to the press — who caused the plan to be dropped. Was a new, activist administration ready to give standing to a counselor who said things could not be done? And why engage in this policy battle if the right questions had been raised (and they had been), the president had heard the CIA's answers, and the worst outcome, if the CIA were wrong, was a quiet guerrilla dissipation?[34]

No, each man was probably right to keep doubts to himself, given an understanding of his problem as a personal survival problem (i.e., job and power survival).[35] The one man who might have killed the invasion was Dean Rusk; only he had the institutional resources, had he sought to use them, to direct acknowledged expertise against key assumptions of the CIA plan. Had he used his intelligence analysts to cloud further the issue of a mass uprising, he might have taken the steam out of the plan. He could have elaborated the scenario of international press coverage of a prolonged civil war and counseled against overt military actions until the Berlin problem was resolved. And a secretary of state with the implicit backing of the New York foreign policy establishment, arguing on these grounds, might well win (and survive), because it was in a sense his job to serve the president by making these arguments. Had he put his job and prestige on the line, he almost certainly could have blocked the plan (although later, he would probably have discovered his resignation "accepted"; no president is willing to be blackmailed on policy by his own appointees).

He did none of these things. It was not his style. He was a survivor, a team player for the long haul with other, more important, battles to join. And his agenda was to preserve, in his own mind (and publicly) an image of himself as the president's senior foreign policy adviser. (It was not an inappropriate self-image. The secretary of state is often described in such terms. Rusk, older than the president and most of the others, had been assistant secretary of state during the Korean War when most beginners around the table—including Kennedy—had still to be trusted with serious responsibility, by anyone, for national decisions.) His self-image and role he retained by reserving views for the president alone: they were not voiced in public confrontation in open meetings.

The natural consequence of fear and pressure was that, "swearing and making the best of it," subordinates ignored orders, corners were cut, and reality was kept from the president. Leaned on with too many demands, or contradictory demands, people calculated what would be on their final exam. CIA field operatives did not convey the president's decision to forbid American involvement, under any circumstances, because they knew high morale and a successful operation were impossible if troops understood President Kennedy might abandon them.[36] Breaking Kennedy's explicit orders, the CIA handlers led the assault because they judged military success depended on it, that was their job, and lapses would be overlooked if the operation succeeded. Under conflicting pressures, Tracy Barnes chose not to brief Stevenson candidly.

Such problems may be endemic: Programs may not work, and subordinates may see why they do not work, yet senior officials are kept in the dark. Social science research at the Department of State, and other studies of bureaucratic behavior, suggest the "official" norms for mutual aid in collective problem solving are often a facade for maneuvers to stay out of trouble.[37] The real norms absorb uncertainties in upward reporting, undercutting bases for open communication, effective top-level monitoring, and collective intelligence.[38] "Cover your ass," "don't make waves," and "keep your skirts clean" are apparently taken by many people in bureaucracies to be good maxims. Bureaucrats may be timid, uncreative, and strategically evasive because they are intimidated, a natural consequence of conventional structures of power and control.[39]

An analogy with a classroom may be useful. Professors typically feel students should speak up and feel free to disagree or express uncertainty. But students may experience reality differently and in fact may speak only to score points. If they are confused, unsure of themselves, feel inadequate or in trouble, they may tend to maintain a bold front, or avoid teachers, and thus (to their mind) avoid a bad reputation or doubts about their ability.

Bureaucratic assessments were more realistic "upward" than "downward"; *subordinates were erroneously taken for granted.* The men at the top made astute assessments of one another. Allen Dulles, for example, presented a

Cuban operation to Eisenhower in such a way that while Eisenhower was never enthusiastic about it, the CIA still received a presidential mandate to begin. Dulles's briefing to Kennedy after his election omitted mention of a "disposal" problem Kennedy would face if he did not stop the CIA. Nor did Dulles provide alternative disposal options to the president (although afterward he implied he might have found ways to effect a quiet disposal).[40] Committed to the plan, believing in it, and wanting to try it, neither he nor Bissell reported the doubt within the CIA that America's hand could remain a secret. Nor did he and Bissell alert the president that the Bay of Pigs had no route for guerrilla escape.[41]

Often underestimated and overlooked because of his quiet and unassuming manner, Dean Rusk also exhibited unusual ability for astute calculation and bureaucratic effectiveness. Unobtrusively, he effected every major retrenchment he wanted by elucidating doubts and sentiments that the president accepted. He produced the D-Day cancellation by the proposal that it be cancelled unless there were "overriding considerations," a deft and reasonable phrasing that accorded with Kennedy's own sentiments. At Rusk's urging, four days before the invasion, the president held a press conference in which he ruled out, categorically, any use of American troops in Cuba. The CIA thought this a sophisticated "disinformation" tactic, but Rusk later used the public commitment he had elicited, on Sunday, as an added reason why American credibility was threatened and required the air-strike cancellation he urged.[42]

While experienced bureaucrats in Washington developed great sensitivity about superiors, their main constituents, they were less gifted when monitoring and appraising behavior downward, within their own agencies. The work Bissell did in Washington (the conceptual mastery, interlocking parts, and mathematical logic of the plan) was impressive. But his predictions and judgments about the behavior of human beings were less impressive and seemed to rely, perhaps a common failing, on the assumption that others down the chain would be brilliant, responsible, and perfectionist about the details of their work.

Bissell had a passion to use intelligence to create order and improve the world. One of his hobbies was railroads. He knew, and could draw from memory, all the major lines in the country. He knew distances and elevations, and on trips he would mentally reroute inefficient lines, calculating elevations, grades, and distances. The lack of absolute perfection in design offended him. When the cost of building the clandestine airstrip at Happy Valley escalated substantially over original estimates, he ordered the man responsible back to Washington and chewed him out: Castro would be overthrown *and* within budget.[43]

Bissell's expert analytical mind, energy, and attention to detail contributed vitally to make the operation possible. Had he personally run everything, the oversights and sloppiness of people who were less meticulous might have been avoided. The different nose assemblies of the B-26s made sense – unless you cared enough and were bright enough to see a problem the alleged defector might face when his plane arrived in Miami. The new aluminum boats with untried outboards would not have hurt the operation had the man on the spot checked them before departing instead of merely assuming they would work. Loading almost all the ammunition on one boat was alright – unless you had the imagination, perhaps the obsession, to worry about extremely bad luck. "Best guess" intelligence estimates, converted to confidence for transmission upward (seaweed instead of a reef, an uninhabited landing site) would have been flagged for their uncertainty and added work undertaken to refine the judgment. But the frustrating reality of a large government operation was that subordinates commonly overlooked details, or assumed (hoped) they would not matter and things would work out.

There is a deeper cause of the treatment of subordinates, misperceptions of them, and oddly naive miscalculation of their responses to the pressures they were under: They were overlooked and taken for granted. I will want to explore this further in chapter 6.

INTELLIGENT AND EFFECTIVE POLICY: EVALUATING PROPOSALS FOR ORGANIZATIONAL CHANGE

The Bay of Pigs invasion was a widely acknowledged fiasco. Operation MONGOOSE abandoned ideals and wreaked violence without an end game while Castro and the Soviet Union, fearful there *would* be an end game, had incentive to collude in a risky (but undeterred) nuclear deterrence gambit which became extraordinarily dangerous for the United States. After such foreign policy failures critics argue: "they should have listened to adviser x" or "they should have recognized fact y." Such criticism can be only ad hoc, but they also suggest that organizational improvements in eliciting and evaluating arguments and evidence might significantly improve the intelligence and effectiveness of major American foreign policy decisions. In this section I want to assess several theories of inadvertent failures in the policymaking process, asking of the case material: Were there arguments (unheard) or available facts (unknown) that would have substantially changed or reversed the president's decisions?

I will assess the following propositions to evaluate whether failings in technical, rational analysis could have been corrected to produce better policies: (a) the decision process failed because it lacked multiple advocacy; (b) the decision process failed because it lacked good institutional memory; (c) the decision process failed because the CIA was poorly organized to provide reliable forecasts; (d) the decision process failed because it was insular and the decision makers exhibited a "groupthink" syndrome.

Failure of Multiple Advocacy

The political scientist Alexander George has recommended that presidents formally assign advocates to argue policy options systematically, as in the courtroom, to assure that both advocacy and criticism are the best the president can obtain.[44] The case material shows, I believe, this would have been a wise idea: Although it probably would not have affected the major directions of policy, nevertheless such procedures would have produced a better invasion plan; and they might have prevented the Cuban Missile Crisis.

Most of the erroneous beliefs and misjudgments associated with the Bay of Pigs and Operation MONGOOSE (chapters 2 and 3) would have been unchanged by a courtroom-like decision process. The president erred, but I doubt even the best technical social science, using the facts available at the time, would have changed his beliefs and judgments. President Kennedy knew the CIA's estimate of the probability of an uprising; Castro enjoyed majority support, there was no assurance of any mass uprising. (Kennedy *chose* to believe he could change this, but his judgment — in the face of ambiguity — was not a factual question.) The *available* arguments that a D-Day cancellation *could* be disastrous were conveyed to Kennedy on Sunday evening; the unforeseen operational problems that combined to make disaster certain — the reef, and the misinterpreted withdrawal order from CIA headquarters — had not yet occurred on that Sunday evening. The hope that America would retain its "fig leaf"? In hindsight this was erroneous, but no one was better positioned than the president to know the facts and assess arguments about the likely behavior of the American press. The belief that Castro, a "psychotic personality," might lose his nerve, was wrong, but it is doubtful that further analysis would have reversed the idea: Castro's fiery provocations appeared manifestly irrational, and who could say what the psychological effects of the invasion itself might be?

But at two major points accurate presentation of available facts, or new arguments, probably would have altered perceptions: (1) Kennedy's wishful image that the Cubans were solely volunteer patriots could probably have been changed to a more realistic appraisal if he had been told candidly of his error; (2) A skeptical analysis of worst-case possibilities would have revealed the guerrilla escape no longer existed. In both cases, the CIA created erroneous impressions, or allowed them to continue; multiple advocacy would have kept the men more honest and forthright with each other.[45]

During Operation MONGOOSE, setting aside the issue of whether assassination was consistent with the CIA's directives, there is no evidence the president's basic decision to battle Castro would have been reversed by available (unpresented) evidence or arguments. But it is possible that the merits of earlier, clearer, and more dramatic deterrent warnings to Khrushchev, consistent with the earlier message-sending methods used in Laos and Berlin, could have been argued, and to good effect.[46]

Poor Institutional Memory

One reason the American government does not learn is the absence of institutional memory. Administrations change, both through elections and, between elections, by personnel changes among a president's appointees.[47] The historian Ernest May has suggested that a systematic capacity to survey historical experience could improve foreign policy decisions.[48] Were there clear failures of institutional or historical memory, and what were their consequences?[49]

If we reconstruct American policy toward Fidel Castro, it does suggest a limited search of precedents, selectively attentive to scenarios of dramatic setbacks (from inaction) or successes (from bold action) that could apply in dealing with the type of man Castro appeared to be. I will discuss four themes: the danger of messianic leaders, the fraudulent idealism of communism, the importance of message sending, and the expectation of inevitable American victory.

The Danger of Messianic Leaders

Kennedy and his advisers belonged to a generation that had bloody warnings seared into personal memory: Hitler's fascist megalomania and World War II shaped their early lives. Kennedy's older brother was killed in the war, and he almost lost his own life in the Pacific theatre. He won public recognition for his book *Why England Slept*. Major Dean Rusk was a staff officer in the China-Burma-India theatre. Lieutenant McGeorge Bundy landed on the Normandy beaches on D-Day plus one.[50]

Hitler, however, was not an anomaly, and their apprehension of charismatic leaders — of whatever political persuasion — who captured imaginations and used violence to shape history was reinforced by later experience. A similar, brutal pattern continued after World War II as other messianic leaders, now of Communist persuasion, battled for power. Millions died violently as Mao's armies fought to victory in China. In the next step, American soldiers paid the price of Mao's victory as this newly consolidated power base was deployed in the Korean War — which (it is important to recall) ended only seven years before President Kennedy was elected.

The Fraud of Communist Idealism

American leaders have always recognized that Communists *preach* ideals. But, in practice, Stalin's brutal and repressive system in Russia appeared to be the invariant result; in each observed case, revolutionary leaders of single-minded ambition who shot their way to power and purged opponents brutally, never surrendered power or risked doing so in free elections. They produced *totalitarian* regimes with secret police and a controlled press, and they suppressed dissent internally and in spheres of international influence (e.g., the violent suppression of the Hungarian uprising in 1956). Talk of "people's democracy" was a sham; Communist elites aided one another (in those days, men perceived a Sino-Soviet bloc), and thus loss of territory was not an isolated geopolitical loss, but a loss of territory to movements that used the best of human ideals as a cloak for the worst of human impulses and collectively challenged the core values of civilized behavior.

Message Sending

"Message sending" to the Russians figured prominently in both the Bay of Pigs and MONGOOSE decisions. Would America be perceived as "tough" or "weak"? Kennedy himself acknowledged that many elements contributed to Castro's success, but if this success were *perceived* to be a Communist advance, American forebearance (especially, deviating from the Monroe Doctrine) could send a message to the Soviets to encourage their assertiveness in other areas. Thus, Kennedy felt he could not accept "visible" defeat in Laos, Berlin, or Cuba else a process begin that would destabilize world order. And the Soviets were thought to respect toughness, to have backed down when confronted by it (e.g., the Berlin airlift crisis), and to have acted aggressively (and with misperception) when America had failed to send messages which accurately conveyed its resolve. The Korean War was thought by many to have been precipitated by public statements that Stalin misinterpreted and that led him to believe the United States would not go to war to defend South Korea against North Korean invasion.

Inevitable Victory

Finally, in the American self-image, America always won, in both major wars (World Wars I and II), Korea, and in numerous past interventions in Latin America (most recently in Guatemala), as indigenous governments collapsed easily. Undoubtedly some Latin Americans were upset by these effective demonstrations of power, but if past interventions gave America a "bad reputation" in Latin America, critics could present no cases in which the long-term costs outweighed the short-term victories — at least in the sense of citing cases where later interventions failed as a result.

Against this background, the potential impact of inadequate historical memory can be tested by asking whether the substantial majority of historical cases were in the *opposite* direction? Was there *clear*, knowable, and preventable error? Probably not. Certainly Kennedy and his advisers, had they thought about it, would have recognized several counterexamples to each lesson — for example, revolutionaries who spoke in universal ideals, but who were essentially nationalistic and constructive in their political goals. (The European underground during World War II, which fought against Hitler's domination, was an important case; many of its leaders, after the war, became influential and constructive in shaping the European Economic Community.)

But it is doubtful that the four basic beliefs would have been reversed. Especially, the assessment of Castro would have been unchanged; as I will review in the next chapter, he did appear to want to challenge American hegemony and to become a dominant political force in the southern hemisphere, and he did appear interested to spread violent revolution. His actions over a two-year period fit the Hitler/Mao model too well for him not to be considered dangerous.[51]

However, I do want to call to the reader's attention an important qualification which bears upon an argument I will make in chapter 6. In the *imagination* Castro fit the Hitler/Mao model, but he was only a dictator on a poor, isolated island without an appreciable navy or air force and surrounded by massive American conventional superiority. He would always lack the military capability to mount and sustain credible invasions, especially if these were opposed by the U.S. navy. If he was dangerous it was because he might be *persuasive* to others, inspire revolutions against repressive governments by their own people. The danger might be real but it was more psychological in its mechanism than Hitler's tanks, and whether one thought such a distinction vitally important (as Eisenhower did, in his equanimity) depended critically on how one assessed the role of imagination in determining power relationships.

However, even without a major difference in policy outcome, better historical knowledge would still have been beneficial. The needs of beginners are dual: They do not have a complete stock of historical scenarios to consult for possible *answers* to policy problems; perhaps more important, they also lack the comparative perspective afforded by potential counterexamples, which informs them of critical *questions* to pose.

Institutional memory (classified, in the early 1960s) about covert operations belonged to the CIA, and Kennedy and his new advisers did not have the personal knowledge to ask critical questions concerning a transfer of the Guatemala plan. In 1954, a skilled ambassador and staff maintained relations with key army officers and others with antipathy to Communism who expected to suffer losses in a Communist state. In Cuba, America could sustain no such presence (diplomatic relations had been broken), and the prominent anti-Castro and anti-Communist elites, the core of any indigenous opposition, were now living in Miami. Castro was an experienced guerrilla, with faith in himself and his cause, and had never lost his nerve when hopelessly outnumbered in his war to liberate Cuba from Batista's control. Nor was the leadership of the Cuban army likely to rattle or defect; most of the troops were untested, but Castro had replaced the high command (recognizing, from the Guatemala precedent, this crucial vulnerability) and these men were personally loyal and experienced guerrilla fighters. At a minimum, such considerations (after the Mafia failed in early April) might have warned Kennedy more vividly against his belief in an antiseptic victory and made him aware that stalemate or a bloodbath might ensue.

Kennedy also needed a review of the CIA's record of planning and execution. Many of their covert operations had not been successful: A CIA attempt to repeat its Guatemala success in Indonesia had failed. Had Kennedy known the full history of CIA operations, he would have recognized that clandestine field agents were notorious for disobedience to Washington's orders, playing the same games of deception with headquarters (e.g., not reporting candidly and fully on their activities) that they played, officially, with the rest of the world. In the 1950s, President Eisenhower's Board of Consultants on Foreign Intelligence Activities had appointed a panel, chaired by Robert Lovett and David Bruce, to conduct a full-scale review of CIA covert operations. The agency recruited young college graduates and sent them around the world to overthrow governments, bribe newspaper editors, rig elections, spend huge sums of money; the coordination and oversight, financial or otherwise, was minimal.[52] The panel's report was highly critical, but there was now a generational lag: Kennedy and his advisers had to know the report existed, and their trusting reliance on the men at the top of the CIA suggests they did not know of this detailed history. The failure also had a personal element: President Kennedy's father, Joseph P. Kennedy, had served on the blue-ribbon panel. But Jack Kennedy, now in his 40s and president, did not ask his father's advice about the CIA's clandestine plans. Later, when he heard of the invasion's failure, Joseph Kennedy's first question was whether it had been run by CIA clandestine operations people. Told it had, he snorted, "I know that outfit, and I wouldn't pay them a hundred bucks a week."[53]

On these matters, the contribution of institutional memory to critical review would have been of vital importance to the president. The CIA's artful manipulation of the president was egregious, albeit bureaucratically sophisticated.[54] The slipshod cover story at the Bay of Pigs produced a chain of events that effectively scuttled the operation even before the first team of frogmen hit the beaches. Control of lower level CIA operatives was weak; at critical times, the men did not obey Kennedy's orders. The first men to hit the beaches were Americans (against the president's explicit order), and the CIA's commanders, in the final hours, were violating orders and en route to beach their boats, with additional supplies, to continue a fight. Again, although still against presidential orders, we now know American CIA operatives continued to enter Cuba during MONGOOSE operations.[55] In 1962, the head of paramilitary operations for MONGOOSE was fired after a confrontation with a murderously angry Robert Kennedy: at the height of the Cuban Missile Crisis, it was discovered, the man had violated direct orders and allowed the MONGOOSE operations he had previously scheduled to continue.[56]

Poor CIA Organization

After the invasion, a popular solution was to split the CIA, divorcing its Plans division (which ran covert operations) from its Intelligence division.[57] The underlying theory was that President Kennedy had been seduced by fanciful CIA promises of mass uprising and these false estimates were produced, consciously or unconsciously, because the CIA planners had a vested interest to believe their plan would succeed and provide intelligence estimates that would sell it.[58]

The CIA reorganization plan was never adopted, apparently for good reason. In reality, we now know its two divisions *were* independent in their appraisals (so much so that Castro's realism about plots against him was evidence, to the Board of National Estimates, that he was paranoid). Bissell's own estimates of indigenous Cuban support were capably made and confirmed by the Taylor Commission. There were errors aplenty, but not errors of bureaucratic organization.

Entrapment in a Small Group

Irving Janis, a psychologist, has argued that the Bay of Pigs decision may have resulted from a syndrome he called "groupthink." In the "groupthink" phenomenon decision makers bind themselves together into a relatively cohesive group to reduce stress and thus introduce systematic deficiencies in their decision making. They do not carefully survey all alternatives, exhaustively search for information, examine pros and cons of each alternative in an unbiased way, or finally face up to the question, "which course of action will best meet all the essential requirements to solve the problem?"[59]

The specific symptoms of the hasty concurrence-seeking of groupthink are in three categories: *overestimation of the group* (illusions of invulnerability and belief in the inherent morality of the group), *closed-mindedness* (collective rationalizations, stereotypes of out-groups), and *pressures toward uniformity* (self-censorship, illusion of unanimity, direct pressure on dissenters, and self-appointed mind guards who act to block troubling issues from being raised or pursued).[60]

Instances of each deficiency can be cited for the Bay of Pigs, the Taylor Commission, and Operation MONGOOSE. Yet assessing the extent to which they were produced by a single cause—concurrence seeking to reduce stress—is a subtle problem. Adequate personal data are lacking to reach a formal conclusion about the weight to be given to such a causal path. However, several observations can be made to indicate that other causal paths were more significant, and can serve to draw together the main points of this chapter's analysis.

First, Janis's "groupthink" analysis was originally proposed when, by the data available in the 1960s, the invasion decision appeared to have been a mindless aberration: 1,200 men were put ashore against 250,000, erroneous assurances (supposedly by the CIA) of a spontaneous mass uprising were never critically evaluated, and the options for dropping the operation were never developed.

Today we know the plan had a more sophisticated rationale than it first seemed. We know of the earlier Guatemala success, the plan for a coordinated Mafia assassination, that the CIA was cautious in the mass discontent numbers it provided, and that the president and most of his advisers did not approve the plan expecting it would surely succeed, and were willing that it fail if it did so invisibly.

Also, we have seen the *primary* cause of activist like-mindedness was political—the nature of the president's own appointments—and this variable was determined before any meetings of the adviser group. There is no basis, in a before–after comparison, to conclude that the general ways these men thought about Communism, Castro, the moral virtue of American foreign policy, the competence of people with opposed views, or the need for tough, activist policies were either produced or changed substantially after January 1961.

Too, we know now that discussions *were* partly critical. Critics *were* persuasive, eventually making the president uneasy enough to whittle down the plan and undercut it. Even before the April 4 meeting that gave unanimous approval, on which Janis specifically focused, critics were *not* suppressed or unheard, they simply lacked ultimate persuasiveness. *Every* key issue later identified as relevant *was* identified and discussed: "noise levels," the Russian response, uprisings, guerrilla escapes, morality. The Cubans in Guatemala—one-for-all-and-all-for-one, with zeal and "team spirit"—were "groupthinkers," but in the White House the president did survey the critical questions, and he heard the answers of his experts.

If one picked a normal, "non-groupthink" baseline for foreign policy decision making, it would probably not be a systematic and thorough review envisioned by Janis but what has been termed a "cybernetic" process.[61] This description proposes that decision makers respond to changes of a prior status quo, that they typically make only a limited canvas of alternatives, and—rather than exhaustively analyze any alternative—they "satisfice" (i.e., carry the analysis to a natural stopping point where they identify a viable solution they are willing to accept). The Bay of Pigs process was such a "limited search," engaged by the need to decide—yes or no—on a packaged proposal. When they were told the Zapata area "was suitable for guerrillas," they made a sophisticated judgment about further debate: *it really doesn't matter.* That is, if America stayed below the threshold needed to trigger Russian military reaction elsewhere and public outcry, there was no point to pursue other questions of whether ultimately the plan would succeed. No one (except the CIA and the expatriates themselves) was committed to its success. The extent of critical scrutiny reflected the issues of power in the case being considered rather than group processes that simply inhibited analytical thinking. (This too, was the assessment made astutely by Dulles and Bissell: if the group believed a sudden or disastrous defeat would not occur, they would agree and give the CIA's plan a chance, even without full confidence it would succeed.)

Similarly, if we compare the MONGOOSE decision and other decisions, the exhaustiveness of the decision process generally reflected substantive political variables (especially fear of the opponent). For MONGOOSE, Kennedy insisted on secrecy and no direct use of American troops—that is, the criteria he thought meant no risk to himself or to America—and within those parameters gave a blank check and demanded the bureaucracy then devise the means to eliminate Castro. To his mind, there was no *reason*—that is, no expected utility—to have further debate. By contrast, I have argued, the Missile Crisis decision process was prolonged and searching—as were the Berlin and Laos crises considered by this same adviser group—because these involved the Russians directly, and Kennedy could find no simple formula for minimal risk by which the decision process could reach an earlier stopping point.

My argument is that the decision was not primarily the result of a small-group entrapment. For example, I list in Table 4.2 the indications that Kennedy was not primarily a "groupthinker," a proposition which Janis himself acknowledges. In fact, the more Kennedy thought about the Bay of Pigs plan, the less enthusiastic and the more ambivalent he became, a "slope" of his enthusiasm curve which is the opposite from what a group entrapment, beginning in January, would be predicted to show.[62]

Table 4.2. Aspects of Groupthink: Kennedy as an Exception

Uncritical Assumption of Virtuous Self
    Kennedy made consistent efforts to change the plans to improve America's moral standing and render America's role "nonaggressive." He invoked a hard-line test of his moral position by requiring that the Cubans formally understand and agree to do it alone.

Uncritical Assumptions of Invulnerability
    Kennedy consistently expressed worries about vulnerabilities and ordered steps to reduce them, at variance with plans presented by the CIA and favored by other advisers: the shift from Trinidad, the D-2 cutback from 16 to 6 planes, the D-Day cancellation. His worries about consequences produced stubborn resistance to the efforts of advisers to elicit American force commitments.

Suppression of Dissidents
    Kennedy formally solicited the views of all his key advisers, appeared equally open to all viewpoints (accepting Schlesinger's memos and going out of his way to solicit his thinking), and was willing to hear dissenting views and evidence (inviting Fulbright to a crucial meeting, soliciting information from a journalist recently returned from Cuba).

Self-Censorship of Doubts
    Active, skeptical, probing in group discussions.
    Initiator, in group settings, of a series of orders (above) expressing explicit criticisms of the plans being presented.

Cohesiveness with Group and Euphoria
    Moody and distracted before giving "go" signal on Sunday. Resists consultations with most group members on D-Day cancellation decision.

As the analysis in this chapter suggests, collectively self-blocking behavior within the executive branch has determinants which are deeper and more pervasive than small-group dynamics. Prior personal (especially anti-Communist) commitment and "subordinate think" are a better characterization of the nexus of inhibition for most of the advisers. Given their backgrounds, roles, and the standard norms, the conduct of most advisers was already determined: the CIA men were advocates, the Joint Chiefs never spoke on political issues, Berle and Mann had advocated the Guatemala operation, Schlesinger was a junior aide. Only four men in the room — Kennedy, Bundy, McNamara, and Rusk — were the uncommitted "principals." Of these four, Kennedy, as we have seen, was not primarily a "groupthinker." What of the three others? McNamara was a fierce and probing critic in his area of expertise in other meetings with these same men. His lack of experience and expertise, not any general, anxious search to blend invisibly into group concurrence, primarily explains reticence in the Cuba meetings: This was not his field.

Thus, to assess whether simple concurrence seeking was a primary cause becomes a question about the two quintessential team players of the Establishment, Rusk and Bundy. Former college deans, they both built careers on ability and the respect of associates — that is, good judgment without being controversial protagonists. But this was an enduring *personal* style — at least a public style — of men who wished to be team players, respectable and noncontroversial. It *manifested* itself in this small group but did not begin here.[63] Moreover, both men, albeit keeping their own counsel in large, public meetings, retained a healthy independence of mind, channeling their criticisms privately, directly to the president on Sunday. Far from being captives of an enthusiastic group consensus, their back-channel advice was independent, and they acted to minimize public controversy and rein in the CIA.

Although an insular, concurrence-seeking, small-group process may have had a modest psychological effect, the perspective of an additional twenty years — as well as the analysis presented in this book — suggests most of the 1961 syndrome correctly observed by Janis is likely caused at a larger, systemic level. Every newly elected administration since Kennedy has also assumed national power with a tendency to overconfident euphoria (Castro did too: the CIA's psychiatrists thought it evidence of a mental disorder). By the 1980s, research has shown that many of President Johnson's early Great Society programs did not work; each economic recovery program announced almost annually in the 1970s did not work, the bold Reagan economic policies in the early 1980s followed the same pattern of initially overconfident prediction. Inherent assumptions of moral purpose, a shared programmatic mind-set, and an "over-mind" fantasy which ignores or attempts to manage the dissent of outsiders — and then a record of overconfidence and substantial error — appear to be common and predictable in the American political system.[64]

Finally, on detailed examination, this was not a cohesive executive branch group. Ambitious men shared a common bond, in their imaginations, with institutions of national power and valued highly their positions in the inner circle, but there was no personal cohesiveness with one another in these early days. Especially, the evidence suggests, a sharp cleavage divided the Eisenhower holdovers, primarily at the CIA (to a lesser degree the JCS) from the "inner" inner circle of new people loyal to Kennedy. The plan was "their" (the CIA's) plan. The politics of this intragroup split likely explains why the CIA game-planned the guerrilla issue, why Kennedy and his own advisers who "placed great importance" on a fail-safe plan nevertheless did not explain this to the CIA and analyze the guerrilla escape plans candidly, and why Kennedy chose to decide the D-Day cancellation issue by conference only with "his" people (Bundy and Rusk).[65]

The System Worked?

At this point, to aid our summary appraisal of the American foreign policy process, I want to evaluate the bold argument of Leslie Gelb and Richard Betts characterizing decisions made during the Vietnam War later in the 1960s. Their conclusion was: *the system works*. They perceived a high level of technically sophisticated, rational analysis provided to decision makers. Successive presidents were consistently told an American victory in Vietnam was unlikely. A continuing presidential purpose—to prevent a visible American defeat—was sustained until the American domestic political consensus changed.[66]

This analysis usefully corrects a popular tendency solely to blame or scapegoat government officials for the Vietnam War (or other aggressive, especially unsuccessful, policies). Gelb and Betts analyze the effects of international "compulsions" to "save face" and "keep your word," but they ultimately point the finger backward, to the American voter and the competitive nature of American politics. Successive American presidents anticipated that a visible "defeat" in southeast Asia would place them at risk of electoral defeat at the hands of voters aroused by opponents who would use such an outcome against them.[67]

For these Cuban cases, did the advising system work? In many ways, in the short term, it did: The CIA's plans for the Bay of Pigs and MONGOOSE, although they did not work, under the circumstances and constraints were probably about the best to be devised rationally. However, the Gelb and Betts thesis is not wholly true, and in each decision loop there was at least one point of critical failure: the (disguised) absence of an "invisible" dissipation of the Bay of Pigs, and the failure to effect a credible deterrent prior to the Missile Crisis.

Yet, testing these ideas of inadvertent errors and technical remedies, I

Table 4.3. Repeated, Self-Blocking Behavior Within the Executive Branch

1. Earlier appointments predetermined policy outcomes.
2. Neither bureaucratically nor personally did anyone accept complete responsibility.
3. Policy meetings were highly ritualized. Sophisticated participants judged no one would learn or rethink views in the light of arguments and evidence that could be presented.
4. Lying within the executive branch and deceptive, politically "sophisticated" behavior produced a system that moved incrementally further from reality.
5. Decision procedures designed to affect choices rather than clarify them inhibited learning.
6. Collective learning was inhibited because subordinates were at personal risk if they told the truth.
7. Bureaucratic assessments were more realistic "upward" than "downward"; subordinates were erroneously taken for granted.

believe we arrive at an important conclusion: Flaws of technical analysis had little effect on the major direction of policy, and the major cause of American policy was motivational. Had he found a way to prevent the costly press publicity attendant on a Bay of Pigs failure, President Kennedy, under the same circumstances, probably would have made the same basic decision again.[68]

In Table 4.3 I list major generalizations concerning the vector of reduced intelligence and effectiveness we have considered in this chapter such as the behavior of presidents and advisers in the executive branch when making major foreign policy decisions.

NOTES

1. And perhaps because, from pride, this new and younger president wanted his administration to do it alone. Dean Acheson did speak to Kennedy about the plan, saying it was obvious that 1,500 Cubans weren't as good as 25,000 Cubans, but he was not directly involved. At the time, he was primarily active with a task force to develop options for the Berlin problem. See H. Parmet, *JFK: The Presidency of John F. Kennedy* (New York: Dial Press, 1983), p. 163.
2. Kennedy, as a matter of courtesy, invited the senator to share an airplane ride to Florida when he discovered, in casual conversation, they both had engagements there. Fulbright used the occasion to give Kennedy a memo opposing the operation. It turned out they both planned to return the same day. A second invitation was extended, and accepted, and just before the plane landed Kennedy told Fulbright he was going directly to a meeting about Cuba and invited him to attend. Fulbright's advice was not solicited by Kennedy before or after this April 4 meeting and Kennedy did not discuss Fulbright's memo with him during either plane trip. See P. Wyden, *Bay of Pigs: The Untold Story* (New York: Simon and Schuster, 1979) pp. 122–123, 146.

    In his oral history Robert Kennedy (Kennedy Library, Martin interview, vol. 1, p. 60) asserted Fulbright later received a more complete military briefing and appeared to rescind or modify his opposition. Fulbright (personal communication) has denied Kennedy's story.

3. A. Schlesinger, *A Thousand Days: John F. Kennedy in the White House* (Boston: Houghton Mifflin, 1965) p. 483.
4. Wyden, *Bay of Pigs*, p. 120.
5. Ibid., p. 165.
6. Ibid., p. 98.
7. T. Powers, *The Man Who Kept the Secrets: Richard Helms and the CIA* (New York: Pocket Books, 1979), p. 135. Note that Helms's comment to Hilsman quoted in Wyden, *Bay of Pigs*, p. 98: "I'm with you on this . . . but I've been cut out." did not candidly explain (i.e., he lied about) Helms's position and personal strategy. It is possible also to analyze the behavior of Bissell, Helms, and Kirkpatrick as career strategies in which positions toward the Bay of Pigs operation were maneuvers to become director after Dulles's departure. See Wyden, *Bay of Pigs*, pp. 95, 324; Powers, op. cit., passim.
8. Wyden, *Bay of Pigs*, p. 98.
9. Parmet, *JFK*, p. 162, reports Bowles did once confront the president personally, but Bowles makes no mention of this in his memoirs.
10. T. Sorenson, *Kennedy* (New York: Harper and Row, 1965), pp. 270–272; Schlesinger, *A Thousand Days*, pp. 435–438.
11. See C. Bowles, *Promises to Keep: My Years in Public Life. 1941–1969* (New York: Harper and Row, 1971), pp. 328–329. Rusk volunteered to tell Bowles if the original plan were to be reinstated so he could take his objections to the president personally.
12. Wyden, *Bay of Pigs*, pp. 120–121.
13. Wyden, *Bay of Pigs*, pp. 71–73.
14. Kennedy also used pragmatism as a criterion. He excluded Douglas Dillon. Dillon, under Eisenhower, was directly involved in Cuban planning. He was now secretary of the Treasury and not invited. He had firm, known, views that the president should be ready to use American forces or should drop the operation.
15. See H. Arendt, *The Origin of Totalitarianism* (New York: Harcourt Brace Jovanovich, 1973) for a general discussion.
16. Wyden, *Bay of Pigs*, "orphan," p. 305; "your operation," p. 204 (italics added).
17. Ibid., p. 8.
18. Schlesinger, *A Thousand Days*, pp. 257–258. The comment was to Schlesinger. As noted above, Kennedy expressed different aspects of his mood and thinking to different advisers; at times, he was likely also more militant than this minimal commitment.
19. Schlesinger, *A Thousand Days*, p. 255.
20. For a discussion of bureaucratic viewpoints and politics see D. Caldwell, "Bureaucratic Foreign Policy Making" *American Behavioral Scientist* 21 (1977): 87–110. and references cited there, M. Halperin, P. Clapp, and A. Kanter, *Bureaucratic Behavior and Foreign Policy* (Washington, DC: Brookings Institution, 1974); G. Allison, *Essence of Decision: Explaining the Cuban Missile Crisis* (Boston: Little, Brown, 1971).
21. A further reason for such behavior was probably the deferential assumption that the president was the "over-mind" of the executive branch, the single rational actor, the judge who would hear all points of view and then decide. Each man understood himself to be playing but one "part" in the process, appropriately presenting his agency's perspective, that is, its responsibility for one set of considerations, one "part" of the problem. See L. Bloomfield, *The Foreign Policy Process: A Modern Primer* (Englewood Cliffs, NJ: Prentice-Hall, 1982), p. 160.

22. Harvard Professor John Plank, recently returned from Cuba, whom Schlesinger asked to brief several participants; quoted in L. Vandenbroucke, "'How Could I Have Been So Stupid?' A Methodological Inquiry into the Decision to Land at the Bay of Pigs" Paper presented at the annual meeting of the International Studies Association-West/Western Political Science Association Meetings. San Diego. (Photocopy, 1982, footnote 63, p. 36.)

23. NSAM 31. This document was circulated after the March 11 meeting at which Kennedy rejected the Trinidad plan.

24. Kennedy manipulated the Bay of Pigs decision process to keep at arm's length the arguments and considerations he did not want to hear; he cut out Stevenson and invited Senator Fulbright to only one meeting; he blocked people with military expertise from the D-day cancellation decision. To the Taylor Commission he appointed men of shared, activist mind set — and no critics of his original decision.

25. Schlesinger, *A Thousand Days*, p. 256. The "tough guy" reference is to A. A. Berle, also an early advocate of Guatemala, 1954.

26. Powers, *The Man Who Kept the Secrets*, p. 135 et passim.

27. Helms might be judged to be right solely by being a uniformly cautious man. It is not clear, then, whether he had better judgment per se.

28. Quoted in Vandenbroucke, "So Stupid," footnote 27, p. 33.

29. Wyden, *Bay of Pigs*, pp. 17–19.

30. Ibid., p. 317.

31. Quoted in ibid., p. 319.

32. See the later discussion of attribution theory (chapter 6) and D. Kahneman, P. Slovic, and A. Tversky, ed., *Judgment Under Uncertainty: Heuristics and Biases* (Cambridge: Cambridge Univ. Press, 1982).

33. Wyden, *Bay of Pigs*, pp. 158–159 discusses the threatened resignations at the CIA following an earlier cut-back in the operation.

34. And the deaths of Cubans, on both sides. But these, it must be inferred, counted for less.

35. See A. Wildavsky, "The Self-Evaluating Organization" in J. Shafritz and A. Hyde, ed., *Classics of Public Administration* (Oak Park, IL: Moore Publishing, 1978), pp. 412–417; C. Argyris and D. Schon, *Organization Learning: A Theory of Action Perspective* (Reading, MA: Addison-Wesley, 1978) for a general discussion of this problem within organizations.

36. Perhaps, too, they did not believe it true and felt they were not expected to pass the message.

37. C. Argyris, *Some Causes of Organizational Ineffectiveness Within the Department of State* (Washington, DC: Department of State Center for International Systems Research, 1967).

38. Argyris and Schon, *Organization Learning*.

39. Wildavsky, "The Self-Evaluating Organization", and H. Wilensky, *Organizational Intelligence: Knowledge and Policy in Government and Industry* (New York: Basic Books, 1967) address these issues. A general review, which does not, however, evaluate the evidence for these general maxims, is D. Katz and R. Kahn, *The Social Psychology of Organizations*, 2nd ed. (New York: Wiley, 1978). See L. Etheredge, "The Hypnosis Model of Power" *Psychoanalysis and Contemporary Science* 3 (1980): 415–451 and "Dual-Track Information Processing in Public Policy Decision Making: Models of Strong Imagination Systems." (Symposium paper presented to the American Psychological Association meetings, Toronto. Photocopy: 1984.) for a suggestion, and discussion, of possible direct effects of hierarchic visual imagery on motivation.

40. A private conversation reported to the author: Dulles said the *only* thing he felt guilty about was his failure to take account of Kennedy's youth and to appreciate that Kennedy's early youthful enthusiasm in November eroded as time progressed. Dulles said that as the older man, he failed a duty to be more perceptive and to develop the options for disposal.

41. Also, nothing crucial went into writing: security against leaks to the press, but also a way to restrict and control the decision process.

    Allen Dulles was considered, generally, a master of bureaucratic infighting, "adept at the arts of polite exchange when murder was in his blood." Powers, *The Man Who Kept the Secrets*, p. 105.

42. Kennedy said, "There will not be, under any circumstances, any intervention in Cuba by the United States armed forces, and this government will do everything it possibly can — and I think it can meet its responsibilities — to make sure that there are no Americans involved in any actions inside Cuba . . . [T]his administration's attitude is so understood and shared by the anti-Castro exiles from Cuba in this country." Quoted in Sorenson, *Kennedy*, p. 298. Kennedy was wrong about his ability, as president, to prevent CIA agents from entering Cuba.

43. Wyden, *Bay of Pigs*, pp. 12–17, 37.

44. A. George, "The Case for Multiple Advocacy in Making Foreign Policy" *American Political Science Review* 67 (September 1972): 751–785; A. George, *Presidential Decisionmaking in Foreign Policy: The Effective Use of Information and Advice* (Boulder, CO: Westview Press, 1980). See also I. Destler, "Comment. Multiple Advocacy: Some Limits and Costs" *American Political Science Review* 67 (1972): 786–790; I. Destler, "National Security Advice to U.S. Presidents: Some Lessons from Thirty Years" *World Politics* 29 (1977): 143–176; I. Destler, "National Security Management: What Presidents Have Wrought" *Political Science Quarterly* 95 (1980): 573–588.

45. But a president who cannot trust his top appointees to be completely honest with him, and on issues of major national importance, has a more serious problem than should be addressed solely by multiple advocacy assignments in the Cabinet Room.

46. We do not, however, have detailed information concerning the deliberations of Soviet intentions. Conceivably, no analyst in American government, given the available information, could have made the case persuasively.

47. H. Heclo, *A Government of Strangers: Executive Politics in Washington* (Washington, DC: Brookings Institution, 1977) reviews these problems.

48. The argument must be assessed partly by conjecture because we do not have verbatim records of the discussions. As well, the men were well educated and well read: many precedents may have occurred to them. See, for example, E. May, *'Lessons' of the Past: The Use and Misuse of History in American Foreign Policy* (New York: Oxford Univ. Press, 1973), p. xii, for a brief discussion of President Kennedy's knowledge of European history.

49. For several efforts to analyze recent experience see, among others, L. Bloomfield and A. Leiss, *Controlling Small Wars: A Strategy for the 1970's* (New York: Knopf, 1969); B. Blechman and S. Kaplan, *Force Without War: The U.S. Armed Forces as a Political Instrument* (Washington, DC: Brookings Institution, 1978); A. George, D. Hall, and W. Simons, *The Limits of Coercive Diplomacy* (Boston: Little, Brown, 1971); A. George, ed., *Managing U.S.-Soviet Rivalry: Problems of Crisis Prevention* (Boulder, CO: Westview Press, 1983); A. George and R. Smoke, *Deterrence in American Foreign Policy: Theory and Practice* (New York: Columbia Univ. Press, 1974), and the broad, quantitative review by F. Beer, *Peace*

Against War: The Ecology of International Violence (San Francisco, CA: W. H. Freeman, 1981).

50. Schlesinger, *A Thousand Days*, pp. 211–212.
51. Too, these considerations had been raised (albeit without a counting of historical cases): Fulbright, chairman of the Senate Foreign Relations Committee, told the president that Castro was "a thorn in the flesh, not a dagger at the heart" and implicitly dismissed the notion that forbearance would undermine the structure of world order.
52. A. Schlesinger, *Robert F. Kennedy and His Times* (Boston: Houghton Mifflin, 1978), pp. 455–459.
53. Ibid., p. 456.
54. And the failure to provide a worst-case, guerrilla-option appendix to the Joint Chiefs for review.
55. T. Branch and G. Crile, "The Kennedy Vendetta: An Account of the CIA's Entanglement in the Secret War Against Cuba" *Harper's* (August, 1975), pp. 49–63.
56. Martin, *Wilderness of Mirrors*, pp. 144–145.
57. G. Allison and P. Szanton, *Remaking Foreign Policy: The Organizational Connection* (New York: Basic Books, 1976), pp. 201–203 discuss this proposal.
58. And the Plans divisions agents and spy-networks in the *field* — who might wish to convey misleading messages to Washington, would not be the only network providing information.
59. I. Janis, *Groupthink: Psychological Studies of Policy Decisions and Fiascoes*, second ed. (Boston: Houghton Mifflin, 1983), p. 298; see also I. Janis, *Victims of Groupthink* (Boston: Houghton Mifflin, 1972).
60. Janis, *Groupthink*, second ed., p. 245.
61. J. Steinbruner, *The Cybernetic Theory of Decision* (Princeton: Princeton Univ. Press, 1974) presents this model. It may be descriptively accurate, but likely reflects many underlying mechanisms: a typically limited sense of personal responsibility, laziness, time pressures, bureaucratic inhibition, low returns to further calculations until after an opponent makes a responding move, etc. I will argue in chapter 6 that the main determinants of the stopping points are power calculations.
62. I do, however, believe that Kennedy and his preselected advisers, under stress, appear to have become "groupthinkers" during the MONGOOSE period.
63. Recall that both men, along with the president, trusted the CIA's assurances of a "quiet" disposal and they probably felt no need to devise a plan that would succeed. This was not a case of *either* approving a plan that would succeed or calling it off; they were willing to approve a plan that might not succeed.
64. See the discussion of imagination systems in chapter 6: it is possible we are observing mood effects caused, subjectively, by the new experience of being "above" and "at the top."
    The theory of small group entrapment also omits history and learning (including the absence of Janis's book and knowledge of its thesis) from the causal equation. The bases of key lessons decision makers needed to learn had not yet, in their experience, occurred. To be forewarned and engage in vigorous intellectual "hot pursuit" of every detail of the CIA's plan, they needed to know CIA experts might seek deliberately to mislead them. This they did not yet realize: the Bay of Pigs disaster had not yet happened, and National Security Adviser McGeorge Bundy — the key man to organize such a review — was dealing with a man he personally admired, an early mentor. Walt Rostow (now Bundy's assistant) had graded papers for him.

65. Janis surely is correct, and Maxwell Taylor would agree with him, that strong individuals who care deeply about issues, have the courage to express their doubts as well as their convictions, and are willing to pursue the truth without support, in face of fears (perhaps realistic) of isolation, rejection, and loss would make vital contributions to any decision process, public or private. Concurrence seekers and people who believe, with a limited sense of personal responsibility, "it really doesn't matter," undermine collective strength. But such solutions, as I will discuss in chapters 6 and 7, demand more of the character, integrity, and autonomy of individuals, and wider supportive changes than in small group processes alone.

66. "the decisionmaking system . . . *did achieve its stated purpose* of preventing a Communist victory in Vietnam until the domestic balance of opinion shifted and Congress decided to reduce support to Saigon in 1974–75 — that is, until the consensus, and hence the purpose, changed and the United States decided to let Vietnam go." L. Gelb and R. Betts, *The Irony of Vietnam: The System Worked* (Washington, DC: Brookings Institution, 1979), p. 24.

67. In a broader assessment, however, the Gelb and Betts thesis falls apart; presidents consistently maneuvered to *prevent* domestic opposition to their conduct of the Vietnam War from arising, to the point of systematic lying and deception. A complete review of the Gelb and Betts book would be a separate project. As chapter 6 will outline, I believe they have misdiagnosed the deeper cause and that the over dramatized system of imaginings (bold overconfidence, fear, and especially the compulsion to dominate events and forces in the imagination) were the principal story. The advisory system, working only analytically, substantially failed both presidents and the nation.

68. Note that the president was *not* trying, in either case, to effect Castro's elimination. He was willing to approve the best acceptable plan that had a *chance*; recall Eisenhower, too, had approved the Guatemala resupply with only a 20 percent estimated probability of success.

Chapter 5 SYSTEM-CONSTRAINED LEARNING

Chapter 4 organized evidence concerning one vector affecting the intelligence and effectiveness of American foreign policy, the behavior of leaders and advisers during the decision-making process. In this chapter I will assemble evidence bearing upon a second vector, the repetition of policy choices. To afford a broader perspective, I will review America's earlier encounters with Fidel Castro in the Eisenhower administration. Then I will expand the historical frame further to argue that individual American foreign policy decisions can be seen to follow a larger pattern and a more general logic (of power relationships) evidencing America's instinctively chosen role in the international political system.

FROM FAILURE TO FAILURE: CUBA AND AMERICA FROM 1958 TO 1960

"What an interesting thing this international chess game is."
—Fidel Castro, 1960 (discussing his choices in American-Cuban relations.)[1]

One way to write history is to be guided by an esthetic theory of truth, seeking to write a story with balance, portraying conflicts as mistakes that might have been avoided had both sides not seen "through a glass, darkly." But in any simple sense, this view of Cuban-American relations is inaccurate: Conflict was inevitable, and could be resolved without violence only were one side, the other, or both to modify its purposes. Thus, what must be appraised critically is that neither side did so and each became impotent to prevent what was, "rationally," its own worst case: for Castro, an American-backed invasion which, if well-executed, had a chance to succeed; for America, a Cuban-Soviet alliance.

I will review selectively the history the two countries created: the main outline of American policy prior to Castro's victory; the sequence of deterioration in 1959–1960; and four aspects of that deterioration which reflected misperception or misjudgment (Castro's abandoning of democratic forms, his hasty efforts to export revolution, his—initially unrealistic—fears of American hostility, and dependency).

Castro's Victory and Its Legacy

In December 1956, Fidel Castro and a handful of men returned to Cuba from exile to begin a revolution. They were to be victorious in two years: Batista's regime collapsed and he fled on January 1, 1959.

From the first, the vital concern in Washington was whether or not Castro was Communist. The evidence argued against the proposition. He was not trained by Moscow. He did not quote Marx nor indoctrinate his troops with Marxist ideology. He criticized both communism ("it kills men by killing their freedom,") and capitalism ("it kills men by hunger"). He promised return to Cuba's constitution of 1940. Initially, the Soviet government predicted that his survival in such close proximity to the United States was unlikely and was unwilling to commit prestige and significant material aid to his support. The Communist Party of Cuba—long-since infiltrated by the CIA—did not consider Castro a member, thought him too undisciplined to subscribe reliably to any ideology, and was wary of his plans for them; they jumped on his bandwagon only at the last minute when his victory became assured.

Under Dulles and Bissell the CIA kept a close watch on dissident groups in foreign countries. Their information concerning Castro was carefully researched: In 1957, when Castro's rebellion numbered less than two dozen men in the Sierra Maestra Mountains, at least one was a CIA agent.[2]

Early American foreign policy became a shifting compromise in battles between factions. Eisenhower's ambassador of the late 1950s, Earl Smith, strongly supported Batista and was his personal friend. Smith believed Castro a secret communist but had no persuasive evidence, and his personal credibility among foreign policy professionals was minimal: a former Wall Street broker and Republican campaign contributor, he also spoke no Spanish. In Washington, key senior posts had changed hands since the Guatemala operation and were now held by individuals more favorably disposed toward change. The assistant secretary for Latin America Affairs, Roy Rubottom, favored Castro's reforms. His chief, Robert Murphy (deputy under secretary of state) could not stomach Batista's corruption and police torture, referring to him privately as a "gorilla."[3] The health of Secretary Dulles, afflicted with intestinal cancer, was failing (he resigned in April 1959 and died five weeks later); his successor (Christian Herter) was a more modest and less domineering personality without Dulles's messianic fervor and belief that even neutrality was "immoral."[4] And a new public mood supported the moderates: Vice-President Nixon was spat upon and his life threatened by an angry mob during a goodwill visit to Latin America in 1958. Dramatically reported in the American press, the incident catalyzed learning, a sensibility that new forces of change were astir on the continent. With different people, a new mood, and persuasive evidence that Castro was not a Communist, cautious forbearance could temporarily shape policy.

The American government's instinctive hostility to Central American revolutionaries was also altered by the vivid and appealing portrayal of Castro presented by the *New York Times*. Castro had anticipated that American public attitudes would be crucial to his success and invited a senior editor of the *Times*, Herbert Matthews, to his camp in the Sierra Maestra. Matthews' enthusiastic report appeared in the *Times* (with front-page headlines for three consecutive days) in February 1957. He wrote:

> The personality of the man is overpowering. It was easy to see that his men adored him . . . Here was an educated, dedicated fanatic, a man of ideals, of courage and of remarkable qualities of leadership . . . one got a feeling he was invincible . . . A great talker who dealt fairly with the peasants, paying for everything they ate.[5]

Matthews' view of Castro as a social democrat created a warm response: Castro suddenly became a North American hero. He presented himself as a moderate and spoke without hostility to America. When a CBS News camera crew visited to do a follow-up story, Castro emphasized that he opposed bloodshed but wished to create an atmosphere in which the Batista government would have to fall. The interview, televised nationally in May 1957, further built Castro's American constituency and bolstered State Department moderates.[6]

American policymakers, however, preferred known, "friendly" leaders to a rebel. The first American plan was to urge Batista to recognize the handwriting on the wall and pressure him to effect economic and political reforms and to end police torture and repression. But Batista (a former sergeant who had obtained power by a coup) had never been interested in popular democracy or economic redistribution and may not have had the power to produce them. The State Department specifically urged democratic elections to give the discontented a greater share of power, but Batista held elections so blatantly rigged that even Ambassador Smith — who claimed to have trusted Batista's "solemn promise" to be honest — said they lacked the semblance of credibility.[7] Believing Americans ingenuous (he faced a growing underground and urban terrorism), Batista accelerated the secret police torture, summary executions, and arrests (followed by permanent disappearances) he thought necessary to maintain order and survive.

Batista's large army, never an effective fighting force, was corrupt, and its typical soldier had no incentive to fight for Batista's survival. A "Big Push" military offense of May 1958 fizzled. His high command was revealed as a "gaggle of corrupt, cruel, and lazy officers without combat experience."[8] Viciously, they engaged in summary executions and took no prisoners. By

contrast, Castro took 433 prisoners, none were mistreated, and these were
turned over to the International Red Cross. Castro spoke warmly of young
officers in Batista's army who were not corrupted but lived for their careers
and their Service. He contrasted them with higher ranks who made themselves
millionaires by vice protection and other crooked practices.[9] Castro was appealing, the kind of man Cubans wanted for their leader.

After the "Big Push" failed, the American government stepped up pressure
on Batista and, simultaneously, began to distance itself to abandon him and
change sides. America stopped his arms supply and declared official policy
to be "noninterventionist." Ambassador Smith was instructed to tell Batista
U.S. troops would not prevent Castro's victory if Batista could not quickly
reform to sustain his own popular support: "the United States would take
no steps to keep Batista in office and would take no steps to remove Batista
from office."[10] The State Department further attempted to increase pressure
for its policy of reform by a private campaign to discourage other countries
from selling arms to Batista.[11]

The American press contributed further to hasten Batista's end. Matthews
of the *Times* aided Castro's cause by stories that implied Castro commanded
a substantial military force. (Castro had tricked Matthews; when he became
a hero in the American press, he had only eighteen men. Castro told Matthews
there were other camps; his aide Ché Guevara dressed their men in different
uniforms and marched them by in different formations during Matthews' interview with Castro.)[12] Cuba's elites believed the *Times* portrayal rather than
the denials in their own censored press; and when the American press also
dramatized the "Big Push" defeat, agreed Batista was hopelessly corrupt,
reported Castro's power growing, and predicted Batista's fall as inevitable,
it helped to create the reality.

The U.S. government did not surrender control gracefully. Its second plan
was to maneuver to block Castro and transfer Batista's power to men who
were known to be friendly to the United States. The CIA scouted the possibilities of a military junta to exclude Castro from power, a substitute president in whose favor Washington could persuade Batista to resign, and a coalition that would limit Castro's real power. It tried to find, but could not find,
suitable candidates.[13]

Castro's victory was based upon the new American-invented prototype, the
Guatemala model. He established an enclave and engaged in psychological
warfare to produce collapse. Contrary to popular myth, he never fought a
major "war." There were no large battles. In the summer of 1958, he had 300
men against Batista's 40,000. When the Batista government collapsed, only
1,500–2,000 Cubans had taken up arms behind Castro's banner.[14] (The size
of Castro's victorious "army" encouraged Dulles and Bissell because it illustrated what an invasion force of 1,200 with the right psychological impact
might accomplish in these countries: it further validated the Guatemala sce-

nario. Castro's victory also tended to scare American policymakers: In the dreamlike world of Latin American politics, without strong political institutionalization, images *were*, often, political reality.[15] A blink and an established government with a formidable military could fall, its power dissipate like smoke. Conventional thinking which linked political power to military strength — 40,000 versus 1,200 — was erroneous.)

From these early events, two plausible but erroneous American lessons followed. First, as State Department liberals perceived their cut-off of Batista to be motivated by sympathy and to be effectively supportive, they hoped Castro might realistically begin his relations with the United States with this same understanding. Second, the State Department judged Castro's new political power to be very conditional. His victory did not come from large numbers of organized followers but from his ideals and because he was in the right place at the right time. If he was untrue to his earlier promises and image, appeared to sell out his nation to the Soviets and establish a dictatorship, they thought him vulnerable to replacement.[16]

Overview of Deterioration

Shortly after his victory in April 1959, Fidel Castro visited the United States. He came to Washington, D.C. at the private invitation of a group of newsmen: he had not been officially invited and President Eisenhower — in a deliberate display of displeasure — extended a golf vacation.[17] But State Department officials met with Castro's ministers (who accompanied him) and expressed willingness to consider requests for foreign aid favorably. Castro instructed his ministers to make no requests, and they never did so.[18] In the following year the American government, without an affirmative response, made over two dozen formal and informal offers of aid and negotiation of differences.[19]

A year after this visit, in early 1960, Castro accepted foreign aid from the Soviet Union, a $100 million trade and aid package announced during a visit by Soviet First Deputy Premier Mikoyan. Thus, as Castro had meanwhile engaged in fierce anti-American rhetoric and spurned American overtures, and now had selected a Soviet benefactor, Eisenhower concluded the man had chosen sides to be America's enemy; he approved the CIA's involvement in covert action against Castro — which became the Bay of Pigs plan — within a month after the Mikoyan visit.[20]

The story of how this break came about can best be reviewed by analyzing the deeper issues at stake from Castro's side. By March 1959, in decisions that now appear internal and not caused by specific American provocation, he began (1) to break free from a traditional framework of Cuban-American relations; (2) to abandon promises for democratic elections and to persecute opponents; (3) to effect social reform promptly by beginning to expropriate property and business ($800 million to $1 billion owned by Americans) without any serious plan for timely payment; (4) to test America's willingness to support nonviolent and rapid change in Latin America; (5) to attempt export of his model of armed revolution; and (6) to prepare his people for an invasion he feared forces in America eventually would launch.[21]

To explore how American-Cuban relations unraveled, I will examine four of these issues in detail: Castro's abandonment of electoral democracy; his early attempts to export revolution; Castro's fears of an American plot; and America's unwillingness to address seriously the problem of dependency.

Abandoning Democracy

Initially, Castro was undecided about a future role; he refused the presidency of Cuba and accepted only command of the armed forces. But he began to give public speeches every two to three days, usually of several hours' length, and to electrifying effect. The crowds adored him and shouted themselves hoarse. He seemed to achieve a mystical, charismatic union of himself with his listeners: "Do we need elections?" Castro would ask. "No!" the crowds shouted. Castro's newly discovered charismatic power, expressed in this sense of mutual union, emboldened him.[22]

Castro decided to take the presidency and to lead Cuba without elections, "until the purposes of the Revolution were achieved." Determined to bond all elements of his country with his charismatic leadership, he became greatly agitated by the experience of formal opposition as if, given the nature of his powerful identification with his people, internal divisions threatened his personal equilibrium. He dealt harshly with opponents. Former Batista officers who had tortured or killed prisoners were executed after public show trials, conducted with public enthusiasm.[23] Former loyal supporters who criticized Castro were driven from office or imprisoned. Many critics, unwilling to live forever in the shadow of Fidel's personality, left for the United States for greater freedom and to solicit American backing.

By these steps, Castro began to appear ominous to American planners; his emerging scenario appeared to be a familiar pattern of evolution to a Communist, one-party state and dictatorship, the alarming pattern of recent messianic leaders who then sought to expand their power, in the next step, by foreign conquests. And that, too, happened.

Exporting Revolution[24]

Castro followed his victory by several attempts to export revolution. He aided bands of other expatriates to mount armed landings, establish enclaves, trigger internal uprisings and overthrow other right-wing dictators; by April 1959, American intelligence knew him to be involved in planning invasions of Haiti, Panama, Nicaragua, and the Dominican Republic.

In April, his first expedition was launched: 102 men—mostly Cubans—landed in Panama and were quickly surrounded and defeated.

In early June, 110 Nicaraguan expatriates landed in Nicaragua from Costa Rica (where they had been trained and financed by President Betancourt of Venezuela); their landing coincided with a landing of seventy men from other political factions who embarked from Cuba. The rebels were quickly defeated.

In mid-June, Cuba launched air and sea attacks against the Dominican Republic. Two hundred and twenty-four men were involved. Trujillo, dictator of the Dominican Republic, was alerted to the sea landings because radio silence was broken, and his air force destroyed the invasion ships by rocket attack (a fate similar to Kennedy's force, almost two years later, when he allowed Castro to retain operational aircraft). Most of the attackers were quickly slain.

In August, perhaps against Castro's personal wishes, about twenty-five to thirty Haitian revolutionaries departed Cuba to overthrow the government of Haiti. Upon landing, they were quickly hunted down and killed.

Washington might have drawn either of two lessons from these violent events. It might have concluded Castro was, at most, a nuisance. He acted impetuously, with poor planning. No mass uprisings occurred in the target countries.[25] He posed no serious danger.

In Washington, however, men responded more to what they imagined were the impulses behind Castro's actions. Now there were data points, they extrapolated the trend, and made a straightforward forecast: Castro was likely to continue such efforts. Thus, the U.S. government continued to refuse arms sales (Castro wanted to purchase battleships and other weapons) and tried to block arms sales to Cuba from all non-Communist sources (successfully in the case of Britain; unsuccessfully in the case of Belgium although Belgian deliveries were destroyed when the delivery ship *La Coubre* exploded in Havana harbor, an event Castro blamed on the CIA).

In retrospect, these early invasions were vastly overconfident and hasty.[26] As we will see, Castro simultaneously wanted support from America in the form of arms sales, a Marshall Plan, and increased sugar purchases. But nothing would make American planners more wary than an early warning Castro intended to incite wars in the Caribbean. Castro's bizarre "invasion" of Panama, especially, vastly underestimated American sensitivity to its security interests in the Panama Canal. Nor did it help Castro's case to speak publicly—as he did—about the "liberation" of Puerto Rico.[27] The major effect of these actions was to increase Washington's wariness and to force Castro eventually to seek Communist sources if he wished offensive (or defensive) weapons.

Overthrow Fears

Initially, the novel situations in which Castro and America found themselves stirred vivid imaginations on both sides: high hopes of culminated romance coexisted with deep fears of treachery. To some in America, Castro was a hero or new-found friend. Yet others imagined his appeal to be a shrewd facade, convinced that he would string America along eventually to emerge in his true colors as a demagogue and Communist enemy. In Cuba, Castro initially told his aides they should not ask America for foreign aid—and this would so surprise Americans they would offer it without being asked. Yet he also feared invasion and duplicity. Awash in scenarios, alert and wary perception of others' imagined secret strategies ultimately led each side to act more from fear than from hope.[28]

To Castro, it appeared realistic, given the Guatemala overthrow, to anticipate Eisenhower might try to overthrow him. We know, now, there was no such plan, but the American government was unable (likely, unwilling) to convey that message. Ché Guevara, Castro's lieutenant, had been in Guatemala City (as a young medical student) in 1954; he and Castro discussed and studied the precedent thoroughly.[29]

Castro's "learning," his prediction of American hostility, was also supported by interpretations drawn from other evidence; Eisenhower's people had appeared to favor Batista until his cause was hopeless (and Castro may not have known of the complex interplay of motives and compromises behind American foreign policy and that Ambassador Smith's views were atypical).[30] Next, they had maneuvered to block Castro from power. Castro's enemies who fled to America were resettled hospitably by the American government in a common area from which attacks could be launched (Miami), and they began to organize and buy arms without effective control by U.S. authorities. By the summer of 1959, terrorist bombs began to explode in Cuban cities, occasional incendiary bombing raids were launched from private American airports, and American officials neither devoted the resources to stop them nor allowed Castro to buy weapons to defend his country. Reality was ambiguous, but was it more reasonable to believe these actions reflected coherent American policy or to believe the State Department's dismayed explanation that these were only unfortunate incidents that Eisenhower, in a free country, could not fully control? Castro, with fire, passionately denounced America for desiring "to castrate" his revolution and Cuba's new independence.[31]

Other evidence before Castro also forecast that, whatever *current* American government policy might be—and the new American ambassador, Philip Bonsal, was genuinely supportive of Cuban social reforms and consistently expressed American desires for friendship and good relations—there were "forces" in America who did want to overthrow him. Vice President Nixon, a likely presidential candidate, had visited Cuba under Batista and praised his "competence." *Time* magazine had supported Batista and now seized upon the public executions of former Batistianos with a moral fervor absent when the tortures and murdering of prisoners took place. Even at Batista's worst, major American critics had never advocated a threat to destroy Cuba's economy (by ending its sugar quota for sales in American markets) to change

Batista's odious policies, but they now did so to attempt to coerce an end to Castro's public executions and to force elections. In 1959, a Senate *Internal Security Subcommittee* staged hearings at which Castro's enemies testified he was communist. True, the Eisenhower administration took pains to be publicly calm and avoid recriminations, but to a man like Castro, the evidence that powerful enemies were building a case against him loomed large.[32]

In retrospect, we can appreciate the problem Castro faced in discussing aid. As he recognized, it was a "chess game." *If* he accepted offers of American aid and negotiation—treated the benevolence as publicly credible—he left himself vulnerable: the United States could string him along, undercut any efforts to prepare his people to resist, strengthen his enemies in exile to create an invasion force, and then invade; or enemies in America could build their case and—with Nixon as president—policy could change suddenly. Castro's other option (and, he thought, the less risky) was to polarize relations, refuse to credit that enticements of aid were sincere, and so strengthen his own control and the anti-American fervor of his people that an invasion could be deterred or defeated. The sympathetic American ambassador, Philip Bonsal, judged in his memoirs that Castro had already concluded by the spring of 1959 that an American invasion was probable—and hence reassurances could not be considered anything but duplicitous stratagems.[33] Castro *thought* he saw clearly the choices and risks.[34]

Dependency

Another source of conflict—unaddressed by American policy—was dependency, a difficult subject for American policymakers to grasp and which they tended to ignore. In Cuba, "dependency" meant Cuba's fate was vulnerable to almost complete unilateral control by Washington. American troops had intervened, and American ambassadors had played major proconsul roles throughout Cuba's history.[35] The Cuban economy depended on American markets for the majority of its imports and exports; American investors were the primary source of private capital and owned major portions of key industries and prime agricultural land. American sugar quota subsidies were a major source of government revenue.[36]

"Dependency" also meant a cumulative, historically produced, psychological drama, a "knowledge" of a zero-sum imaginative reality: America loomed large, and Cubans were comparatively diminished. American decision makers had little memory for the relevant history. But Castro's speeches recalled each past wrong: every intervention, every American manipulation. The Platt Amendment, which earlier in the century had presumptuously asserted America's legal right to supervise Cuban policies, lived on in the image of his current "America." The unwillingness to forget history blocked learning and recognition of any changed American attitudes.[37]

The psychology of this dependency problem apparently was lost on Eisenhower, never an arrogant man. He saw America and Cuba as great trading partners, thus the mutual advantages were obvious, and mutual friendship and good relations the obvious attitude for any sensible man in touch with reality. As long as Castro was not a Communist, he had nothing to worry about. To Eisenhower it was a genuine mystery what made "that bearded fellow," as he sometimes referred to Castro, so upset, especially when America offered to be generous in foreign aid to help him.

Eisenhower's vexed perplexity was not his alone. In the late 1950s, American political elites had little experience with Black protest or domestic radicals. As America had not been invaded since 1812 and was a "superpower," the agitating vulnerability and demeaned status of Cuba — with its continuing image of American condescension — was not a problem they could appreciate readily. But probably, at a deeper level, they did not *want* to understand it either. The self-image of a world leader was comfortable, America's hegemony was understood as merely expressing a genuine, responsible benevolence. Too much would have to change to credit Castro's reversed image of a condescending, hostile America. American leaders *knew* their self-image to be objective reality and, like a therapist with an upset patient, Castro's exercised psychological problems were deemed his to sort out. (But it is probably true that most American leaders would have welcomed a cure: the inferiority complexes, resentments, and sensitivities made Cuba exasperating to deal with.)

Castro put forth a solution to the dependency problem; he wanted to make himself, and Cuba, a leading power in Latin America, build up his military to deter an invasion, and change his trade and aid relations. He would seek to establish foreign aid as a right (to forestall going hat-in-hand to Washington and being subjected to lists of changes America might want to discuss while they considered whether to be generous).

Initially, he tried a peaceful approach. In 1959, while ruling out bilateral aid requests, he tested America's attitude by enthusiastically proposing (at an Organization of American States meeting) a $30 billion Marshall Plan, funded by America, to aid development throughout Latin America and thus accord Latin American peoples status equal with those of Western Europe. His Marshall Plan speech was a sensible test of whether America had a new attitude to Latin America and would be a friend of rapid reform.[38] (As his own initiative, such a public proposal would — if accepted — heighten his prestige in Latin America and further his heroic identity.) Castro also proposed that America expand its sugar purchases from Cuba and raise the price it paid, thus implicitly (as "purchases" rather than aid) increasing his revenues without making Cuba appear a "hat-in-hand" benefactee. He also solicited American agreement to sell him arms.

But the Eisenhower administration was less than interested in such changes from a traditional framework. The Marshall Plan speech was icily rejected with the clear message Castro was presumptuous to propose it.[39] His hints of indirect aid, at American initiative, were ignored. Arms sales were blocked because Castro had not been peaceful. America intended to be wary of Castro until it better understood his intentions and how they would fit with American plans. It took the position he should settle down, grow up, and stop behaving like a juvenile delinquent with a bizarrely romantic fantasy about more violent revolutions.[40]

Review: Motivation and Understanding

For the purpose of analysis in later chapters, I want to underscore several features of this history.

1. Castro's hubris led him to overconfidence and risky misjudgment. He would have won democratic elections by an overwhelming majority; spurning them, he strengthened his enemies. His efforts to overthrow governments in Haiti, Panama, Nicaragua, and the Dominican Republic were also badly planned, vastly overconfident, and premature.

2. Castro was wrong about the most probable American actions. Prior to March 1960 there was no administration intention or plan to overthrow him. To be sure, Richard Nixon had agitated for an invasion since early 1959, but this was not Eisenhower's policy nor Herter's. Perhaps it could be said that Castro had learned too quickly, learned the rule but not the exceptions: he did not understand the complexities and inconsistencies of American foreign policy, did not recognize he could now be an exception to the Arbenz (and other interventionist) precedents, and failed to recognize that neither the extravagant praise Batista had enjoyed nor the vituperative rhetoric of the American right fully represented the character of American policy at the time.

3. Knowing its own history, the United States did not act realistically and effectively to calm Castro's fears as it should have done if it wished good relations. By treating Castro as either an overwrought adolescent (to be "calmed down" by a kindly ambassador) or a madman, it acted consistently with a benevolent self-image but failed, specifically, to give the verifiable guarantees that Castro would have needed to find a kindly ambassador credible.

In part, such American failures of empathy and imagination arose because policymakers did not use their own psychological experience. Earlier in the 1950s, Americans' imagined fears of a foreign enemy approached the point of hysteria during the McCarthy period, even at a very *low* level of good evidence: no large network of anti-American agents exploded terror bombs throughout the country, no foreign-based planes routinely bombed cities and destroyed crops with impunity, no groups of enemies were known to be arming, unimpeded, in a neighboring country. Yet Cubans were subjected to this treatment by former Batistianos who had fled to the United States. It was an extraordinarily presumptuous attitude to think there could be good relations — or even effective reassurance — by words alone when terror bombs were exploding in Havana and the American right and Batistianos were, with impunity, flying in from American airports to drop incendiary bombs. American inaction, and a slightly ingenuous American viewpoint that these were "minor" incidents, were policy responses badly out of touch with reality in Cuba and overestimated the power of Washington's viewpoint to be the standard to define reality.[41]

4. The American government became caught up in a public drama driven by simple, yet unrealistic, images and associations. For example, it never bargained with Castro about the thresholds to be honored to guarantee his survival. Cuba's quota of sugar sales to the United States was suspended in the spring of 1960 — de facto economic warfare designed to destroy support for the Castro government — without prior bargaining, and this simple Dr. Jekyll/Mr. Hyde switch reflected the absence of well-planned prior use of coercive diplomacy.[42]

Moreover, Castro's acceptance of $100 million in aid from the USSR was deemed at the time — wrongly — to show his regime was "dominated" by international Communism and that his decided course was to become a "puppet" of the Russians.[43] In fact, after the Cuban Missile Crisis, Castro confirmed the earlier assessment of his politics, that is, that he was always his own man. Having effected a Soviet guarantee of his survival, and pledges of massive aid, Castro next turned on the indigenous Cuban Communist Party, purged over half of its members, and has for over twenty years assured that, whatever the dominant rhetoric on his island might be, the primary loyalty of the Cuban Communist Party will be to himself and to his brother.[44]

In assaying both of these overreactions it is probably worth noting that the dramas of international relations reported (and created) in the American press, once an aid to Castro's cause, later worked against him. The drama of the Mikoyan visit was contentious, highly publicized, and created a reality which made the Eisenhower administration vulnerable to political cost if it did not seem to respond effectively to a challenge.

5. The American government learned too slowly and, in retrospect, it is probably correct to say that Castro was not considered important enough by Eisenhower — that is, powerful or dangerous enough — to produce more rapid learning. Ultimately the United States did take actions which, had they been taken two years earlier, would have achieved more positive results and possibly prevented the deterioration to violence and strong Soviet ties. Castro's $30 billion test in 1959 was met in spirit by Kennedy's 1961, $20 billion Alliance for Progress. Only after a potential Soviet deal was set in motion, in 1960, did American officials become serious about proposals to end the private war and offset the expropriation costs of American property. Had they been so concerned even a year earlier, there would have been a base for wider negotiations of Cuban-American relations. And in 1962 Kennedy pledged not to invade Cuba. These, with verifiable guarantees, were the quid pro quos that should have been offered two years before.[45]

THE INTERNATIONAL POLITICAL SYSTEM

I want to pull back, at this point, to place the types of American foreign policy decisions we have observed into a broader perspective. Detailed stories, drawn from several decision cycles, give the impression major foreign policy outcomes depend upon personalities, organizational routines, or details of press coverage. Yet the principal outcomes of policymaking processes remain substantially invariant across decades (Table 5.1).

As the historical inventory in Table 5.1 shows, recent American interventions belong to a larger managerial pattern. Many (North) Americans are unaware of this history, but the recurrent pattern of American interventions in the Central American region is striking; the United States intervened with troops on forty-three separate occasions in the nineteenth century. Then, in the first third of this century, U.S. military interventions occurred in Cuba, Panama, Mexico, and Honduras. The United States occupied the island of Haiti for more than nineteen years, set up a military government in the Dominican Republic from 1916 until 1924, and launched two major interventions in Nicaragua.

The historical record suggests a more general cause and that the fear of Communism is not a unique justification for American use of troops — and violence. In fact, the agitation of *any* revolutionary disorder has risked an American suppressive response. Since its Monroe Doctrine was unilaterally promulgated in the early nineteenth century, the American proprietary response has been to eliminate — and at a low threshold of sensitivity — any major rival in the region. In the mid-nineteenth century, the British Empire aroused American proprietary responses. Spain's influence was the target of the Spanish-American War. Japan became another rival who stirred action in Nicaragua, in 1909, when President Taft believed that country might accord either Japan or Britain the right to build what ultimately became (after an American-sponsored revolution) the Panama Canal. During World War I a new German menace moved to the fore. Bolshevism became the foreign threat to American hegemony when, in the 1920s, Mexico was feared by some to show signs of increasing USSR influence.[46]

Since the 1950s, American policymakers have continued to attempt to direct events, often using economic power and economic aid. Beginning in the mid-1960s, military aid increased (both substantially and in proportion to economic aid) in the belief that strong indigenous military establishments would be progressive forces (or at least preserve order), and, since the 1950s, America has learned to use covert activities to reduce public controversy further.[47] But when immediate action has been required, troops have been used. (Lyndon Johnson promptly sent 20,000 American troops to the Dominican Republic in 1965 to "prevent another Cuba"; the Reagan administration sent American troops into Grenada in 1983 to overthrow a government of

Table 5.1. Selected Chronology: U.S. Military and Covert Interventions in Latin America*

19th Century
  43 interventions, including Spanish-American War (1898)

1903–1914   *Panama*
             Protect American lives and interests during independence war with Colombia
             and the construction of the Panama Canal

1906–1909   *Cuba*
             Restore order and protect lives after revolutionary activity

1912–1925   *Nicaragua*
             Prevent attempted revolution: remain to promote peace and stability

1914–1919   *Mexico*
             Respond to Villa's raids (included Pershing's expedition into northern Mexico
             and 9 subsequent brief incursions)

1915–1934   *Haiti*
             Maintain order during period of chronic threatened insurrection

1916–1924   *Dominican Republic*
             Maintain order during period of chronic threatened insurrection

1917–1922   *Cuba*
             Protect American interests during an insurrection and subsequent unsettled
             conditions

1918–1920   *Panama*
             Perform police duty during election disturbances and in subsequent unsettled
             conditions

1926–1933   *Nicaragua*
             Help put down revolutionary activity (included forays against the "outlaw" San-
             dino in 1928)

1954   *Guatemala*
             Assist overthrow of Arbenz government (CIA)

1961–1962   *Cuba*
             Attempt overthrow of Castro at Bay of Pigs; Operation MONGOOSE follows
             to "raise the cost." At least two assassination attempts coordinated with the
             Bay of Pigs invasion use Mafia intermediaries; 6 during MONGOOSE phase
             activate QJ/WIN and others with direct CIA control

1961   *Dominican Republic*
             Collude in assassination of right-wing dictator Trujillo to "prevent another
             Cuba" (CIA)

1965   *Dominican Republic*
             Intervene to "prevent another Cuba" during civil disorder

1967   *Bolivia*
             Help track down Ché Guevara (Special Forces & U.S. space satellites).
             Guevara killed by Bolivians

1971–1973   *Chile*
             Carry out covert operations to "make the economy scream." CIA involvement
             in assassination of the elected Marxist president, Allende

1980–?   *Nicaragua, Honduras, El Salvador*
             Commence "secret" wars against revolutionaries. Use of Argentine and Israeli
             "cut-outs." Buildup of American military infrastructure in Honduras

1983   *Grenada*
             Carry out invasion to overthrow Marxist government

---

*Excludes 23 minor troop incursions of less than a year, 1901–1933.

Sources: U.S. Senate (1962) in Ronning (1970), pp. 25–32; Fain et al. (1977).

radicals.) For 150 years the pattern of decision has been consistent: When inattention is disrupted by challenge, the American response has demonstrated, in the words of the historian Walter LaFeber, " . . . a willingness to use military force, a fear of foreign influence, and a dread of revolutionary instability."[48]

The policy events we have observed, then, appear *not* to be the inadvertent result of intellectual arguments or facts that a decision process failed to include. Primarily, while being concerned about learning, we have been witnessing instances of a broader pattern of behavior by a system, and behavior of presidents and decision makers who are, themselves, actors inside a system.[49] But what could *cause* a system's decision makers to behave in this way? I turn to this question in the next chapter.

NOTES

1. Quoted in H. Thomas, *The Cuban Revolution* (New York: Harper and Row, 1971, 1977), p. 1270.
2. Ibid., pp. 938–939.
3. Ibid., pp. 948, 1206–1207, 1211–1212 recounts the policy battles. The memoirs of E. Smith, *The Fourth Floor: An Account of the Castro Communist Revolution* (New York: Random House, 1962) provide his version, but oddly exculpate Eisenhower and Herter. P. Bonsal, *Cuba, Castro and the United States* (Pittsburgh: Univ. of Pittsburgh Press, 1971) provides an unusually sympathetic and perceptive account, although his characterization of the history of American foreign policy does not explain the many crucial decisions (e.g., to eliminate the sugar quota) which were not discussed with him in advance (although he was the ambassador) and concerning which there was no direct bargaining. Smith was correct that Castro *became* a self-described Communist, but there is still no persuasive evidence he held those views prior to the end of 1962 when it was clear that his survival depended upon the Soviet Union's protection, as it has since.
4. For a discussion of the nature of such personal differences, and supporting evidence, see Lloyd Etheredge, *A World of Men: The Private Sources of American Foreign Policy* (Cambridge, MA: MIT Press, 1978).
5. Quoted in Thomas, *Cuban Revolution*, p. 919.
6. Ibid., pp. 909–924, 937; see also T. Draper, *Castro's Revolution: Myths and Realities* (New York: Praeger, 1962), Appendix; H. Matthews, *Castro: A Political Biography* (London: Allen Lane, 1969).
7. Smith, *Fourth Floor*, pp. 154–155. Details of the "perfectly fraudulent" election are discussed in Thomas, *Cuban Revolution*, p. 1014, but glossed over in Smith. Castro sought to block the elections by issuing Revolutionary Law Number Two, on October 10, 1958, calling for capital punishment of all candidates.
8. Thomas, *Cuban Revolution*, p. 997 et passim. Castro's intelligence was also superb (ibid.). There have been persistent rumors that bribery of Batista's military was used to good effect.
9. Ibid., p. 999.
10. Smith, *Fourth Floor*, pp. 94–95.
11. Ibid., p. 100.
12. Thomas, *Cuban Revolution*, p. 920; Draper, *Castro's Revolution*, Appendix.
13. Thomas, *Cuban Revolution*, pp. 1015–1019; Smith, *Fourth Floor*, pp. 165–166.
14. We may also admire a further case of learning between professionals. To plan

the Bay of Pigs, Bissell adapted Castro against Castro. His novel scheme (not part of Guatemala) was to bring journalists to the beachhead and feed them false stories to create an impression that the momentum of events was against Castro; it cleverly adopted Castro's own public media strategy. Moreover, Castro's own success bolstered the CIA's confidence. Estimates of military strength are provided in Thomas, *Cuban Revolution*, p. 1042.

15. S. Huntington, *Political Order in Changing Societies* (New Haven, CT: Yale Univ. Press, 1968) provides a good discussion of this concept. It might illustrate this concept to note that during the 1960s Fidel Castro established a Radio Free Dixie in Cuba—analogous to the Radio Swan used against himself—and apparently believed that he could easily foment rebellion against state governments in the southern United States.

16. P. Bonsal, "Cuba, Castro and the United States," *Foreign Affairs* (January 1967): 260–276; Bonsal, *Cuba, Castro and the United States*, pp. 28–33. et passim.

17. On Eisenhower's attitude and Castro's visit see Thomas, *Cuban Revolution*, p. 1210.

18. Thomas, *Cuban Revolution*, p. 1213.

19. P. Blackstock, *The Strategy of Subversion: Manipulating the Policies of Other Nations* (Chicago: Quadrangle, 1964), pp. 239–240.

20. A review of events is provided in Thomas, *Cuban Revolution*, pp. 1262–1270 et passim.

21. J. Dominguez, *Cuba: Order and Revolution* (Cambridge, MA: Harvard Univ. Press, 1978), p. 145 et passim; Thomas, *Cuban Revolution*.

22. In the spring of 1960, a group of Princeton-based academics confirmed the phenomenon. They studied public opinion in Cuba with a cross-section sample of 1,000 Cubans drawn primarily from urban areas. They found 86% of adult Cubans supported Castro; 43% they called "fervent": L. Free, *Attitudes of the Cuban People Toward the Castro Regime in the Late Spring of 1960* (Princeton, NJ: Institute for International Social Research, 1960), pp. 5, 6. Castro's people were found to have enormous confidence in his powers: on a scale of 0 to 10, the average subjective rating of their "quality of personal life" five years earlier was 4.1; in 1960 (at the time of the survey) it was 6.3; but for 1965 they envisioned 8.4 (ibid., p. 1). The director of the study personally briefed Allen Dulles of its results a week before the Bay of Pigs operation. (B. Wedge, personal communication.) I have been unable to determine whether Dulles told Kennedy of these results, but they were consistent with the CIA's general estimates of Castro's majority support.

23. Miro Cardona, the first prime minister of Cuba after Batista's fall, resigned over the retroactively legalized death penalty, the violations of civil liberties, and Castro's increasing move to one-man rule.

24. For these accounts I have relied primarily upon C. Ameringer, *The Democratic Left in Exile: The Antidictatorial Struggle in the Caribbean, 1945–1959* (Coral Gables, FL: Univ. of Miami Press, 1974), pp. 270–283.

25. Although, to be sure, the rebels were never able to establish a foothold as Castro had done.

26. These also helped to convince the Kennedy Administration that Trujillo of the Dominican Republic was so retrograde that he would encourage Communist advances; it eventually collaborated indirectly in his assassination, an action which likely received additional justification because Trujillo attempted to assassinate Betancourt of Venezuela, one of the liberal, progressive supporters of Kennedy's Alliance for Progress. See the review in U.S. Senate, Select Committee to Study Governmental Operations with Respect to Intelligence Activities, *Alleged Assassination Plots Involving Foreign Leaders* Senate Report 94: 465. November

20, 1975 (Washington, DC: Government Printing Office, 1975). It would be incorrect to term American foreign policy reactionary; in the Trujillo case, and also (later) in the Diem case in South Vietnam, it has sought to replace rightist foreign leaders who blocked reforms deemed necessary for anti-Communist purposes.

27. The Puerto Rico threat is reported in A. Berle, "The Cuban Crisis: Failure of American Foreign Policy," *Foreign Affairs* 39 (October 1960): 44.

28. Bonsal, *Cuba, Castro and the United States* passim and Thomas, *Cuban Revolution* passim.

29. Thomas, *Cuban Revolution*, p. 1060.

30. Ibid., p. 1060.

31. Ibid., p. 1077.

32. Bonsal, *Cuba, Castro and the United States*, pp. 28–33 et passim.

33. Ibid., p. 67.

34. Ibid., p. 112.

35. E.g., Thomas, *Cuban Revolution*, p. 1062.

36. Bonsal, *Cuba, Castro and the United States*, pp. 231–245, discusses the role of sugar.

37. Thomas, *Cuban Revolution*, pp. 1206–1207 et passim; Bonsal, *Cuba, Castro and the United States*, pp. 246–288, discusses the historical background to Castro's feelings. See also J. Plank, "The Caribbean: Intervention, When and How" *Foreign Affairs* 44 (October 1965): 37–48 for a thoughtful general discussion and contribution to historical memory.

38. Thomas, *Cuban Revolution*, p. 1213.

39. Ibid.

40. "He thought of himself as riding a wave that would engulf the future in Cuba, the United States and Latin America. He saw himself as the heroic pioneer of the future." Bonsal, *Cuba, Castro and the United States*, p. 65.

41. The language used by participants to discuss relations between America and Cuba, imagining an interpersonal relationship, was also far too simple and unrefined ("friendly," "dependent," "pro-communist") to be an adequate linguistic model for the ambiguous, multileveled, and complex, emotion-charged relationship that existed and evolved on both sides. Chemists have developed an elaborate notational system to identify complex organic compounds, and the absence of an analogous technical characterization in international relations may produce too hasty thematic analyses based upon interpersonal analogies.

42. Bonsal, *Cuba, Castro and the United States*, pp. 145–153. Note also (p. 132) that discussions were not undertaken with the Soviet Union. See the general discussion by A. George, D. Hall, and W. Simons, *The Limits of Coercive Diplomacy* (Boston: Little, Brown, 1971) who seek to draw lessons from past experience.

43. In 1959 the U.S. accounted for 74% of Cuban exports and 65% of its imports. Thus, at the $100 million threshold, if it applied its own test, the United States was the dominant political force on the island and would remain so. Dominguez, *Cuba*, p. 149.

44. Ibid., pp. 212–213, 306.

45. Thomas, *Cuban Revolution*, pp. 1263, 1270, discusses these last-minute offers which emerged after discussions for a Soviet-Cuban deal became known.

46. R. Millett, "We've Done It All to Them Before in Central America" *Washington Post* (August 7, 1983), C1, 4; W. LaFeber, *Inevitable Revolution: The United States in Central America* (New York: Norton, 1983) passim.

47. LaFeber, *op. cit.* provides an excellent overview. See also J. Chace, "Deeper into the Mire" *New York Review of Books* (March 1, 1984), pp. 40–48.

48. LaFeber, *op. cit.*, p. 18. Logically, one might desire a search for counterexamples, identifying all "potential" intervention cases to show the American response has been invariant. However, it seems to have been so, and with only two exceptions. Thomas Mann, a specialist in American foreign policy toward the region, told the Kissinger Commission: "United States policy of opposition to attempts by states hostile to our form of government to impose their systems on independent American states . . . was first announced by Monroe in 1823 . . . [and] on only two occasions has the US failed to follow this policy. (His references are to Fidel Castro and to the Nicaraguan and El Salvador Marxists in the 1980s.) T. Mann, *Testimony* in National Bipartisan Commission on Central America, *Appendix to the Report of the National Bipartisan Commission on Central America* (Washington, DC: Government Printing Office, 1984), p. 680.

49. This conclusion is not to say that variations of personality are unimportant. In the history we have considered, Nixon would have preferred earlier intervention and used American troops to finish Castro decisively (the advice he gave to Kennedy). Eisenhower likely would have approved the Trinidad plan with a guerrilla escape but gone no further. Kennedy might have pursued only peaceful Alliance for Progress competition if he had not found the capabilities for an expatriate invasion awaiting him (i.e., the lead-time before Castro acquired MIGs was too short for the option of "deniable" invasion to be developed *de novo* beginning in 1961). If learning would involve motivational change, the degree of learning the American political system is capable of integrating into its responses is limited, albeit genuine. Etheredge, *World of Men*, provides evidence of sources of personality variations. Note that study addresses the problem of explaining variations about means, not the means (which might be considered the system baselines).

Chapter 6 DUAL-TRACK DECISION MAKING AND THE AMERICAN FOREIGN POLICY SYSTEM

In chapters 4 and 5 I drew lessons from a sequence of American government decisions to identify blocks to foreign policy learning. That review also concluded that recurrent policy outcomes could not be explained by technical flaws in bureaucratic organization or rational analysis procedures.

In this chapter I will complete the process of reorganizing the historical material to identify recurrent, learning-relevant patterns, and will then turn to the question of causation. Specifically, I will assess attempts to explain foreign policy choices and errors as a result of "natural" errors in cognition. Then, I will draw upon this discussion, earlier chapters, and recent behavioral science research concerned with how ambitious men experience the nature of power to propose a new theory: that American foreign policy is shaped by two channels (rational analysis and imagination-derived thinking about power relationships), and that it is via a second channel of strong imagination systems that political information is understood, foreign policy is created, and from which — by consequence of the functioning of the mind within a distinctive larger-than-life drama — learning is blocked, and, further, that similar American policies are repeatedly adopted, by similar processes, which run aground in local reality.

THE ORGANIZATION OF POINTS OF VIEW

As a first step to develop this integrated explanation, I invite the reader's attention to five patterns of thinking reflected in the case material.

Decisions reflected subjective "positioning," adoption of a point of view. Policy derives from an enterprise larger than analytical reasoning, a choice of interpretation, and a personal point of view. As in the solution to a set of simultaneous equations, a policy is a joint expression of who one is, what the important values and purposes are conceived to be, who others are, and what role is imagined for America. As we have seen, bureaucratic identities typically created — and limited — the interpretations and viewpoints of men in lower roles. But personal identity directly entered the equation at the senior level.[1] Dwight Eisenhower, for example, positioned himself "above" these

141

problems and was less buffeted, "hysterical," and empassioned than men whose personalities and lesser stature and sense of mastery located themselves amidst tense, consequential battles with uncertain control. He opposed Communism, and he would probably have authorized an expatriate invasion of Cuba. But he was not obsessed to eliminate Castro, he did not credit alarmist projections of rapidly spreading Communist revolution, and he did not fear that, should he fail to take action on a minor irritant, he would thereby mislead the Soviets to test his personal resolve in areas of vital American interest such as Berlin. "Boys," he simply would say to Dulles and Bissell (when they would brief him about their difficulties in preparing the operation they had wanted to mount), "if you don't intend to go through with this, let's stop talking about it."[2]

Eisenhower's confidence and equanimity probably were a result both of his personality (he was a secure man) and his experience as the victorious Supreme Allied Commander in World War II. After the successful defeat of Hitler's armies, it would have been far-fetched to imagine that a histrionic Latin American leader of a poor island nation, without a navy, posed a consequential threat. American conventional forces in the Caribbean were overwhelming. Nor was Eisenhower an activist with idealistic zeal; unresponsive to such appeals himself, he was personally skeptical that Castro could foment revolutions in other countries easily.[3]

Eisenhower's calm style contrasted to that of more typical American politicians — for example, Nixon and Kennedy, tenser and younger men still competing for prominence, success, and the presidency. Both imagined a world of greater threat, of compelling necessities for tough and masterful action: Castro loomed larger in their imaginations.

Eisenhower's calm also derived from his standing as a genuine national hero. He had been drafted to run for the presidency, did not compete for it from a position of relative obscurity. He was elected, and reelected, by overwhelming majorities and enjoyed public confidence: It was an asset, and a support for forbearance and patience, the two relative unknowns lacked.[4]

Policy thinking was overconfident. People imagined they knew more than they did, and their plans worked more easily in their heads than in reality. In political life, legitimacy may come from the pretense of knowledge. If one admits there is something to learn, one thereby admits he does not yet know the answer. When public standards for evidence and serious argument in a political system are low, a competitive, Darwinian advantage accrues to men who are verbally impressive and pretend to confident knowledge of the outer world that they do not possess.

Overconfidence may be a general human trait, and this fact has been cited as a general explanation of one factor in foreign policy error. In recent years, research has supported the proposition that many people have overconfident estimates of the validity of their current knowledge.[5] CIA political analysts, specifically, have been asked by researchers to estimate the confidence of their knowledge of simple facts (which is larger, Greenland or Australia?) and typically overestimate the probability they have given the correct answer.[6]

We have seen that President Kennedy and the CIA planners made many overconfident assumptions about the Bay of Pigs plan. Nothing about that operation — except the technological trickery of the Pinar del Rio diversion — turned out as bright people imagined, before the event, that it would.

A contributing cause of a flawlessly imagined implementation was probably that most men were without extensive and varied experience with these problems; as beginners, they could work only with their imaginations. At points where men had extensive, realistic experience, their planning was attentive to detail and of higher quality. The Bay of Pigs logistics plans, on paper, were excellent: 72 tons of supplies off-loaded on D-Day; 415 tons to arrive within ten days; then another 530 tons; then another 607 tons. Weaponry was well chosen, the men well trained, and they inflicted casualties at an impressive 20 : 1 ratio until their ammunition ran out.[7] The logistics of MONGOOSE, and the tight management and press control to keep it secret for a decade were also impressive.[8]

This contrast, between simple and overconfident images of beginners and the integrated, detailed, and realistic analyses of experienced men, underscores a characteristic of learning in foreign affairs. Subjectively, learning is not a shift from ignorance to confident knowledge. It can be observed as a shift from too simple and too confident generalizations — often boldly advanced and staunchly defended — to complex, integrated understandings grounded in realistic attention to detail. (For example, as I proposed in chapter 3, a shift analogous to that from an impressionistic earth, air, fire, and water conception of elements of the physical universe to the periodic table.) Thus, one source of foreign policy overconfidence and failure is simply that the United States is not sufficiently imperialistic: no administration intervenes frequently enough in other countries to learn to do it well before it leaves office.

That the American president is typically a foreign policy "beginner" is a structural feature of the American political system. A president need have only *domestic* political experience: To win the presidential nomination, he and key aides must spend years building contacts, talking and listening, getting to know the names and concerns of thousands of convention delegates, interest group representatives, and donors. They spend a lifetime developing a sense of the "touch and feel" of the American political system and its news media. But American leaders (and too, their domestic publics) have relatively little personal basis to judge the people, the systems, the reactions of other countries. Predictably, simple fantasies — and passionate debates around them — can take hold more readily.

Simple emotional themes and avoidance of complicated, unpleasant truths. Dissonance reduction has been proposed by psychologists as a mechanism widely used to organize viewpoints.[9] The theory predicts that, once we know certain elements of a decision maker's beliefs, attitudes, and allegiances, we may often predict other elements by asking "what, given these, would it be most *comfortable* for this man also to believe?"[10]

A story from the fall of 1960 suggests the type of process psychologists have found may occur internally and automatically. The CIA's chief in Guatemala flew back to Washington to discuss a serious problem he did not want to solve on his own responsibility. The young Cuban males in his charge, isolated in the secret camp, had no contact with women; increasingly they went AWOL to find them. He could not effectively confine the men, thus he had a security problem: Should they talk too freely with the prostitutes they hired, especially after they had been drinking, this might expose the operation.

The man explained his problem to Richard Bissell and Tracy Barnes over dinner. He thought it necessary to hire security-cleared prostitutes for the men; as this solution required authorization and proper budget authority, he wanted Bissell to make the decision. At this point in the discussion, Tracy Barnes quickly excused himself and left the table for several minutes. Whatever the "order from Washington" would be, Barnes did not want to be in a position to admit, later, that he knew.[11]

This byplay is a model for a deeper, internal process that pervades these two years. Intelligent men, psychologically, chose to avoid truths *and* in patterns suggesting, at a deeper level, they *did* know already what reality would be if they faced it. They stopped asking questions at exactly the point where the realistic answers would begin to be uncomfortable to know. Richard Barnett has called it a national security manager's "need not to know."[12]

For example, many participants identified with President Kennedy and secretly imagined the president's true commitments were to themselves and their own positions or well-being. Faced with contrary evidence they retained such beliefs. No one was willing to consider that he and the president had fundamentally different inner sympathies; when the supposition was vital and problematic, they did not test it. Cuban leaders in New York, told three times American troops were prohibited, required formally to assent to the condition, still did not believe it. Many (favorable) advisers "knew" the president was committed to the operation's success and would use troops. But after a key Pentagon meeting, Schlesinger confidently imagined it was *he* and the president who were of one mind in sharing major doubts. Many years later, in his memoirs, Chester Bowles still believed he and the president were "extremely close" in their foreign policy views and attributed Kennedy's persistently different actions only to his failure to "think through" bad advice.[13]

The desire to avoid uncomfortable truths was also reflected in the simple road maps through complex issues offered the president by the strongest proponents and opponents. A. A. ("Let'er rip") Berle believed Castro was a Communist revolutionary, a power clash was inevitable, the operation was morally justified, and it was likely to succeed.[14] Schlesinger and Fulbright propounded a different but equally straight and simple viewpoint: Castro's future was unknown but unlikely to be a serious political threat; the invasion's American sponsorship would not be secret; it would undermine American prestige; it would fail or produce a prolonged civil war.[15] Each strong advocate "lined up" all considerations in a point of view to support, consistently, his conclusions. Notably, the simpler and more consistent the scenario for interpretation, belief, and action urged on Kennedy, the stronger — pro or con — the advocacy.[16]

Finally, the organizing power of emotional themes to supercede analytical thought is evident in the evasion of President Kennedy. He wanted the Bay of Pigs to be American support for idealistic Cubans — not American "aggression" — and he did not ask tough questions about realities in Guatemala or pursue Barnes's report that Miro did not believe the American troop restrictions. Ambivalent about the "CIA's" operation, he did not ask for a military briefing, remember crucial details, or ask for military staffing of his D-Day decisions. In MONGOOSE, he ordered both secrecy and the elimination of Castro, and did not want to analyze responsibly whether both objectives conflicted, once again, with what his subordinates could produce.[17]

Policy thinking was primarily defensive. The psychologist Abraham Maslow has asserted that a hierarchy of motives determines human behavior.[18] When basic (lower) needs are threatened, the individual ignores opportunities to pursue other needs and values, and becomes preoccupied — even obsessed — with meeting the basic needs. Security needs — survival of the self and of anything the self identifies with itself — are among the basic needs that can readily become preoccupying, to the exclusion of other values.[19]

A pattern emerges if we view the Bay of Pigs and MONGOOSE decisions from this perspective. Men, at each turn, first identified threats to the survival of themselves or things they cared about, then organized (interpreted) the decisions they faced primarily to respond to these threats. They adopted points of view to manage these "security" risks they defined, and discounted other aspects of the problem. More than it first seemed, the 1960–1962 sequence of decisions — underneath the aggressive postures and bold rhetoric — also emerges as a series of maneuvers organized to cope with fear, the apprehension of future imagined consequences.

President Kennedy experienced threat from every direction: what Castro might do, what the Russians might do, what critics — especially Republicans — would do if he cancelled and left himself vulnerable. At each point, his primary motive was to identify and manage the threats. Later, the increased violence and savagery of MONGOOSE was deemed a necessity to cope with the increased threat posed by Castro's success.[20] After the Cuban Missile Crisis, President Kennedy said privately he would have been impeached if he had not adopted his bold and tough posture.[21] The CIA's planners, committed to their plan, misled the president and other officials, fearful that to tell the complete truth would risk their plan's rejection. Helms avoided the decision process to keep his job. Schlesinger, intimidated, resorted to private memos rather than speak out — and lose — before others with tough, virile stances who were his senior in rank.

As we have seen in chapter 4, the fears of ambitious men who wanted to keep their jobs was a consistent determinant of behavior during the decision process. Thus we may observe that foreign policies *and* the policymaking process reflected a *defensive* logic. Survival and security were more salient than potential gains. The image of men acting boldly to pursue positive values should be supplemented by the image of men maneuvering defensively, in reaction, to manage current and future threats to security and survival.[22] Especially during MONGOOSE, under stress, the lives of Cubans became "nothing to lose," the men abandoned ideals and did what, to their understanding, "must be done."

Opponents' behavior was often explained by referring to their predispositions, America's by referring to its situation. Another common cognitive mechanism is also reflected in the case material, a tendency to attribute the cause of behavior of other people (nations) to their predispositions, while thinking of one's own (America's) behavior as a response forced by the circumstances.[23] Such differences in the perception of causation have been studied by psychologists and appear to occur frequently. For example, a professor might attribute the cause of a student's late paper to an inner characteristic of the student (poor work habits) but explain his own delay in submitting a paper for publication to situational factors (the complexity of the task and competing pressures and demands upon him).

In the case material we have seen a tendency to explain Castro's behavior by his predispositions (for example, that he was extraordinarily ambitious, mad, a Communist — or all three; even moderates in the Eisenhower administration treated him as an immature juvenile delinquent to be calmed down and "brought around"). Russian behavior, in precipitating the Cuban Missile Crisis, was also attributed to Khrushchev's ambitions rather than to American actions or threats.[24] And, throughout, the American self-concept was of righteous behavior, the resort to violence or threat being forced upon it.

Perspective on Cognitive Processes

Each of these last patterns we have just considered has been proposed as a possible source of choices, and an autonomous source of error, in foreign policy perceptions and judgements. Each of these processes for organizing viewpoints can be established as a naturally occurring human tendency in experiments. Transferred "naively" and intuitively to foreign policy decision making, however, they may run the risk of being used unreflectively, applied to situations erroneously, and producing a mismatch which results in unrealistic, ineffective policy.[25]

These processes do occur in the case material, but I believe the proper judgment is that they do not occur autonomously and produce policy simply and directly. My reasoning is as follows. First, we may observe that each mechanism had exceptions; many men were bold but some men (e.g., Helms) were cautious. Many men were fearful ("hysterical") but some men (e.g., Fulbright, Eisenhower) were sanguine. Many blamed Castro or Khrushchev for their aggressiveness but others (principally outside of government circles) blamed America's threatening actions. The mechanisms by which the mind of the individual — and especially the minds of the majority — *selected* a mechanism and came to rest wants explaining to give a satisfactory explanation.

Second, these mechanisms were not adopted or maintained unreflectively — as on an individual's private checklist following an experiment. Both in the Cabinet Room and in the press, Cuban policy was debated loudly over an extended period. One would have needed to be deaf not to know, accurately, that one's own views were subject to challenge. Thus to posit simple *unreflective* processes ("if only they had recognized it, it might have been different") is an inadequate explanation. Where these decided men "came down" requires a theory of political judgment with more elements than an unreflective failure to recognize that there were other alternatives with evidence to support them.

I believe the answer is that specific cognitive mechanisms were not adopted autonomously but by individuals — the majority — when these were consistent with a strongly held sensibility concerning power.[26] It is to an explication of what, to the majority, I believe that sensibility to have been that I now turn.

INTEGRATION: POLICYMAKING INSIDE A LARGER-THAN-LIFE DRAMA

My purpose in this section is to propose a theory that the phenomenon we have observed represents a distinctive and strong system of imagination, a personal way of knowing about political power. It is a characteristic of tough, ambitious, shrewdly calculating men who vie for power and status behind a public veneer of civilized and idealistic concern.[27] I will draw upon research and literature independent of the current case material to explain this system of experiencing political reality.[28] I will then return to the case material from recent American foreign policy to discuss how this interpretation of hardball politics allows us to recognize the three vectors of blocked learning to have a common source.

Two Imagination Subsystems in the Experience of Power Relationships

The defining feature of a practitioner of hardball politics is the simultaneous existence of two different and unintegrated experiences of the self. Each is linked with a companion imagination system of larger-than-life drama that arrays other people and nations — regardless of physical reality — in this drama above or below the relevant sense of the self (viewpoint) of the knower.

In the foreground of the mind is a "lower," depleted, insecure self. Here is a sense of low self-esteem and of self-doubt, a strong propensity to feel inadequate and ashamed, continuing worry about social acceptability, discomfort with intimacy, fear of genuineness, candor, and self-revelation, insecurity and apprehension about (vaguely defined) impending disaster. But above and in the background there exists a wholly different, relatively split-off sector of the mind, a "grandiose self."[29] This sector includes fantasies and drives for grandiose accomplishment, total recognition and admiration, complete dominance of events of the world, and a complete self-confidence. It is a highly charged sector, and much of the individual's life is organized by it as an effort to establish himself subjectively in the ongoing social and political drama so that he will achieve recognition as its director, superior to the other participants.[30]

Moving from this basic description of two selves (and associated dramas) of a hardball-politics decision maker (HP), let me now elaborate the outline, jointly aligning personality tendencies and characteristics of hardball politics in a discussion of eight themes: ambition for the self; deficiencies of love and superficial interpersonal relations; twinship images of hardball opponents; weak ethics and disconnected moral restraint; defective humor; aggressiveness, tactical manipulativeness, and vanity; moderately dreamlike and emotionally organized mental processes; and hyperactivity.

Ambition

One could view the job of a politician or president solely as a tedious, stressful, overly demanding, ethically compromising, uncertain job, a psychodrama role forcing the individual to act out public fantasies and anxieties and be the target of everyone's complaints. But to the HP, in his internal psychodrama, it is inconceivable that anyone would want anything else, or any other associations, as the fulfillment of a life.[31] Looking upward, the HP manifests what is known as "idealizing transference" to the institutions (and especially to the major symbols and highest offices of those institutions) of which he is a part. This aspect of the internal topography of upward ambition reflects faith there is something above worth being ambitious for. The "higher" the office, the more it is idealized as a location of prestige, honor, recognition, and power, the more desirable it seems. The HP feels an almost religious awe of these offices, his upward distance to personal salvation is a political distance.[32]

It is important to be clear that what the HP wants primarily is to realize the experience of directorship atop the unfolding social and political drama of his times. He seeks a position of power less to use power to accomplish certain specific goals than for the personal gratification of being engagé and a top dog. Although he may genuinely dedicate himself to certain ideals of grandiose accomplishment, these typically are stylistic and symbolic, and seldom involve thoughtful and well-elaborated programs.[33] The major story is that, above all, he wants to succeed; he imagines a better society to follow (he is vague about details) once his own will occupies the idealized "over-mind" location of high office.

This "upward" ambition has the character of a single-minded obsession, fusing a desire for personal integration (and salvation) within a political quest. (In the American political scene, to be in the White House or as close to it — even to the Oval Office — as possible.) It organizes an entire life in its service.[34] But it is a quest whose consummation is always in the distance and there is little genuine pleasure in the striving.[35] The tragic fact is that in his ambitious "upward" quest for personal salvation and fulfillment, the HP is not a satisfied man; he is caught up in the push and pull of an ambition that gives him little rest or deep satisfaction. Simpler pleasures pass him by; he is a man made for more important things.

The upward striving of the HP involves also what is known as "mirror transference."[36] That is, he relates implicitly to most other people (i.e., of lower status) with the expectation and need that they confirm his grandiose strivings, give him public recognition that shows him as he wishes himself to appear. He seeks an echo of applause, love, and unbounded admiration and respect coming back.[37] And he is certain such response is out there, albeit latent and mobilizable, that "in their hearts," in their "hearts and minds," the people, the silent majority, know he is right and eventually will respond.[38]

It is difficult to say whether the HP seeks love, or unbounded admiration, or status, or unlimited power or success; these connotations become joined in high political office. He is on a public ego trip; in fact, he wants all simultaneously. The "public" is not important to him in a genuine sense; he perceives them not as autonomous fellow human beings of equal status and respect with whom he works collaboratively in a specialized role, but as a supporting cast of subordinate parts in his own drama. He will aspire to be a "public servant" only if this status means he will be in a higher status role "looked up to" by the public. Favorable publicity and recognition are, of course, important to the HP "rationally," in order to be elected, but his vanity requires these for more than their strategic value.

Thus, the ambition of the HP involves two kinds of biased drama simultaneously. He subjectively experiences both an idealized goal above himself and — below — a potentially attentive and supportive mass public. In both cases there is probable overdramatization and distortion: the harsher reality is that the majority of a congressman's constituents do not bother to remember his name, and in a pluralistic society, and world, universal acclaim is a chimera, perhaps even for an American president. It is likely that the HP's hopes and fantasies, this selective absence of reality testing in his epistemology, are useful to society since they help to sustain his lifelong quest and the dutiful and energetic performance of his roles.

One particular feature of ambition in the HP is worth additional comment: He vastly overestimates the probability of achieving fulfillment of his long-range grandiose project.[39] He has an almost religious confidence in his own eventual success. Such inner certainty that he will be recognized by future events as the conquering hero is an invaluable aid to perseverance in the skirmishes and setbacks inevitable in the political arena. The HP (as we shall see in detail later) bases his long-range plans substantially on the strength of these internal fantasies and not upon rational assessments derived from external evidence. He will leave his mark upon history, and he is not deterred by ambiguities and low probabilities of success. Success *must* be accomplished.

Deficiencies of Love

The interpersonal relations of the HP are superficial; he has little genuine love and affection for others.[40] He does not become involved (even in marriage) to an extent that would divert him from pursuing his own ambitious self-interest, and he does not let sentimentality or genuine emotion get the better of him. There often is a facade of cordiality and considerable skill at ingratiation, glad-handing, and interpersonal relations — a kind of "Hiya fella, how are you?" (to person A), "Hiya fella, how are you?" (to person B), "Hiya fella, how are you?" (to person C). The essential that is absent is qualitative, true caring for another unique person's welfare, relating to other people as ends rather than as means. The HP operates with cool, even cold, detachment.

There is, however, one area of interpersonal relations — technically, narcissistic object choice — where this inner distance does not apply: In ordinary English, it is the area of loyalty. With people who support or potentially support his grandiose striving, the HP develops intense emotional involvement.[41] But such relations are vampiresque (he does not form strong bonds of mutual respect and love with autonomous individuals) and he denies such people (including, e.g., wives and staff) independent lives, molding them to live for him and expecting them to serve his ambitions. Fundamental disagreement is perceived as disloyalty, and disloyalty engenders a powerful and violent rejection by the HP.[42]

Such a style of interpersonal relations can be quite functional in hardball politics. The HP has "permanent interests but no permanent allies" (in the phrase sometimes used in a *realpolitik* prescription for American foreign policy). He does not let his ambition become encumbered by love or loyalty or personal friendships. He can shift coalitions instrumentally without regret, continuing in the pursuit of his own success and reparative vindication.

Mirror Images of Opponents

The image of opponents evidences what is technically a "twinship transference:" the HP experiences other people as essentially like himself, replicas of his own psychodynamics.[43] All participants are expected to be "grown up" (*sic*), to know their self-interest, to look out for "number one" first, and to engage in shrewd, rational calculations in the service of hardball maneuvering for domination, status, and power in the world. He thereby experiences himself to inhabit a fearful, insecure, and dangerous arena, a competitive, Hobbesian world. Other men in the arena are experienced to be as ambitious as he is himself, untrustworthy when egotistical self-interests diverge sharply. He expects others have secret desires to be opportunistic, to outmaneuver and defeat him, dominate and control him, to string him along, trip him up, win away his constituents, expand their spheres of influence, stab him in the back (although this latter is only figurative in American domestic practice these days).[44] And as there is some truth in this—other hardball players *are* like himself—this intuition-based knowledge can stand him in good stead because there *are* people who will try, opportunistically, to outmaneuver him, undermine him, steal his constituency, dominate and control him, string him along, trip him up, or stab him in the back. To ambitious men of this type, then, both foreign and domestic opponents will be expected to press advantages, to be vigilant for weakness, and to take advantage of vulnerabilities if they find an opportunity. Moreover, the presumption of shrewd, self-interested calculation by others eliminates moral qualms: others are imagined to know the risks they are taking in a political arena.

Of course, no politician can afford to be completely treacherous, and there are game rules, norms of accommodation, surface camaraderie, and ethical sensitivities among the powerful.[45] And fortunately not all of American society, politicians, or countries, play hardball, but the hardball politician lives in an uncertain subsystem, a "cold, cruel world" of "dog eat dog."[46] Power politics is partly a collective and uncomfortable *folie à deux*.

Weak Ethics and Disconnected Moral Restraint

The ethics of the HP differ from ordinary morality. He does not have a strong and principled superego.[47] Rather the ideals of his grandiose self (and the fears of social shame and exposure of his insecure, depleted self) join to provide a substitute for ethical restraint. He plays hardball without moral qualms about his typical lack of candor, dissembling, his hypocrisy, or manipulativeness, his using of other people, his wars or invasions for national interest (i.e., to further national power), his covert activities, his "leaks" of information to the press which unfairly damage his opponent's reputation, and so forth.[48] The HP always seeks an edge on what he would achieve by ethical means; while fear of exposure will be a deterrent, his character structure does not inhibit him. And he fears, perhaps with some justification, that in playing hardball "nice guys finish last." "This is not an honorable undertaking conducted by honorable men through honorable means," Secretary of State Henry Kissinger—in the Nixon administration—lectured one of his idealistic subordinates.[49]

But this is not to say the HP lacks a sense of morality. The fantasies embedded in the grandiose self include an almost religious sense of moral justification. The HP feels greater moral virtue to be identical with his higher location in his grandiose dreams. He imagines he will be a high status benefactor to mankind, and achievement and retention of power thus become the sine qua non, his greatest moral guide. He experiences a "higher purpose" served by his day-to-day hardball escapades. In its most rationalized form the HP gives a name to this vaguely specified higher virtue which supersedes normal morality and ethical conduct, *"raison d'ètat,"* *"staats-raisen,"* "public interest," or "national security."

There are, however, constraints of shame and embarrassment to cope with and, feeling potentially ashamed, the HP does much of his scheming in private and conducts most of his deals in back rooms. He has a penchant for secrecy. And players believe everyone else is calculating and maneuvering backstage. No one is believed to have integrity or to be open, candid, or trustworthy except as a semblance, a strategy. But while the secrecy is sometimes functional, in the hardball power drama it does not arise only from this source. Rather the HP is also afraid to tell the truth about his hardball politics because he presupposes instinctively (and perhaps correctly) that full public knowledge would risk public rejection.[50] What the HP fears most is that such rejection would result in subjective separation from the higher idealized images (i.e., high office) in the larger-than-life drama within which his life is located.

Defective Humor

An additional characteristic of the HP is a defective sense of humor.[51] He lacks a playful, warm detachment about himself and the conduct of human affairs. He takes himself seriously. If he has a sense of humor it favors being unkind about someone else: "Gerald Ford can't walk and chew gum at the same time," said Lyndon Johnson. The pure form is best captured by Hobbes's theory of humor, that it expressed coolness and dominance, perhaps a touch of malicious superiority, rather than a playful amusement.[52] And the HP does not much care for jokes or funny stories told about himself.

Cold, Condescending Aggression and Vanity

The HP handles many interpersonal and political situations with tactical shrewdness because he retains an aloof inner distance, a lack of major emotional investment in anything save winning. But just as personal disloyalty will stir his wrath, so does a challenger, particularly of lower status (hence unworthy and, comparatively, underestimated) who unsettles the fantasy and threatens the grandiose location and control he is driven to effect. Under such challenge he experiences cold, imperious rage and an aggressive drive for control and reparative revenge, for punishment of those lesser men, upstarts so insolent as to question his natural superiority and benevolent wisdom.[53] Theodore Roosevelt dispatched American troops into Cuba in 1906 and wrote in a private letter, "Just at the moment I am so angry with that infernal little Cuban republic that I would like to wipe its people off the face of the earth."[54]

The fact of emotion-charged vanity increases the sensitivity to "face" and avoidance of embarrassment in the world of power politics. Professional politicians are cautious not to express such ridicule openly (although ambitious aides often will do so in anonymous leaks to the press). The tact of professional diplomats is especially helpful in dealing among such men without arousing complicated emotions of insult and revenge.

The inner nexus of such cold, imperious vanity and anger is the psychology of the grandiose self. One patient in psychoanalysis expressed this typical stance when he was leaving a job and his employers were speculating about a suitable replacement. The thought went through his mind of saying, "How about God?"[55]

But the people who lack an independent power base and are dependent upon the HP, his staff, often get the full force of his vanity and frustrations. He can be a bully and petulant, taking as a personal affront any deviation from perfection and any sign his staff has not absolutely dedicated their lives to him. He gives them little autonomy. Nietzsche's theory appears correct: "One will seldom err if extreme actions are ascribed to vanity, ordinary actions to habit, and mean actions to fear." The HP is especially likely to act from both vanity and fear.[56]

It should be clear, however, that stubbornness, imperial determination, and aggression to effect control of what are seen as lesser men are not always dysfunctional.[57] The capacity to persevere in a course of action despite travails, opposition, and criticism can be a formula for success, whether creating a revolutionary movement or "toughing out" the attacks of critics. HPs have a Darwinian advantage in the competitive quest. And once in office, critics of the direction of policy are more readily ignored: To the HP the *advantage* of being a leader is to be able finally to ignore lower status critics.

Partial Regression: Slightly Drunken, Emotionally Organized Thought

The HP is engaged by power, his mental life preoccupied with it. He cannot get away from it and relax because the concern is part of his personality. He directly, physically, experiences "forces," "threats," and "pressures" moving him to act in various ways. In technical terms, his mental processes are partly regressed and primary process. The HP may have the gift to fashion bold visions or alarums from such material, but he usually lacks the detached executive control to be a first-rate artist; proportion is lacking and often he is only vague, emotionalistic, dull, and vacuous. The HP has a "veil of ambiguity and indirectness"; there is a slight drunkenness to his thought when he thinks or declaims about important issues.[58] His thinking seems to reflect underlying emotional themes and, in perspective, he appears caught up powerfully in a world of his own imagining.

It should be clear that the term "slight drunkenness" is used here in a specialized sense. Power exists in the mind, and the conventional subculture of hardball power is a subculture of mental processes widely shared. The primary process dramatizations of the HP put him in touch with, and allow his intuition to guide him within, this subculture. It is functional; in fact, someone without his sensitivity might be unable to succeed in hardball politics. He would be like Plato's former prisoner in a cave who, returning to the world of shadows and semblances, it unable to perform effectively because his eyes are not attuned to the lack of light.[59]

I do not wish to be misunderstood: The HP can be shrewd, and often effective, in the capture of high office. It is simply that analytically rational intelligence operates in connection with a larger part of his mind that functions as if he were sleepwalking: manipulating vaguely defined, emotionally laden, symbols; adopting dramatic poses; exhorting; attacking; reassuring; defending; declaiming. This is the nature of public rhetoric in hardball politics.[60] What rationalist accounts of such ambiguity and emotionalism (which see such traits as mere stratagems) omit is the deeper cause that men with ambition are psychologically predisposed to be caught in their own imaginations and speak with this slight drunkenness of mind.[61]

There are other important senses in which the HP's mental processes, while common among politicians, are regressed. As discussed above, he lives partially in a world of strong imagination, of empowered abstraction, of viscerally experienced threats, forces, and pressures; as well, his ambition typically involves major psychic investment in his internal dramatization with grandiose fantasies, substantial overestimation of his probability of ultimate success, and his biased perceptions idealize too much (upwards), stereotype too simply (others as like himself), and misconstrue the lower status public as (at least potentially) fully attentive and a responsive cast of supporting characters. In a psychiatric taxonomy his is in part a "borderline" character (Table 6.1).

Hyperactivity

There is a final characteristic of the HP syndrome closely allied to grandiose striving: hyperactivity. When he is engaged in, or associated with, projects he considers heroically important, his being becomes flooded with nervous energy. He walks fast (typically with the grandiose fantasy that his project

Table 6.1. From Within: The "Hardball Politics" Imagination System

Normality	Borderline (HP)	Psychosis
Integrated subjective self	Structural split into two selves (grandiose/depleted)	Complete fragmentation of subjective self
Mature self-esteem	Grandiosity/shame	Full delusional constitution of grandiose self; cold paranoid grandiosity/omnipotent persecutor
Mature self-confidence	Imperial, absolute self-confidence/hypochondria, continual worry about well-being, insecurity	Full delusional constitution of grandiose self; cold, paranoid/omnipotent persecutors and malevolent forces
Mature ambition	Compelling drive to merge with ("attain") idealized powerful offices; solipsistic claims for attention; fears of inadequacy	Full delusional constitution of grandiose self; cold paranoid grandiosity/omnipotent persecutor
Genuine love, warmth with autonomous individuals	Partial withdrawal of object libido; partial narcissistic bonding (loyalty/disloyalty)	Complete withdrawal of object libido; narcissistic bonding
Secondary process (secularized) reality testing and creative use of primary process under ego control	Partially distorting idealizing, twinship and mirror stereotypes; vague awe, primary process "religious" feelings, reified abstractions, and experiences of forces, pressures, power; habitual ambiguity and indirection; marked libidinal intrusions into speech and thought	Massive projection and transference; full deterioration of reality testing; uncontrolled intrusion of primary process, incomprehensible, illogical, fully emotionally expressive speech and thought
Mature, playful humor	Deteriorated humor	Absent
Capacity for enthusiasm	Episodes of hypomanic excitement	Auto-erotic tension state

is essential to preserve the well-being and functioning of the world, that it will come part or degenerate if he ceases).[62] He over-schedules himself. He works long hours, seldom with time to relax or enjoy recreation. The importance of his own projects may produce so much physiological arousal that he needs to turn to alcohol to calm himself.

Coda

Individuals whose inner worlds are complex, larger-than-life power dramas of enormous grandiosity and apprehensive vulnerability, while they have a basic skeleton in common, are not identical. Some are motivated simply to live out their wish to occupy the role of a high-status benefactor, others have such fantasies infused with genuine ability and socially useful content, a genuine idealism of heroic accomplishment to produce a better world. (But it is, of course, not a world to be produced now by truth, compassion, fairness, the freeing of individuals from warping roles, and the rearrangement of norms. It is a vision predicated on the scenario of grandiose competitive accomplishment, dominance—in the imagination, integration of the self by being above others—and survival of the self against countervailing forces: utopia first requires domination; political control precedes ethics.) The subjective intensity of such a power drama varies in degree and is not a complete description either of all determinants of hardball practice or of other aspects of personality.

Compassion and the Hardball Politics Practitioner

This review of hardball politics has drawn upon a psychiatric humanism which diagnoses as pathological, by comparison with its ideals, the behavior I have described. The rationale is that the two "selves" are seen to be parts of a potentially integrated whole; therapy is thought to be a more effective nurturant than the pursuit of worldly ambition to effect such spiritual healing. But this diagnosis—which suggests why psychologists, with a larger perspective, are skeptical of the limited "realism" in international politics—also implies, within a psychiatric mode, compassion for what one sees as the problems of the HP (a compassion which the HP, with his scorn of weakness— including, often, a misinformed view that psychology is only a "soft," liberal viewpoint—seldom would reciprocate).[63] How much sympathy and compassion to accord the hardball player who makes others victims of his irrationalities will have to be left to the reader. But it would be appropriate to recall Ernest Jones's summary of Freud's image of man and to note also that the HP himself is driven by imperatives whose origins are a mystery to him (and especially suffers physically from stress and psychogenic illness when success is problematic or he encounters setbacks), and that his political agendas (an effort at self-therapy—a lifelong quest to integrate his depleted self with the image of a charismatic idealized self) are seldom wholly successful: "The images of the innocent babe or unfolding plant have been replaced," Jones wrote, "by more sympathetic and living ones of creatures pathetically struggling 'with no language but a cry,' to achieve the self-control and inner security that civilized man has so far attempted in vain to attain."[64] Yet the fused quest to effect both inner security and national security simultaneously can be deadly as well as tragically unrealistic.

The prayer for beneficent transformation of the world and the syndrome of its hardball practices is an old one. "From pride, vain-glory, and hypocrisy; from envy, hatred, and malice, and all uncharitableness, good Lord, deliver us" reads the litany of *The Book of Common Prayer*.[65] In his 1837 Phi Bet꞉

Kappa address at Harvard, Ralph Waldo Emerson spoke eloquently about the disheartening effects of "business as usual," pointing out that "Young men of the fairest promise, who begin life upon our shores, inflated by the mountain winds, shined upon by all the stars of God, find the earth below not in unison with these, but are hindered from action by the disgust which the principles on which business is managed inspire."[66] An inspired goodwill and "patience" were Emerson's prescriptions to idealistic youth. Yet 124 years later, in 1961 — and almost 150 years later in the mid-1980s (as I will discuss in the next chapter) — there was still no effective remedy for this condition.

A THEORY OF AMERICAN FOREIGN POLICY

> *U.S. officials were inclined to believe [national security] justifications however misled or misinformed they might have been.*
> —C. Blasier, *The Hovering Giant: U.S. Responses to Revolutionary Change in Latin America*[67]

On the Cuban beaches, in 1961, the American-sponsored expatriates shot and wounded a twelve-year-old boy wearing the uniform of Castro's militia, who sought to defend his homeland against capitalist invaders. On the afternoon of D-Day, the Brigade's political commander, Manuel Artime, spoke to the boy: "I started explaining to him what communism meant . . . that he was only a little part of the big machine; that it was a regime that would destroy anybody who opposed its policies . . . "

Manuel Artime himself had only forty-eight hours remaining before he was abandoned . . . a little part in a big machine. His men dying and Castro's forces pressing forward, he clung to faith in the American president he idolized, waiting, any moment, for the awesome deus ex machina of American jet firepower to blaze across the skies above the mosquito-infested Zapata swamps. It never came.

And shortly the American government would begin the next phase of its hardball campaign to eliminate a Communist opponent — more assassination contracts, the "boom and blast" of MONGOOSE.

There is a common logic when national policies have the form of a hierarchical power drama.[68] Both American planners and Castro treated people like little parts of big machines, both became agitated and driven, when in positions of superiority, to neutralize or destroy anybody who seriously challenged their position.

The "hardball" style has often advertised itself as a simple, dispassionate rationality and realism. My suggestion is that there is nothing dispassionate about hardball politics save its impersonal callousness and lack of compassion. The dispassionate, calculating, sophisticated talking is a facade: a surface expression of an extraordinarily complex system of powerfully charged imagination accompanied by fierce tensions, arrogance, stark fear. There is a logic to power, but no technical rationality to the knowing of it. It is a system that belongs to a different psychological realm altogether: maximize technical rationality in a process with unchanged imaginations, and there would be little noticeable difference in the conduct of American foreign policy.

Let me now proceed, formally, to integrate the argument. Like the shape of iron filings on a sheet of paper which reveals the shape and power of a magnet beneath, the strong imagination system we have surveyed produces the form, and repetition of, three vectors of blocked learning: (1) characteristic policies; (2) characteristic self-blocking behavior within the American executive branch's policy process; and (3) a characteristic syndrome of errors of judgment and perception.

Vector 1: The Form of Policy

The American government since World War II has not been empire-minded to the same degree as many other regimes in history; there are important distinctions and discriminations to be made. Nevertheless, I think we best understand American foreign policy toward leftist revolutionary challenges to governments within its (self-designated) sphere of identification and influence as expressing, in the main, the impulses and motives I have just described.

The principal American policy, in fact, is not intervention but "business as usual" inattention; any lower-status country, without power, which has not yet become a "trouble spot" is taken for granted. The depth of analysis and search in the American decision process is limited, and only when another major power which *genuinely* threatens America is involved (e.g., the Missile Crisis) is there motivation for extensive, consequential thought.

When a leftist revolutionary process begins, a standard American policy sequence (see the discussion of the 1980s in the next chapter, Table 7.2) unfolds, accompanied by agitated debate (with overdramatization) and producing an increasingly activist policy designed to restore a sense of control with respect to this growing, public challenge. Events thousands of miles distant suddenly arouse "hysteria" in American policymakers, overconfidence in their power to manage events, and a feeling of necessity to do so.[69]

I have outlined the core elements of this policy structure in Table 6.2, elements reflecting the presence of this top-down drama: overconfidence, fear, defective ethics, slightly drunken and emotion-charged talk, depersonalized and scornful hostility (regardless of the merits of the revolution), deteriorated humor, and feverish activism.

Table 6.2. Hardball Politics: A Repeated System of American Foreign Policy

Main Characteristic: Inattention to lower status nations between crises.

Reaction engaged via revolutionary challenge from below

I. *Ambition and Overconfidence*
   1. Escalating violence employed to preserve a dramatic role (above) of unchallenged domination and control. "Light at the end of the tunnel" faith, albeit without externally validating evidence and without a rational plan for an end game.

II. *Fear and Suspicion*
   1. "Domino theory" national security threats are overdramatized.

III. *Defective Ethics*
   1. Ideals poorly integrated and abandoned readily. Absence of principled restraint.
   2. Depersonalization leads to "technocratic" rationality. Deaths and injuries to foreigners, especially of low status, enter rational calculations as "nothing to lose."

IV. *Emotionally Organized Thought*
   1. Discussions, especially if public, will appear slightly drunken, that is, confident yet decoupled from reality, use emotion-laden symbols consistent with an imagined role of rightful American dominance, and possess only a modest ability to afford clear analysis of local realities.

V. *"Cold," Scornful Aggression*
   1. Policies are designed to prevent America's "visible" (i.e., dramatically consequential) defeat—or the "visible" success of an illegitimate challenger. Rational, "coercive diplomacy" designed simply to negotiate specific changes or limits in behavior is not used.

VI. *Deteriorated Humor*
   1. Absence of modesty and good humor.

VII. *Hyperactivity*
   1. Activism, particularly increasing to the point of obsession as earlier policies prove ineffective and challenges grow.

Vector 2: Behavior Within the Policy Process

If we recognize the national security world to be, as I have suggested, a subculture with a highly charged sensibility of power drama, I believe we can understand more clearly a common cause of the self-blocking behavior reviewed in chapter 4.[70]

Primarily, one finds highly ambitious men, decided in the rightness of their views (to the point of overconfidence) and preferring like-minded advisers. The deepest fear of the highly ambitious is to be excluded from the inner circle at the top, and they dissemble, engage in self-censorship, and mute the emotional force of their communication upwards. Individuals have strong fear of appearing weak or tender-minded in such circles and engage in self-censorship of any reservations that might appear to reflect these traits, leading policy discussions to further bias toward the hardball sensibility.

Also characteristic of such a system will be a tendency to disregard (and take for granted) the "invisible," lower status subordinates who will implement any plans. There will be defective ethics, ready dissembling and manipulation, and morality will only be discussed in pragmatically utilitarian (rather than principled) terms. There will be angry rejection of the disloyal and scorn for any perceived weakness.

I have listed these and other characteristics of the foreign policy process in Table 6.3. It is, perhaps, not a reassuring picture: The system can, I believe, work better when men of unusual maturity, responsibility, and strength of character serve in top posts — such men would be needed to supplant the natural tendencies of such a system, with its powerful attraction to the highly ambitious.

Vector 3: Characteristic Tendencies to Faulty Perceptions and Judgments

Finally, if we reconsider the pattern of misjudgments and misperceptions I have suggested (chapter 2), these, as well, may be seen to be expressions of the imagination system I described in the previous section: that is, to be assessments made likely as an effect of the underlying presence of a "hardball" dramatic sensibility for thinking about America's position in the world

Table 6.3. Hardball Politics: Self-Blocking Characteristics of the American Policy Process

I. *Ambition and Overconfidence*
   1. Decided world views.
   2. Too hasty preference for like-minded advisers.
   3. Majority confident of successful use of force.

II. *Fear and Suspicion*
   1. Strong fear of being excluded from access to power leads to inhibition and self-censorship, especially by subordinates.
   2. Fear of expressing "soft" views.
   3. Strong fear of press exposure.

III. *Emotionally Organized Thought*
   1. Tendency, in a top-down system, to ignore subordinates and take them for granted in planning.

IV. *Defective Ethics*
   1. Dissembling and strategic maneuvers within the policy process.
   2. Limited sense of personal responsibility for outcomes.

V. *"Cold" Aggression*
   1. Strong rejection of the "disloyal" (e.g., Bowles).
   2. Scorn of weakness (liberal idealists "lack balls").

VI. *Hyperactivity*
   1. Accompanied by exaggerated sense of the import and importance of one's work.

and the nature of power in international relations. I suggest the following proposition: *At each point where the policy process stopped at what was, in retrospect, a misjudgment or misperception, it did so because the stopping point was a node of the hardball dramatic sensibility.*

Thus, it will be a typical — a naturally occurring and continuing — feature of American foreign policy in its return engagements to be overdramatized and oddly wired in the following ways: overconfidence; exaggerated fears; self-deceptive ethical pretensions; symbolic entrapments and a substantial disconnection between the terms of discussion and the local realities in which the covert actions (and wars) are conducted; overconfident activism. I have outlined such tendencies resulting from the dual-track nature of American foreign policy in Table 6.4. (In the next chapter I will return again to these issues to illustrate how this overlay repeats itself in the current return engagement in the 1980s.)

One of the features of this framework may deserve to be especially underscored. Because of the two "self systems," grandiosity and vulnerability coexist. That is, the more tense and "hardball" the decision maker's own personal tendencies and participation in this general system, the greater will be the "domino" fear. "Light at the end of the tunnel" policies (believed even without an end game or rational plan) coexist with "domino theory" fears that the entire structure of order could come part. Both are linked, predictable features of the characteristic American template.[71]

While there are personal differences — Eisenhower is the modest and integrated man in the case material — I want to emphasize the primary determinant of this thinking is systemic, the use of imagination to understand political power. One needs, in the imagination, to create a sensibility of American power and place in the world: the hardball system is, in part, an instinctive way ambitious, power-oriented men do so personally (and for one another), and the tendency of this syndrome to overdramatization and characteristic error, and to block further improvements in intelligence and effectiveness, is a risk of any great power.[72]

I do not want to imply that behavior and thought in the American foreign policy process were organized and overdramatized along these dimensions, and American foreign policy driven, to a point of madness. Kennedy did not live in a world of delusion, but only part way there, in a world of compelling upward ambition and ideals.[73] His "hardball" system was not the extreme form; that was Hitler: megalomania ("a Thousand Year Reich"); paranoia about enemies (Jews were polluting; Jews and the French were sinister, plotting, dangerous, to be eradicated); amoral aggressiveness (military domination and world war). Kennedy's was a moderated form of imagination entrapment and its logic of policy response: idealistic ambition (New Frontier, a world constructively managed by U.S. power with his leadership); a perceiver only of challenges and dangerous challengers (he spoke of Castro only

Table 6.4. Hardball Politics: Characteristic American Tendencies to
Errors of Judgment and Perception

I. *Ambition and Overconfidence*
1. Substantial overconfidence in success, even without evidence or a rational plan (a mystical "light at the end of the tunnel" faith).
2. Overconfident faith in mass public support for American-defined purposes in the target country. Overconfident faith in eventual public vindication through success at home.
3. Substantial underestimation (and scorn for the ability and learning rates of) lower status opponents.

II. *Fear and Suspicion of Opponents**
1. Strong fear of ambitions of other rival nations (e.g., Castro, Soviets) and of America's domino vulnerabilities, worldwide, if weakness is displayed.
2. Strong fear of vulnerability to Republicans and other aggressive domestic opponents if there is "failure" through perceived weakness.

III. *Defective Ethics*
1. Uncritical belief in the coincidence of American policy and moral virtue.
2. Compassion (and, to an extent, reality) disappears in a "nothing to lose from trying" obsession for success.
3. Strategic dissembling and press manipulation to out-maneuver genuine democratic accountability.

IV. *Symbolic Involvements*
1. Use of ambiguous phraseologies and characterizations with modest power to clarify issues and forces in local reality.
2. Tendency to overdramatize and to capture one's own imagination. In policymaking, this leads to the self-absorbed belief that American viewpoints effectively define reality.
3. Direct experience of sinister, malevolent forces.

V. *Hyperactivity*
1. Unrealistic faith that a plethora of activist programs, begun "when the hour is late," will restore control.

---

*Note that fear is a function of the insecure self, overconfidence a function of the grandiose self. Hence the two will not, a priori, be thoughtfully integrated (as in the months before the Cuban missile crisis when the anxious search for missiles coincided with confidence they would never be introduced).

as "a cancer we cannot live with for another ten years"); a cool, self-deprecating wit (but not Adlai Stevenson's warm gift of humor); a pragmatic, toughness. Yet I fear we misunderstood the causes of international violence, the commonality of humanity, the nature of the mind, and the deeply personal — and even intimate — path of the personal learning and growth required of genuine statesmen (who can be larger than such systems, master them, and direct them to constructive purposes) if we fail to appreciate that such differences of degree lie along common dimensions.

NOTES

1. See C. Geertz, "Deep Play: Notes on the Balinese Cockfight" in his *The Interpretation of Cultures* (New York: Basic Books, 1973), pp. 412–453, for an example of levels of analysis that can be applied to such dramas as international conflict and arms races. See also R. Jervis, *Perception and Misperception in International Relations* (Princeton, NJ: Princeton Univ. Press, 1976), pp. 239–271; L. Etheredge, *A World of Men: The Private Sources of American Foreign Policy* (Cambridge, MA: MIT Press, 1978); the classic article by D. Pruitt, "Definition of the Situation as a Determinant of International Action" in H. Kelman, ed., *International Behavior* (New York: Holt, Rinehart & Winston, 1965), and D. Ball, "The 'Definition of Situation': Some Theoretical and Methodological Consequences of Taking W. I. Thomas Seriously" *Journal for the Theory of Social Behavior* 2 (1972): 61–82.

2. P. Wyden, *Bay of Pigs: The Untold Story* (New York: Simon and Schuster, 1979), p. 31. Compare Robert Kennedy's tense and driven approach.

3. F. Greenstein, *The Hidden-Hand Presidency: Eisenhower as Leader* (New York: Basic Books, 1984) provides an able discussion of Eisenhower's sense of mastery.

4. That Eisenhower took a calmer view is not to say he was correct; my intention is that a subjective stance, not "objective" facts alone, determine a policy.

5. D. Kahneman, P. Slovic and A. Tversky, ed., *Judgment Under Uncertainty: Heuristics and Biases* (Cambridge: Cambridge Univ. Press, 1982); Jervis, *Perception and Misperception*, pp. 187–191.

6. R. Cambridge and R. Shreckengost, *Are You Sure? The Subjective Probability Assessment Test* (Washington, DC: Central Intelligence Agency, 1978).

7. See L. Bloomfield and A. Leiss, *Controlling Small Wars: A Strategy for the 1970's* (New York: Knopf, 1969), pp. 138–142 for a review of logistics and comparative weaponry at the Bay of Pigs.

8. What it takes to be an expert, rather than only to sound like one, is exemplified in Robert Amory's view of Colonel Hawkins, who was enthusiastically endorsed for his prior combat experience by the JCS. Amory, the DDI (deputy director-Intelligence) at the CIA was the counterpart to Bissell, who was the DDP (deputy director-Plans). Amory fought in 26 assault landings during World War II, many as small as the Bay of Pigs. He later said, "Hawkins made one [beach-head assault] in his whole goddamn life, and that was Iwo Jima, which was three divisions abreast. He was a very able soldier and Marine, but he didn't know beans about what a small, self-contained beachhead would be like." It is also true that Hawkins lacked experience with planning large night assaults on uncharted beaches: The American military did not do that. In fairness to Hawkins, the night assault idea was forced upon him at the last minute after Hawkins was already committed to the operation, rather than being his understanding of the operation he was recruited to plan. See Wyden, *Bay of Pigs*, p. 69.

9. A useful compendium is R. Abelson, E. Aronson, T. Newcomb, M. Rosenberg, and P. Tannenbaum, ed., *Theories of Cognitive Consistency: A Sourcebook* (Chicago: Rand McNally, 1968).

10. A thoughtful discussion of applications to foreign policy decision making is Jervis, *Perception and Misperception*, chapter 4 and pp. 356–372. See especially his discussion of defensive avoidance.

11. Bissell "passed the buck" back: he laughed, said he certainly was not going to authorize American government funds, and simply added with a smile, "I don't

want to hear any more about it. Your job is to get things done down there." The story is told in Wyden, *Bay of Pigs*, pp. 52–53. The president of Guatemala proved sympathetic to the plight of Latin males, his government provided funds, and the CIA established a "chit" system with extra chits awarded the men for good conduct. Ibid.

12. R. Barnett, *Roots of War: The Men and Institutions Behind American Foreign Policy* (New York: Penguin, 1972). See especially his emphasis on "managerial" styles of thought, a useful corrective to Marxist interpretations. See also A. Maslow's perceptive essay "The Need to Know and the Fear of Knowing" in A. Maslow, *Toward a Psychology of Being*, 2nd ed. (New York: Van Nostrand, 1968), pp. 60–67.

13. C. Bowles, *Promises to Keep: My Years in Public Life, 1941–1969* (New York: Harper and Row, 1971), p. 449.

14. A. Berle, "The Cuban Crisis: Failure of American Foreign Policy" *Foreign Affairs* (October 1960): 40–55; and B. Berle and T. Jacobs, ed., *Navigating the Rapids, 1918–1971: From the Papers of Adolf A. Berle* (New York: Harcourt Brace Jovanovich, 1973).

15. Other balanced, emotionally-consistent views opposed to invasion might hold that: (a) Castro was not a Communist; (b) if he were a Communist, America had forced him to become one; (c) being a Communist reflected genuinely high ideals.

16. Cognitive complexity may thus be inconsistent with the emotional force required for policy prescription and political action. See also the discussion of cognitive complexity in the work of P. Tetlock, "Integrative Complexity as a Variable in Political Decision-Making." Paper delivered at the annual meeting of the International Studies Association. (Photocopy: March, 1980).

17. This was also a tactic — no excuses — to dramatize a message to the bureaucracy.

18. A. Maslow, *Motivation and Personality* (New York: Harper and Row, 1954).

19. See also C. Alderfer, *Existence, Relatedness, and Growth: Human Needs in Organizational Settings* (New York: Free Press, 1972); Etheredge, *A World of Men*.

20. The Bay of Pigs' scenario intended for Castro — to be set upon from all sides with uncertain information and control — was not far removed from Kennedy's own circumstances.

21. See the general discussion of Kennedy's views in this regard in N. Lebow, "The Cuban Missile Crisis: Reading the Lessons Correctly" *Political Science Quarterly* 98 (1983): 431–458.

22. The less anxious, idealistic liberals may have been motivated by moral vision, ideals, and hope.

23. See D. Kahneman et al., ed., *Judgment Under Uncertainty* for a discussion of this "attribution" error.

24. Note these could be reasonable (even if not correct) inferences because decision makers could remember, or observe, the same "objective" circumstances and find Castro's hostile behavior distinctive: Batista did not behave this way; nor did other liberal reformers in Latin America (for example, Betancourt of Venezuela). Other "plausible" Cuban leaders (such as its former prime minister, Miro Cardona, now in exile and head of the American-sponsored liberation government) were friendly. Vary the leader, vary the national policy — at least on the surface, the analysis could make sense.

25. Jervis, *Perception and Misperception* is a principal theorist of this school. I want to avoid doing him a slight disservice by referencing his research while discussing *autonomous* cognitive error. He also writes of motivated mechanisms and has been

primarily concerned to expand the theoretical universe of articulated possibilities rather than to propose a general theory.

26. For example, to blame Castro *and* to consider him dangerous was to *justify* an American policy and a vision of American power in the world.

27. The most rigorous research in this line of investigation is reviewed by D. Winter and A. Stewart, "The Power Motive" in H. London and J. Exner, ed., *Dimensions of Personality* (New York: Wiley, 1978, pp. 392–447. This section draws heavily upon the work of others and the reader is referred to my "Hardball Politics: A Model" in *Political Psychology* 1 (1979); 3–26 for a systematic bibliography. Modern works on power motivation and characteristic modes of thought, with reference to American policy making include H. Lasswell's pioneering *Power and Personality* (New York: Norton, 1948); A. George and J. George, *Woodrow Wilson and Col. House* (New York: Dover, 1964); J. Barber, *The Presidential Character* (Englewood Cliffs, NJ: Prentice-Hall, 1972), especially his discussion of the active-negative character; F. Bailey, *Strategms and Spoils: A Social Anthropology of Politics* (Toronto: Copp Clark, 1969); D. Winter, *The Power Motive* (New York: Free Press, 1973); R. Caro, *The Power Broker: Robert Moses and the Decline of New York* (New York: Knopf, 1974); D. Mayhew, *Congress: The Electoral Connection* (New Haven, CT: Yale Univ. Press, 1974); M. Halperin, P. Clapp, and A. Kanter, *Bureaucratic Behavior and Foreign Policy* (Washington, DC: Brookings, 1974); C. Bernstein and B. Woodward, *All the President's Men* (New York: Warner, 1974); J. Newhouse, *Cold Dawn: The Story of SALT* (New York: Holt, Rinehart & Winston, 1973); D. McClelland, *Power: The Inner Experience* (New York: Irvington, 1975); L. O'Connor, *Court: Mayor Daley and His City* (New York: Avon, 1975); B. Mazlish, *In Search of Nixon* (New York: Basic Books, 1972) and his *The Revolutionary Ascetic: Evolution of a Public Type* (New York: Basic Books, 1976); Ole Holsti, "The 'Operational Code' as an Approach to the Analysis of Belief Systems. Final Report to the National Science Foundation." (Duke University: Photocopy, 1977); R. Tucker, "The 'Georges' Wilson Re-Examined: An Essay on Psychobiography" *American Political Science Review* 71 (1977); D. Halberstam, *The Best and the Brightest* (New York: Random House, 1972); S. Hersh, *The Price of Power: Kissinger in the Nixon White House* (New York: Summit Books, 1983).

Specialists will recognize that I am moving beyond a personality based explanation and, via the concept of larger-than-life drama, addressing the integration of individual behavior within systems. I propose a reversal of Lasswell's classic dictum and also suggest public events arouse and engage private motives. H. Lasswell, *Psychopathology and Politics* (Chicago: Univ. of Chicago Press, 1930). My argument is that participation in the over dramatized and oddly wired sensibility of power serves various functions, including problem solving, e.g., M. Smith, "Political Attitudes" in J. Knutson, ed., *Handbook of Political Psychology* (San Francisco: Jossey-Bass, 1973), pp. 57–82. I should emphasize that my argument addresses the national security sub-world as it responds to the return engagements observed in this book and, amidst my borrowings, do not wish to imply that those I cite would agree with, or are responsible for, the solution I suggest to explain the three vectors.

28. B. Tuchman, *The March of Folly: From Troy to Vietnam* (New York: Knopf, 1984) has written a similar analysis about the same problem. I believe she is correct to locate power motivation as a key solution to the problem, although think the present theory better developed and easier to integrate with other lines of investigation, for example, psychoanalytic "self" psychology; the suggestion of a

genetic epistemology via hardwired effects of strong and hierarchical visual imagery. See D. Bear's invited address to the International Society for Political Psychology, Toronto, 1984 (unpublished) for an outline of such possible integrations and L. Etheredge, "Dual-Track Information Processing in Public Policy Decision Making: Models of Strong Imagination Systems" Symposium paper presented to the American Psychological Association meetings, Toronto, 1984 (photocopy) for a general discussion.

29. This duality is not readily assessed with conventional measures of self-esteem as the HP is ashamed to reveal low self-esteem and in part experiences enormously high self-esteem. For a discussion of several methodological issues and evidence for high manifest self-esteem among the politically active, see P. Sniderman, *Personality and Democratic Politics* (Berkeley, CA: Univ. of California Press, 1975). Psychoanalytic characterizations of this phenomenon are suggested in H. Kohut, *The Analysis of the Self* (New York: International Universities Press, 1971) and his *The Restoration of the Self* (New York: International Universities Press, 1977).

30. Early childhood antecedents appear complex and are not fully documented. They seem to include a mother whose indulgence is self-involved ("narcissistic" in psychoanalytic terminology); that is, the child, rather than being related to as an autonomous person, confirmed and loved for himself, is valued as a being who can fulfill the mother's own aspirations through heroic accomplishment. Thus the child is both empowered while (following Lasswell) he is deprived of power as an autonomous individual. See Kohut, *The Analysis of the Self*; L. Pye, *Mao Tse Tung: The Man in the Leader* (New York: Basic Books, 1976).

31. Ambition drives such men even in the face of extreme objective risk. Commenting on the attractions and the enormous risks of the office of Caesar, M. Grant, *The Twelve Caesars* (New York: Scribner's, 1975), p. 257, observes: "In view of the alarming perils involved, it may seem difficult to understand why anyone could be eager to become ruler of the Roman Empire. Yet signs of reluctance were not greatly in evidence. Even in the third century A.D., when a would-be usurper scarcely needed to be a statistical expert to note that the average reign ended rapidly and violently, candidates for the throne still proliferated on every side."

32. One of the important therapeutic tasks in the integration of the HP is realization that such dramatizations are in his own mind, albeit shared by others in the system to create its reality. This may be especially difficult to achieve among politicians because HPs and others with similar traits in the news media join in a "collusion of grandiosity" to define and sustain their collective and mutually reinforcing idealized fantasies of "high" public offices as "objective" social reality. See V. Volkan's work, esp. *Primitive Internalized Object Relations: A Clinical Study of Schizophrenic, Borderline, and Narcissistic Patients* (New York: International Universities Press, 1976), p. 269; O. Kernberg, *Borderline Conditions and Pathological Narcissism* (New York: Aronson, 1975), pp. 51–85; J. Gedo and A. Goldberg, *Models of the Mind* (Chicago: Univ. of Chicago Press, 1973) on disillusionment therapy. On efforts mutually to reinforce the prestige of the position they occupy and the institutional ladders they climb, see Mayhew, *Congress*.

33. C. Bowles, *Promises to Keep*, p. 29, for example, laments Kennedy's disinterest in the drafting of the Democratic Party platform on which he ran.

34. In terms of psychological theory, ordinary stimulus-response punishments do not extinguish the HP's long-term behavior, although they may hurt his feelings.

35. The HP, in other words, does not enjoy his work. Contrary to what one might expect in a politician, most British prime ministers have not much enjoyed associating with other people. See H. Berrington, "The Fiery Chariot: British Prime Ministers and the Search for Love" *British Journal of Political Science* 4 (1974):

345–369; Kohut, *The Analysis of the Self*, pp. 120, 144, 199.

36. Kohut, *The Analysis of the Self*, pp. 96–98; 251–253 et passim.

37. There may be a need, too, to receive this comparatively and competitively, by constantly seeking out and winning against challengers and opponents. See also H. Kohut, "Thoughts on Narcissism and Narcissistic Rage" in *The Psychoanalytic Study of the Child* (Chicago: Quadrangle, 1971).

38. There is the anticipated reward (via the mirror transference) of future, perhaps eternal, fame and vindication "in the eyes of history." The reference to "hearts and minds" is to a phrase which is part of this syndrome in the case of America's Vietnam policy. See L. Gelb and R. Betts, *The Irony of Vietnam: The System Worked* (Washington, DC: Brookings Institution, 1979). "Silent majority" refers to a phrase used during the Nixon Administration.

39. Kohut, *The Analysis of the Self*, pp. 150–151. However, the observation of political life that "great power is in general gained by running great risks" may be correct. If so, the inherent inability of the HP to believe his personal failure is a realistic possibility may eliminate inhibitions to his upward ambitions that would deter more "normal" men. Hubris may lead to great successes as well as to great tragic disasters. The problem of assessing overconfidence and attitudes toward risk is subtle because, while the HP, in one sector of his mind, worries constantly about failure, in another sector of his mind he is convinced it will never occur. The above quotation is from Herodotus, *The History of Herodotus*. Translated by G. Macaulay. (London: MacMillan & Co., 1904), p. 151. See also the discussion of risk taking by a military HP, Gen. Douglas MacArthur, especially his decision for the Inchon landing and underestimation of the Chinese Communists in the Korean War in J. DeRivera, *The Psychological Dimension of Foreign Policy* (Chicago, IL: Charles E. Merrill, 1968), pp. 175–180. See also Kohut, *The Analysis of the Self*, pp. 150–151.

40. Kohut, *The Analysis of the Self*, pp. 9, 85–88, 97.

41. Ibid., p. 3. To retain power "Daley has intuitively known from the beginning (that) a man must surround himself with servitors, people who are totally loyal and utterly dependent on the man, Daley, for their own well-being." O'Connor, *Court*, p. 11.

42. Ibid., p. 123 et passim.

43. The congressional expert, Richard Fenno, observes: "One of the dominant impressions of my travels is the terrific sense of uncertainty which animates these Congressmen. They perceive electoral troubles where the most imaginative outside observer could not possibly perceive, conjure up or hallucinate them." Cited in Mayhew, *Congress*, p. 35, note 2.

   During the Watergate cover-up case, President Nixon was often called upon by critics to apologize and ask forgiveness. A hardball practitioner such as Nixon would know (believe) this would not work.

44. Hersh, *The Price of Power* provides a recent discussion of behavior in the national security process in this light. The Nixon administration was more extreme in this regard than the Kennedy years. A general discussion of pervasive, mutual mistrust in the foreign policy process is C. Argyris, *Some Causes of Organizational Ineffectiveness Within the Department of State* (Washington, DC: Department of State. Center for International Systems Research, 1967). See also the sensibility of the self-blocking people portrayed in A. Wildavsky, "The Self-Evaluating Organization" in J. Shafritz and A. Hyde, ed., *Classics of Public Administration* (Oak Park, IL: Moore Publishing Co.), pp. 412–427.

45. See the distinction between normative and pragmatic rules in Bailey, *Strategms and Spoils*, p. 5. See also S. Huntington, *Political Order in Changing Societies*

(New Haven, CT: Yale Univ. Press, 1968) on political development and "arts of association."

46. Unpleasant consequences for a polity and the international political system tend to follow, as James Madison noted in *The Federalist* #10 (J. Cooke, ed., Cleveland and New York: Meridian Books, 1961), p. 59: "an attachment of different leaders ambitiously contending for pre-eminence and power . . . [has], in turn, divided mankind into parties, inflamed them with mutual animosity, and rendered them much more disposed to vex and oppress each other than to cooperate for their common good." Madison did not discuss the breathless dramatizations of the mass media, but his analysis would apply as well.

47. Kohut, *The Analysis of the Self*, p. 232.

48. See Halperin et al., *Bureaucratic Behavior* for an inventory derived partly from personal observation.

49. R. Woodward and C. Bernstein, *The Final Days* (New York: Simon and Schuster, 1976), p. 194. See also Etheredge, *A World of Men*. Dean Acheson made a similar point: Some goings-on in Washington would make the Borgias envious, he thought. He also thought it necessary for a Secretary of State to have "a killer instinct." Another former State Department official thought an ideal preparation for understanding the territoriality, coalitions, in-group secrecy, demands for loyalty, and tough style in national security circles was to have been a member of a juvenile street gang. Acheson is cited in G. Allison, *Essence of Decision: Explaining the Cuban Missile Crisis* (Boston: Little, Brown, 1971), p. 180.

50. Kohut, *The Analysis of the Self*, p. 232.

51. Ibid., pp. 199, 238; H. Kohut, "Forms and Transformations of Narcissism" *Journal of the American Psychoanalytic Association* 14 (1966): 243–272.

52. T. Hobbes. *Leviathan*. C. Macpherson, ed. (Baltimore, MD: Penguin, 1968), p. 126: "Sudden glory is the passion which maketh those grimaces called laughter: and is caused . . . by the apprehension of some deformed thing in another." Hobbes also felt people laughed from delight in self-congratulation. His unpleasant theory is not always true, but perceptive and of local validity if taken as the observation of one of the major observers of politics.

53. H. Kohut, "Thoughts on Narcissistic Rage"; J. Nehemiah, *Foundations of Psychopathology* (New York: Oxford Univ. Press, 1961), pp. 165–166; Etheredge, *A World of Men*, p. 82.

54. Quoted in T. Bailey, *A Diplomatic History of the American People* 10th ed. (Englewood Cliffs, NJ: Prentice-Hall, 1980), p. 500.

55. Quoted in Kohut, *The Analysis of the Self*, p. 149. On competitive "credit-claiming" see Mayhew, *Congress*.

56. F. Nietzsche, *Human, All Too Human: A Book for Free Spirits*. Trans. by P. Cohen. (New York: Russell & Russell, 1964).

57. See O. Fenichel, *The Psychoanalytic Theory of Neurosis* (New York: Norton, 1945), p. 279, on the relation of stubbornness to narcissism.

58. Kohut, *The Analysis of the Self*, pp. 97, 184.

59. Plato, *The Republic*. In E. Hamilton and H. Cairns, ed., *The Collected Dialogues of Plato* (New York: Pantheon, 1961), p. 749.

60. M. Edelman, *The Symbolic Uses of Politics* (Urbana, IL: Univ. of Illinois Press, 1964); D. Graber, *Verbal Behavior and Politics* (Urbana, IL: Univ. of Illinois Press, 1976); and D. Nimmo, *Popular Images of Politics* (Englewood Cliffs, NJ: Prentice-Hall, 1974) discuss these issues.

61. See also R. Robins's introduction to R. Robins, ed., *Psychopathology and Political Leadership* (New Orleans: Tulane Univ. Press, 1977), pp. 1–34 on (potentially visionary) primary process shifts in the discourse of political leaders.

62. The HP is trying to hold himself together in the face of stress. See Kohut, *The Analysis of the Self*, pp. 152–153; also A. Wallace, "Stress and Rapid Personality Changes" *International Record of Medicine* 169 (1956): 761–764. MONGOOSE would qualify as an example.

63. The present analysis suggests how an understanding of psychology may afford a larger perspective, but I do not mean to endorse tender minded analyses.

64. E. Jones, *Sigmund Freud: Four Centenary Addresses* (New York: Basic Books, 1956), p. 145.

65. Church of England, *The Book of Common Prayer* (London: Oxford Univ. Press, 1960), p. 70.

66. R. Emerson, "The American Scholar" in B. Atkinson, ed., *Selected Writings of Emerson* (New York: Modern Library, 1950), p. 63.

67. C. Blasier, *The Hovering Giant: U.S. Responses to Revolutionary Change in Latin America* (Pittsburgh, PA: Pittsburgh Univ. Press, 1976), p. 229.

68. My argument is for a system of epistemology and motivation, that is, a hard-wired effect of hierarchic imagery on brain function. See also Etheredge, "Dual-Track Information Processing."

69. As the process intensifies, in the imagination authority tends to be fused as one, and all radicals and revolutionaries tend to be lumped together. This unified top-down schema is one of the bases of the "domino" fears of contagion.

    If one wishes an oversimplified account, it is that American policymakers understand power in dramatic terms, and act, as if they were Freudian analysts, interpreting any challenge to established authority as a symbolic challenge to all established authority, hence a direct threat to themselves.

70. I want to emphasize that my use of the word "imagination" is technical, and I do not mean to imply any individual is misperceiving the reality of power relations within such a system. For example, I do not believe Arthur Schlesinger, Jr., was wrong to anticipate scorn and exploitation of his vulnerability to retaliation if he were a public opponent of the plan in the inner circle; he probably was correct.

71. Richard Nixon and Alexander Haig may serve as examples of men who, comparatively, have been unusually ambitious, hardball, tense, and prone to domino fears. Note that, via this theory, the fearfulness of domestic critics does *not* come from memory of the "who lost China?" debate in the 1950s — it is instinctive, visceral "knowledge," and historical experience only serves to substantiate what is already understood about the world.

    The syndrome I outline is, I believe, consistent with (but broader than) D. Ellsberg, *Papers on the War* (New York: Simon & Schuster, 1972).

72. The unnerving thought that the entire structure of domestic and international power is, in substantial degree, based upon hierarchical drama may also be a sensibility which emerges at the top; and sometimes it is true: A blink, and social order *might* disintegrate — as it did for Arbenz (or Batista) — by only a token challenge.

72. A complete analysis would add that Kennedy's liberalism also fueled his idealism and, at war beneath the surface, produced ambivalent policies and drew him back, especially when public exposure threatened to ram together the opposing tendencies he sought, uneasily to serve and manage within himself. The inner conflict made him a better, albeit more self-doubting, man. Nixon would have sent in troops. Kennedy was too liberal and decent to be effective (devastating) in his violence, but too ambitious, competitive and "hardball" to leave Castro alone. See Etheredge, *A World of Men* for evidence concerning sources of ambivalence in American foreign policy.

Chapter 7 RETURN ENGAGEMENT: THE 1980s

We began with the question of learning and arrived at the problem of repetition. In the last chapter I proposed a solution that three principal features of American foreign policy are jointly produced for this class of problems, by entrapment within a system of dramatic sensibility inherent to the world of power-oriented men (especially of upwardly mobile ambition) which blocks learning and repeats despite failure. It creates as *symptoms* of its presence characteristic patterns of policy, of misjudgment and misperception and of collectively self-defeating behavior within the policy process. It is a system of motivational imperative yielding compassionless policies, vicious in their consequences, afflicted by cyclical inattention and without rational long-term follow-through, lacking integrity with the ideals it professes; and a system which at least once has threatened America and the world with a nuclear war.[1]

My discussion of this strongly imagined system, an intense experience of living within a world of larger-than-life drama, was not directed at the level of individual psychology, although individual psychology certainly sustains it, and individual personality variations can be consequential in their effect. The root cause is the mind's own construction of the government of a powerful state, created and experienced domestically as a solid presence above individuals' sense of themselves. Conventional political socialization catalyzes the mind to create a sensibility of larger-than-life drama and thus, making "high" office and leadership of such a drama especially attractive to those with upwardly mobile ambition, aids selectively to locate in the national security world a disproportionate number of men (and, occasionally, women) who participate to an unusually strong, vivid, and sincere degree in such a drama and also — for fear of exclusion — mold their talents and constrain their better instincts to its service.[2]

This system, I suggest, is the cause of diverse observations which otherwise appear unconnected. Political scientists have noted that cold-blooded (allegedly "rational") calculations of international and domestic power determine policy. Psychologists have puzzled at how error-prone and ineffective the results have been. Organizational theorists have been impressed by the lack of rational, long-term plans and policy integration and by the power-

170

oriented gamesmanship which afflicts the national security decision process.[3] As we have seen, each set of different characterizations is right. I suggest they have a common source, with rational calculation ability in a peripheral role and applied to motives and dramatic necessities, designations of costs and benefits, a sense of limited personal responsibility, and assessments of reality known (intuitively) via the overdramatized imagining that characterizes this shared responsibility.

AMERICAN FOREIGN POLICY AND UNREFINED IMAGINING

I will make three further observations concerning the creation of American foreign policy primarily via this second, imagination determined, track, and then move to the present day.

First, in debate about Central American policy, the American political system has been in a situation where a disjunction between the domestic character of government and the foreign policy it produces, in local reality to Central America, tends to block realistic political discussion. To most Americans (especially to the now-frayed Democratic coalition), government has been, domestically, a progressive force. Thus, the imagery of U.S. policies in Central America as repressive and indecent (and an agitated expression of values most Americans, themselves, would reject if their government were to adopt them domestically) is the reverse of popular experience. There is a disjunction between frames of reference; in America, one cannot readily play the role of a trusted and responsible leader and discuss America's foreign policy by a seemingly radical characterization.

Second, dramatic images and simple themes dictated by the instinctive dynamics of the mind are common in popular debates.[4] But two distinctive features of the American political system allow simple a priori images to be sustained in its foreign affairs.

1. The American political system is not designed to assure cognitively or emotionally complex learning.[5] Political institutions were reasonably well-constructed to solve domestic conflicts based on interest group politics; simple *agreement* among powerful domestic actors that a solution is fair, or at least one they can live with, is, de facto, a viable political solution. But in America's international relations, no feedback system is well connected to introduce realism into the internal political process: neither potential victims in other nations, nor potential beneficiaries, are voters. Politicians who rely upon standard political signals, the preferences and votes of their domestic constituents, do not find a reliable guide to produce satisfactory solutions to foreign problems.

2. An era of fortuitous success in Western European policy has obscured the general weakness of American foreign policy learning concerning other areas of the world. America's insular political process can produce effective

policy attentive to foreign realities when unofficial mechanisms, and a match between political cultures, sustain realism: Both conditions have been available for the localized arena of American policy toward Western Europe since World War II. These decisions have more typically reflected the actions of men who were well-informed about the nations and situations they faced. There has been a foreign policy establishment, a network of influential men based in New York and affiliated with the Council on Foreign Relations, which created and sustained such policies, whose members could be regularly recruited to policy positions, and who supported one another while they served in office. Tied by cultural history and ideals, the prominence of European history and languages in schooling, the experiences of family vacations, the daily ties of international financial and business relationships, the members of this European-centered network linked knowledge to political influence and to foreign policy.

The categories and theories of America's political culture also generalized successfully to this vital Western European theatre (and their use was reinforced). Western Europe is a morally and politically simpler area of the world for Americans to understand: decision makers could pursue American security interests, work through established governments which are democratic (and in countries whose elites wish them to be), and champion freedom, stability, and economic growth in the same coherent package without troubling trade-offs. The Marshall Plan reconstruction of Western European economies after World War II and the NATO alliance against the Soviet Union effectively served American security, political stability, economic growth, and other shared values. But such an American template, transferred elsewhere, does not organize realistic viewpoints and choices for successful policies in areas of the world with other principles of cultural and political organization; instead, it has produced policies impeded by irrelevant categories.[6]

Third, critics typically argue that American decision makers have not *understood* the local nature of conflicts. My conclusion is that these critics are incorrect and misdiagnose the problem. Local ignorance does not continue because decision makers were unaware of this argument or inadvertently failed to produce a policy process to give them this understanding. They *chose* to establish policy at a sufficiently "high" level of political "sophistication" at which there is no *need* — and little use for — detailed, local knowledge. Given a global political drama, and the top-down problem of a revolutionary challenge to established governments (especially linked in *any* way to the Soviet Union or Marxist ideological formulas), the policy of the drama — containment or elimination — is instinctive: America, on a world stage, plays a game of yardage and territory, a drama of will, to be won by America or its challengers. Whether there is a 10% Communist causal component or origin of arms, or a 70% component, the territory is eventually won or lost in toto. Thus, it is not only irrelevant but *dangerous*, in a world of ambitious political actors, to become embroiled by such local considerations. These, in a cloud of complexity, would detract attention from the larger drama. That the resulting policies run aground in local realities is America's risk, a fate inherent to the second track of imagination-based policy.

I now turn to America's return engagement in the 1980s to suggest how the lessons we have drawn from history clarify the system of highly dramatized and Washington-centered imagination that is again at work.

The Carter Years

America's engagement with Central American revolutions now centrally involves two countries, Nicaragua and El Salvador. El Salvador is an enclave (8,260 square miles, about the size of Massachusetts) on the western coast of the Central American isthmus, bordering Guatemala to the north and enclosed by Honduras on the east and south. Nicaragua (57,000 square miles, about the size of Iowa) borders Honduras (to the north) and Costa Rica (to the south). Population (in the early 1980s) was 4.7 million in El Salvador and 2.8 million in Nicaragua.[7]

Nicaragua

Nicaragua was ruled by a single family, the Somoza dynasty, after 1936, when American troops left and the American-created and trained National Guard, headed by the first Somoza, began to rule the country. The Somozas were consistently appreciated in Washington as American "friends," a term defined operationally as being always willing to accommodate the American ambassador. Typically for the region, the distribution of wealth and income has been very unequal: In 1978, 5% of the population received approximately 40% of the national income, and the Somoza family controlled half of the country's agricultural production. Social conditions were appalling, including high (and preventable) rates of infant mortality (about 120/1,000 live births) and widespread malnutrition among the urban and rural poor.[8] The greed, corruption, and nastiness practiced by the regime gave it no good reason to want genuine electoral democracy.

In 1961, inspired by Fidel Castro's example, a group of about twenty university students formed the original Sandinista National Liberation Front (FSLN), named for the nationalist hero (termed an "outlaw" by American officials at the time) who led a guerrilla fight against an American marine occupation in the late 1920s. The Somoza government contained this challenge before 1978; several times it virtually wiped out the FSLN, and the group attracted little open public support.[9]

A variety of changes produced the successful Sandinista-led overthrow of the last Somoza in July 1979.

First, the regime itself became more hateful. It created public outrage following the massive earthquake of 1972 that levelled Managua; millions of dollars of humanitarian aid poured in, but almost all of it was diverted to the pockets of the Somoza family and the military. The devastated victims received almost nothing — and knew it — as the National Guard sold the emergency food supplies for personal profit and the Somoza family and its friends made huge real estate killings by buying land needed for rebuilding.[10] The catalyst to national mutiny occurred in January 1978 when the Somoza regime murdered Pedro Joaquin Charorro, editor of the opposition newspaper *La Prensa*. The Sandinistas, like Castro in his day in Cuba, were the most visible symbol of organized opposition and had the internal organization to move quickly to expand their ranks.[11]

Had they felt assured of reliable, incremental progress, most Nicaraguans would probably have preferred ameliorative solutions to engulfment in revolutionary violence. The American press, as it typically does, has experimented with simple images portraying the anti-Somoza revolution to be an heroic, mass overthrow of an oppressive government. But there were also systemic causes for the overthrow, especially for its success in 1979. By the late 1970s the world economy had also changed, and the Nicaraguan government and the masses, jointly, were victims, thrown into mortal combat by conditions neither controlled. A world economic recession, an enormous rise in interest rates and the cost of international debt service, and the sharp rise in oil prices sharply reversed economic growth, drove per capita income steeply downward, and especially pressured the poor for whom loss of income imperiled life and well-being in economic systems without basic welfare programs.[12] Table 7.1 illustrates the magnitude of this shared effect throughout the region.

Thus a causal (and moral) analysis of the revolution includes American administrations and Congresses which, as all Central American economies declined precipitously, were in the "inattention" phase of the policy process and did not choose (rationally) to make available the measure of resources to avoid exacerbated antagonisms. The American press, when it writes of how the odious wealthy in Central American countries do not redistribute their wealth,

Table 7.1. GDP Decline from Peak Year to 1983

Country	Peak Year	GDP per capita
El Salvador	1978	− 35%
Honduras	1979	− 12%
Guatemala	1980	− 14%
Nicaragua	1977	− 38%

Source: National Bipartisan Commission (1984), p. 49. GDP = Gross Domestic Product. It is unlikely the numbers are precise and averages derived by simple division understate the modal decline.

omits that neither do many who were substantially better off, and able to do so, in America and many other nations.

Initially, the Sandinista rebellion fared poorly against the heavily armed and professionally trained National Guard. But it received vital international support: Fidel Castro was instrumental (between March 1978 and March 1979) in the unification of guerrilla factions. President Carazo of Costa Rica permitted use of his country as a safe haven and staging area. Financial support (and arms) came from many foreign supporters, including Venezuela, Cuba, Colombia, and Panama (which served as a route for transshipment of Cuban arms). None of these regimes was subjected to military reprisals by the United States for its actions.[13]

By January 1979, the Carter administration, following the normal American policy sequence (Table 7.2), judged Somoza's days were numbered, cut off arms shipments, and began to position itself for relations with his successors.[14] A climactic meeting of hemisphere foreign ministers on June 21, 1979, produced an Organization of American States resolution condemning Somoza and calling for him to step down. Venezuela took the lead to sponsor the resolution and the Carter administration did not oppose it, although it cast about for alternatives to a Sandinista victory, unsuccessfully soliciting OAS support for a peacekeeping force that would effect formation of a broadly based provisional government to dilute Sandinista influence.[15]

Somoza's collapse did not occur as bloodlessly as Batista's. As the war spread, the American-trained and -armed National Guard was ruthless, unconstrained by law: 50,000 people (in a country of 2.7 million) were killed and 100,000 wounded.[16]

The original Government of National Reconstruction, which took power in July 1979, was composed of three Sandinista leaders and two prominent representatives of non-Sandinista democratic groups. It promised to hold free elections, but—as in the case of Castro—that promise was not fulfilled. By August 1980 the Sandinistas had engineered removal of non-Sandinistas from the central leadership and announced there would be no elections until 1985, when these would no longer have a "bourgeois character."[17] It also became clear that the Sandinistas were seeking to build new, mass party organizations and establish national political unity tied to their leadership. They developed mass organizations for major campaigns to improve literacy and health (and were aided by Cuban doctors and teachers); the campaigns were genuine, and impressively successful.[18]

The FSLN directorate, with nine members, has appeared to operate in a collegial style without primacy by a single leader. All nine have said they are "Marxist Leninists," although it is not clear what it means to use this label or to declare (as one leader has done) that "*Sandinismo* and Marxism-Leninism are inseparable."[19] But it is clear that the FSLN, vitally concerned with national security, has wanted to consolidate its power and direct the nation

Table 7.2. Normal Sequence of American Foreign Policy:
Right-Wing Governments and Revolutions in Central America

Stage 1: Inattention between crises
a. Subjective disavowal of responsibility for, or identity with, character of governments re-ceiving aid
b. Primary emphasis on military aid (since the Johnson administration), coupled to belief that a strong indigenous military strengthens civil order during a political and economic development process

Stage 2: As a guerrilla movement develops, pressure on the indigenous government to reform is increased, but not enough
a. American administration takes the position that the right-wing government will become democratic and progressive because the handwriting is on the wall, economic aid is increased, military aid more so
b. American administration advocates electoral democracy with belief that democratic elections will create a more responsive government and establish a national consensus to defeat the guerrillas
c. Series of overconfident assessments in Washington predict that the government is just about to get serious reform underway (American press experiments with stories portray-ing the revolutionaries as heroes.)
d. *In extremis*, U.S. may back coups or assassination attempts to eliminate highly intran-sigent dictators (Trujillo, Diem)
e. Government does not reform and, several months before the end, America cuts off aid to position itself for relations with the new government. Last-ditch efforts search, un-successfully, for coalition alternatives to a revolutionary victory.

Stage 3: New revolutionary government is "felt out" to determine if it will reestablish a traditional framework of relationships
a. Interpretation is ambiguous because since 1954 revolutionary movements have presumed American hostility and have learned to move with increased rapidity to polarize public opinion (with anti-American rhetoric) and effect rapid military buildups to deter American covert or overt invasion
b. Revolutionary government begins aid to revolutionary movements in other countries on a small scale
c. A "breakpoint" occurs, typically with manifest evidence that democratic elections will not be promptly held and there is a growing symbolic (e.g., arms acquisition) tie to com-munist ideology. (Typically, arms sales from American sources have been denied.) Tran-sition period hope to effect tolerable relations has not succeeded

[Stage 3.5: American government formally recognizes two problems: short-term problem of revolution and its spread, long-term problem of eliminating deeper causes of revolution in poverty, injustice, unresponsive governments, etc. Plans are set afoot to get a long-term (constructive) solution on track while the immediate problem is handled]

Stage 4: American government begins covert operations to "raise the cost" to the regime and if possible to overthrow it
a. Initial operations are accompanied by faith that the people do not really want the new government, especially if Marxist, and will link up with American-backed forces
b. When the idealistic component fails to effect the anticipated popular response it is dropped, and a "nothing-to-lose" calculus leads to efforts to "make the economy scream" even though there is no realistic end game
c. Expatriates, recruited for the harassment campaign, are led to believe America will back them to victory, even though there is no realistic American plan or expectation this will occur

Stage 5: Within several years after an American victory (more recently, defeat), the long-term program to effect change in underlying conditions which produce revolutions comes apart (e.g., Alliance for Progress, Mekong River Development Plan)

Stage 6: Inattention begins again

by its own vision, without the divisive public controversy, compromise, and entree for CIA-fostered dilution of their power they apparently fear might result from American-style democracy. *La Prensa*, still a voice of criticism, has been subject to prior censorship for substantial periods, and at times critics have been physically harassed. The record suggests, however, that the regime enjoys substantial majority favor for its accomplishments. Its humanitarin idealism has been genuine: In three years, from 1980 to 1983, it supplanted the callous indifference of the Somoza dynasty to the health of the people and eliminated polio, reduced 120,000 cases of malaria to 7,000 and reduced the infant mortality rate by 30%. The political debate in the country remains open, passionate, and diverse. Amnesty International reports no significant evidence of torture or disappearances of persons in Sandinista Nicaragua.[20] By any measure of performance, it is the best government Nicaragua has ever had and (excepting Costa Rica) a far better government for the majority of its people than the other governments in the region which have been American allies.

The Carter administration initially sought to avoid a strong tie between Nicaragua and the Soviet Union or Cuba, sent a gracious and supportive ambassador (Lawrence Pezzullo), and provided substantial aid.[21] Total U.S. aid from 1979 to 1981 came to $117 million, more than five times the aid provided the Somoza regime from 1974 to 1979.[22] The Carter administration also actively supported disbursements to Nicaragua of $102 million from the World Bank and $189 million from the Inter-American Development Bank during these years.

However, the Sandinista government was instinctively mistrustful of the United States and sought to apply earlier lessons from the fate of Arbenz and the covert operations against Castro (and Allende in Chile).[23] The government moved quickly to organize its population for national defense and to expand its armed forces: By 1984 there was national conscription, 48,000 troops on active duty, and perhaps as many as 200,000 men and women in training for the popular militia. Weapons were widely distributed, creating the threat of a prolonged, bloody, defensive war should there be an American or American-backed invasion. (By comparison, Somoza's National Guard at the height of the civil war had only 15,000.) Soviet weapons were acquired at a pace suggesting the Sandinistas feared they had limited time; massive supplies of Soviet-bloc arms arrived together with Soviet and Cuban advisers who effected a choice of weapons professionally judged by Pentagon analysts as good choices for defense. The military forces, by 1984, had acquired heavy tanks and assault helicopters, 1,000 trucks and armored personnel carriers, mobile rocket launchers, heavy artillery, and hand weapons and ammunition to equip ground forces fully. In addition, thirty Nicaraguan pilots were trained in Bulgaria to fly MIG jets and these pilots, and their planes, were stationed in Cuba.[24] This conventional capability (now the largest in the region) serves two obvious purposes: combatting the CIA-funded *contras* and deterring an invasion by American troops or any combination of regional right-wing governments.[25]

The breakpoint in U.S.–Nicaraguan relations came with the first election of President Ronald Reagan. In the fall of 1980, just after his election and before his inauguration, rebels in El Salvador began what they called a "final offensive," hoping to achieve victory before President Reagan assumed office. Nicaragua, for the first time, began massive transshipments of Soviet-bloc arms to aid the rebels, and the Carter administration moved to cut off aid to Nicaragua. Thus the standard American policy sequence (Table 7.2) again moved down the same path.

Its new military capability has also given Nicaragua the capacity to deploy this armed force against its rightist neighbors. El Salvador is probably safe from a direct attack; there is no direct route for a Nicaraguan land invasion of El Salvador, and the American navy could readily block the Gulf of Fonseca. Honduras probably could not be defeated at the present time, but if the indigenous guerrillas made rapid gains the situation might change, especially if the Nicaraguans brought into play their thirty MIGs now stationed offstage on Cuba and received aid from Cuba.[26] If it had reason to do so, Nicaragua could rapidly conquer Costa Rica, which has never created a military force of its own. There is a case for an American military "shield" — and deterrent messages — if American policy wishes to prevent these eventualities, however likely or unlikely.[27]

Background and the Carter Years: El Salvador

The story of revolution in El Salvador parallels, in substantial degree, the story of Nicaragua. About 200 families control the country and its wealth (not fourteen, as in popular legend), disparities are severe, callous indifference of the wealthy for the "subhuman" peasants has been a continuing feature of the country's life; at least two-thirds of the population lives in extreme poverty; illiteracy and malnutrition are widespread in the countryside.[28]

An American theory of political development once held that economic development would produce political development, especially democratic modernization.[29] That theory is no longer in good repute among social scientists: El Salvador is a country (like Nicaragua and many others) where the opposite result occurred. As did Nicaragua's, El Salvador's military governments in the 1970s became even more brutal and repressive while the economy expanded.[30]

Briefly, following the Sandinista victory, this situation appeared to change; in October 1979, a group of young officers overthrew the government of Gen. Carlos Humberto Romero and replaced him with a five-man civilian junta which pledged land and other reforms. Their motive, from most analyses, was not reform per se but to prevent a spread of revolution. But the result illustrates a deeper fact of political power in El Salvador (and elsewhere in

Latin America); its official "government" is not a government in the (North) American conception. It is able to act only when the ruling classes of the society find it in their interest to give their support. After this reformist coup, other elements in the military and other ruling groups quickly blocked reforms; within three months, three of the civilian members of the junta had resigned in frustration (one of the members, Social Democrat Guillermo Ungo, is now a leading spokesman for the guerrillas), and the semiofficial murder squads of the ruling classes increased their campaign of mass terror and intimidation.[31]

The misleading categories used in American public discussion bear further comment: in the American template, "governments" control societies; their decisions are legitimate and binding. But in El Salvador, "government" does not have an equivalent role and the current president (Duarte, at the end of 1984) occupies a symbolic position in a public sideshow in a society where the substantial power is exercised by Cosa Nostra–type families and private armies linked with military coalitions. There is no tradition or expectation of military deference to civilian control. (Nor is the military of El Salvador organized in a top-down fashion: It is a network of personalized coalitions, often with stronger ties within themselves than to official commanders.)[32] High turnout in elections traditionally has not reflected citizens' faith that elections empower a democratic government; in El Salvador, voting is compulsory.[33]

The "death squads" of El Salvador are the brutish expression of ruling classes the Kissinger Commission (discussed below) has oddly championed as incipiently democratic and progressive. Several American conservatives — including the political scientist Jeane Kirkpatrick, United Nations Ambassador during the first Reagan administration — have written that right-wing governments in Central America are "authoritarian," apparently imagining them to be strict, law-and-order governments. But this American-based conception is inappropriate: the powerful men in El Salvador are not "law-and-order" authoritarians, nor do they respect the individual rights that American conservatives value. They are murderers: From October 1979 until January 1984, the Roman Catholic Archdiocese of San Salvador documented by firsthand testimony more than 40,000 murders of civilian noncombatants.[34] This terrorism, murders typically accompanied by torture and hacked-up and mutilated bodies left for public display, is unimpeded by law. The national battle does not pit the principle of law and order (the side of government) against the principle of revolution (the side of the guerrillas): Prosecutors and judges have been intentionally killed, and the lives of others threatened (by people who are credible); the "security" forces have not allowed any convictions of murders of El Salvador citizens. Public remonstrances by the Carter and Reagan administrations have been judged (correctly) a bluff and have been distinctively impotent.

Terror has been directed against all nonrightists who are politically active.

The armed forces have pledged to "relentlessly persecute" political leaders of the left and have done so. (For example, six leaders of the left political coalition, FDR, were publicly kidnapped by government security forces during a press conference in November 1980, tortured, mutilated, and murdered; the incident was not even investigated.) Leaders of the (legal) Christian Democratic Party have frequently been killed; ninety Christian Democratic mayors, for example, have been assassinated since 1979. Anyone who criticizes such political murder or advocates major reform or negotiation with the guerrillas does so at realistic mortal risk. In the rural areas, the murder teams have conducted random executions in areas suspected of being favorable to the guerrillas.[35]

The El Salvador rebels — avowedly Marxist-Leninists and (given the circumstances, understandably) hostile to the United States — have received substantial aid from Nicaragua and, via that route, from Cuba, the Soviet Union, and Eastern Europe.[36] Since the spring of 1981 the flow of arms from these sources is probably small, the revolutionaries have ample funds to purchase weapons on the international black market without relying on ideologically motivated sources, and — perhaps the most important source — a major domestic black market for American-supplied weapons and ammunition now operates in El Salvador.[37] But it seems clear that there is genuine, consequential support, especially sophisticated communication capabilities and expert tactical advice, by Soviet and Cuban specialists, and sites within Nicaragua are used by the guerrillas as locations for strategic planning.[38]

In a country of 4.7 million people, the deaths (50,000+ since 1979) have been numerous, primarily of civilians at the hands of the murder squads.[39] The active combatants are a small proportion.[40] By early 1984 the El Salvador military had grown to about 37,000 men.[41] The guerrilla forces also are growing and now number about 12,000.[42] The guerrillas are well trained, do receive support from among the population, and now effect a casualty rate (killed or wounded) of government soldiers of about 15% a year.[43] They have also expanded their own counterterror, aimed at government officials, the economy, and the land reform and other programs designed to build government support. About sixty-three murders of civilians by guerrillas were recorded in a fourteen-month period ending in July 1983.[44] The long-term prospect for the regime appears poor without massive American aid: the traditional ruling elites have few friends among the masses; the ratio of troops to guerrillas is far less than the ten-to-one typically said to be needed for victory in a counterguerrilla war, and the progressively intentioned Duarte government elected in 1984 probably lacks the power to produce major change — either for progressive reform or to curb the death squads (which is a major goal of the rebels and a requirement for any negotiated settlement). The Duarte government is also subject, readily, to right-wing replacement should it attempt to acquire power or begin serious negotiations.

Policy and the Reagan Administration

The first Reagan administration, under its first secretary of state, Alexander Haig, began immediately to plan the elimination of what it conceived to be Communist power in the western hemisphere. It launched a major propaganda effort similar to the campaign which (in 1954) preceded the overthrow of Arbenz. Haig dramatized the issue of Communist-bloc weapons in the hemisphere, the threat of spreading revolutions, warned that "vital interests" of American security were at risk, and threatened to "go to the source" (i.e., Cuba).[45] The administration substantially increased aid (especially military aid) to the El Salvador government. Against Nicaragua, Operation MONGOOSE was born again with the CIA, under director William Casey, creating, equipping, inspiring, paying for, and directing *contra* forces to attack Nicaragua from bases in Honduras and Costa Rica.[46]

Initially, this highly visible crusade ran into trouble. The American elite press, opposed to the direction of policy, counterattacked against the allegation of a primarily Communist-inspired revolution and left the public justifications dubious. *Newsweek* took the lead to inform the American people about the administration's "secret war" in which 15,000 troops were assembled to engage in commando raids, seek to destroy the economy, and if possible establish an enclave inside Nicaraguan territory.[47] Initially, Argentina was used as a "cut-out" to train guerrilla forces for use against Castro, and provide training and arms for operations in Central America, without requiring congressional approval by involving the CIA directly. The Senate Intelligence Oversight Committee blocked the early, aggressive anti-Cuban initiative and forced the resignation of the new deputy director-Plans, Max Hugel, who had been "less than candid" in disclosing the plans.[48] The right-wing Argentine government unexpectedly invaded the Falkland Islands and, despite the efforts of General Haig to mediate the resulting miliary conflict with England, the cooperative Argentine relation with Washington cooled after the government was defeated.

Secretary Haig's controversial public style—White House mail began to run ten to one *against* the administration's policies—produced impressive tactical learning.[49] He was dismissed in the summer of 1982, replaced by the stylistically bland and respectable George Shultz, and, while continuing its same policies, the Reagan administration astutely calmed its rhetoric, maneuvered around symbolic sensitivities, and neutralized its critics in the media and Congress.[50] It ceased to discuss its policies in public, except rarely and in the most general slogans. After the proxy war against Nicaragua was described in the press, the White House declared that such "secret" things should not be discussed in public.[51] It skillfully outmaneuvered potential congressional opposition to effect a major U.S. troop buildup in Honduras under the guise of training exercises. To build a consensus (or at least disarm his critics while the commission met), President Reagan appointed a National Bipartisan Commission in 1983, whose existence blocked rising criticism until the early spring of 1984. (I discuss the commission's report below.) Israel was used as a "cut-out" to provide weapons and aid in a channel that would outflank the congressional appropriations process and make it difficult for liberal supporters of Israel to inquire into, or criticize, the "plausibly deniable" arrangements.[52] Sophisticated planners encouraged "private" funds from rightist groups in America to outmaneuver Congress and assure continuing aid to the *contras* (reportedly, about $17 million of aid).[53] The realistic and perennial power drama fear — that opponents would be "scapegoated" if El Salvador was "lost" — was manipulated to weaken congressional criticism.[54] By the late summer of 1984 American "advisors" created the strategy and tactics of the El Salvador military, America trained the troops, and America was paying most of the cost of the war.[55]

As of the fall of 1984, press reports indicate the Reagan administration wants victory (or, at least, to avoid visible defeat) in El Salvador.[56] It is divided in its objectives toward Nicaragua; a smaller "moderate" faction apparently hopes to use the new Operation MONGOOSE to exact economic devastation and a death rate of indigenous defenders in Nicaragua sufficient to end support for the El Salvador revolution (and this, perhaps more consequentially than its material cost, might affect their morale). A hawkish faction is said to want the complete elimination of any substantial "Marxist-Leninist" role in the government of Nicaragua, is unwilling to "learn to live" with less, and — although without a realistic end game — may be expected to press for both increased psychological warfare and military activity, although would likely prefer Honduras to take any major combat role.[57]

The Reagan administration initially pressed for open, democratic elections in Nicaragua, and then reversed itself to demand postponement of elections held in November 1984 so that opposition groups could have more time to form and campaign openly. The baseline of silence about the Somoza regime's electoral practices suggests that the agitated argument about Nicaraguan electoral practices has been triggered not by questions of principle but as a mechanism of control, i.e., probably with the expectation that growing American-exacted damage will make support of El Salvador's rebels so unpopular that any elected government would thus be more amenable to reduce support of the rebels and anti-American rhetoric. As in the case of Castro two decades earlier, however, there has been little doubt that the Sandinista electoral victory in the fall of 1984 did reflect the wishes of the majority of the people and that, at best, only its large margin of victory would have been modestly reduced by fuller participation of exile groups backed by the United States. Thus the loud — and to a substantial degree unwarranted — administration discrediting of the election can also be seen as a maneuver to prepare American public opinion for a continuing war.

Because the administration has not produced good results, pressure has mounted (as it did for Bissell) for more direct American management. America's candidate for the presidency of El Salvador, Duarte, in 1984 received $2.1 million of "secret" funding to assure his electoral victory—an extraordinary sum for an election in such a poor country;[58] mining of Nicaragua's harbors (directed by American CIA commanders) occurred in the spring of 1984;[59] direct tactical command by the CIA has been increasing.[60] A temporary congressional suspension of official American aid to the *contras* was primarily symbolic, did not address either the cut-out mechanisms or the free flow of "private" funding, and is unlikely to hamper a decided Executive branch's policies.

One fact should be noted concerning the Reagan administration's professed willingness to negotiate an end to conflict: Press reports consistently suggest that many hard-liners within the Reagan administration simply desire to destroy the Sandinista government (and have seen "nothing to lose" from attempts using the CIA).[61] It seems probable, then, the United States has had no wholly trustworthy negotiating proposal in dealings with the Sandinistas that could, if accepted, assure that the regime can survive at peace.

THE KISSINGER COMMISSION REPORT

In 1983 President Reagan appointed a National Bipartisan Commission on Central America (the Kissinger Commission) to study this latest return engagement. My analysis will be that the commission used analytical intelligence in a secondary role and recommended policy which reflects instead the imagination syndrome outlined in chapter 6. Thus, its scenario for American policy is unlikely to work because the *Report* has, as a result, little connection with the local realities of Central America.

I have chosen to discuss the commission *Report* because, in conjunction with the earlier discussion of American policy, it illustrates my thesis by the public nature of the commission's work. That is, the standard theories (discussed earlier) of inadvertent error are implausible explanations of how the *Report* was derived: procedural threats to rationality, inaccessible knowledge of history, small group loyalty and insularity, simple unreflective thought and unchallenged assumptions do not account for the commissioners' *Report*. To be sure, no radicals were appointed to the commission, and in this sense the original appointments determined its findings. But the appointments did afford diversity within the range of variation consistent with being considered responsible American leaders; the twelve commissioners were drawn from both political parties (and included Robert Strauss, former national chairman of the Democratic Party, and Lane Kirkland, president of the AFL-CIO).[62] Most commissioners had established careers and major constituencies independent from the Reagan administration. They were men of distinction and accomplishment. Nor was the commission an insular group shielded from multiple advocacy. It heard testimony from almost 200 Americans representing diverse constituencies and viewpoints (and received written submissions from 400 more), heard from 300 officials and witnesses abroad (and met with the government of Nicaragua). Central American policy was being widely debated in the press. The commission heard the critics of current policy.[63] That it did not *accept* their views cannot be attributed to such perennial and wishful diagnoses as criticisms that were "unheard" or even "not understood" in a formal sense.[64]

Overview

The commissioners' viewpoint is the standard policy analysis in similar reports stretching back twenty-five years.[65] They recognized two problems. The short-term problem is to contain spreading revolution. The long-term problem is to eliminate the deeper causes of revolution: poverty, injustice, economic disarray, cruel and unresponsive governments.

The commission's principal conclusions may be summarized in five points:

1. The "miserable" conditions of life of most people in the region have invited revolution: "If reforms had been undertaken earlier, there would almost surely have been no fertile ground for revolution."[66]

2. These conditions have been "exploited" by hostile outside forces — specifically Cuba, backed by the Soviet Union and now operating through Nicaragua — and these "will turn any revolution they capture into a totalitarian state, threatening the region and robbing the people of their hopes for liberty."[67] Indigenous revolutions themselves would not be a security threat to the United States, but they become a threat when these "aggressive outside powers" use them to expand their own political influence and military control in our hemisphere.[68]

3. Without rapid progress for political, economic, and social reforms, peace in the region will be "fragile or elusive."[69]

4. But unless the insurgencies are stopped, constructive American-led political, economic, and social progress can only be fragile or elusive: "Once an insurgency is fully under way . . . it has a momentum which reform alone cannot stop. Unchecked, the insurgents can destroy faster than the reformers can build."[70]

5. America has a humanitarian interest to alleviate suffering and a national interest to "strengthen democratic institutions wherever in the hemisphere they are weak."[71]

From this analysis the commission recommended, with great urgency, military aid to shield existing governments, suppress insurgencies, and buy time for long-term reforms it proposed. It specifically urged substantially increased military aid to El Salvador, and it predicted the days of the El Salvador government were numbered without massive American aid.[72]

Within its assumptions, the rational policy analysis done in Washington was intelligent and superb. A refined and sophisticated inventory of more that fifty aspects of Central American societies provided for a long-term plan to reshape almost every major characteristic of those societies. Diverse policy tools would include a literacy corps, scholarships, training in public administration, reforms of the judicial system, extension of health care, rescheduling of foreign debt, improvement of international trade. And the *Report* is politically astute about its domestic constituencies: major domestic groups can find their concerns acknowledged and recognize an expanded role in an $8 billion aid package envisioned over the next five years: banks and financial institutions are guaranteed loan rescheduling, business groups will find support for private venture capital, humanitarian organizations have their involvement funded, universities can develop ties and training programs, fervent anti-Communists will find greater military aid endorsed while liberals find recommendations to bolster "genuine democracy," link aid to human rights progress, and design "humane" antiguerrilla programs that do not rely upon government death squads and terror of the civilian population.

My plan is to analyze the commission's findings selectively, illustrating how the continuing overlay of imagination, discussed in chapter 6, makes the *Report* an ineffective guide. I will also suggest that different images were, on the objective evidence presented, more plausible.[73] I will use as my principal source the evidence and staff analyses provided the commision and included in its official publications. My focus will be: (1) overconfidence; (2) exaggerated fear and experience of vulnerability; (3) emotionally organized (and nonempirical) use of language; (4) an unrealistic, Maxwell Taylor-like prescription for the American policy process which overlooks a likely breakdown in the intellectual and moral integrity of the commission's planning.

Overconfidence

The commission's viewpoint envisions America in a managerial role, boldly transforming Central American societies to become liberal, democratic, progressive, and prosperous — more like the United States. This well-intentioned ethnocentrism is not so crude as the jingoism of an earlier day; the language is responsible, reflecting the managerial, problem-solving instincts of leaders in an economically advanced society.[74]

In El Salvador, the commission's short-term strategy is to transform the entire political system. Death squads must end, democracy must be created and supported, reforms must move swiftly, the guerrillas must be defeated. To accomplish these results "the U.S. government must rely on the abilities and good faith of the government under attack."[75]

The commission's term "good faith" is the best place to begin discussion of the problem of external validity. The evidence (reviewd earlier) shows that the opposite of pro-democratic good faith is a characteristic of El Salvador's ruling classes. Castro's "handwriting on the wall" produced no progress. During the relative peace and growing prosperity of the 1970s, El Salvador became, as the commission notes elsewhere, more brutal and oppressive.[76] And in the late 1970s, when the Sandinista victory produced a reformist coup in El Salvador, the reformist government found itself an impotent sideshow and resigned in frustration within three months. Social, economic, and political reforms in the 1980s have been slow and undertaken under massive pressure from Washington. (One should not be misled by overconfident, activist official assurances that impressive reforms are just about to occur: The speed with which reform *can* be accomplished if there is a seriously committed political system is demonstrated by the Sandinista program in Nicaragua carried out when they too have been at war, in their case against American-sponsored *contra* forces roughly the size of the antiregime forces in El Salvador.) Forty thousand murders, including many members of the democratic left, are not the mark of ruling classes whose attitudes are favorable to social progress and democracy. In reality, one is dealing with long-standing attitudes, men who believe the American military shield reflects America's own anti-Communist interests, and whose correct lesson from recent history is that America is so locked in by its own power-drama logic that threats of aid cutoffs are a bluff. The right in Central America has probably learned faster than the American government.[77]

Moreover, the practice of mass murder and terror reflects the brutality of ruling groups genuinely terrified for survival, not simply terrified of revolution but also of genuine democracy. In the situation of massive inequality in which the wealthy are located, and given their past practices and attitudes, allowing any genuine acquisition of power by a democratic government is revolutionary. There is no large middle class to mediate the alternatives.[78] At this point the commissioners should have asked themselves what incentives they offer to men who have committed 40,000 murders of civilians (each victim with a family, neighbors, and friends) to surrender power to the populace they have terrorized?

The overconfident ambition of the *Report* extends to idealized imaginings about the people of El Salvador and their faith in official (and American) promises. Just as the "hearts and minds" of Cuba's people (or Vietnam's) were once thought eager for American leadership, so El Salvador's peasants are imagined willing to forget the past, to believe that the real nature of power and the character of those who hold power has changed only because a sideshow election has given a decent man, Duarte, the title of president and to merge, trustingly and enthusiastically, with Washington's vision of progress.

The commission's bold imaginings of successful American control are also contrary to America's own historical experience in Latin America. The Alliance for Progress's military "shield" only worked when a country evidenced a strong elite consensus favorable to economic and social reform. Rightist client governments are championed by American administrations as *just* on the verge of reform: it never works out.[79] But, I would argue, American administrations nevertheless act on the overlay because the American imagined scenario must be *made* to work if the American image of its own constructive leadership and masterful control is to be sustained.

Exaggerated Fear and Experience of Vulnerability

It seems implausible to imagine that small, poor, Central American countries threaten American national security. Yet that was the mind-set of the commission members, and they tried to suggest plausible reasons to explain the fear:

1. A series of developments which might require us to devote large resources to defend the southern approaches to the United States, thus reducing our capacity to defend our interests elsewhere.
2. A potentially serious threat to our shipping lanes through the Caribbean.
3. A proliferation of Marxist-Leninist states that would increase violence, dislocation, and political repression in the region.
4. The erosion of our power to influence events worldwide that would flow form the perception we were unable to influence vital events close to home.[80]

The commissioners did not calibrate their imaginations by specific scenarios to justify their fear of a serious threat to America. But even if the Mexican government should be overthrown (and that is not a present issue), it is difficult to see new "large resources" that will need to be added to the hundreds of billions of dollars already spent annually.[81] Even if a Mexican government were someday overthrown by revolutionaries willing to ally with other countries south of its borders, it remains mysterious why a concert of poor countries would bother to begin an easily defeated attack upon the U.S. mainland.

The second alleged danger, interdiction of shipping, assumes a scenario in which these small countries would want to commit suicide by war on the American navy. Such a remote threat is probably forestalled best, if the commission wished to do so, not by the fervent activism of its programs but, in a straightforward, tough-minded way by specifying to Nicaragua and a Marxist-Leninist El Salvador, privately, the types of weapons (e.g., a substantial navy) they may not acquire and then forthrightly destroying such capability if it should be acquired beyond the limits drawn.

Possibly more realistic is the third fear of widened intraregional conflict. Assuming the El Salvador government is overthrown, it is conceivable that this regime, and the Nicaraguan government, would wish — all other things being equal — jointly to aid revolutionary movements in Guatemala and Honduras. The hostility of those regimes has been long-standing, and in the event of continuing American support for the *contras* the long-term security and

peace of both Nicaragua and a new El Salvador government would be well
served by eliminating hostile rightist governments and CIA staging areas on
their borders.[82] At the moment, however, the Nicaraguan government would
have difficulty mobilizing its people for a sustained aggressive war (any major popular support will probably be created by American policy itself via
the continuing economic destruction of the American *contra* forces.) But with
America's new infrastructure and capacities to move large numbers of its
troops into Honduras, the Nicaraguan government would be mad to begin
a war, and thus there apppears no basis to suppose a realistic threat by
Nicaragua to its neighbors. Guerrilla warfare in both Guatemala and Honduras will probably not succeed if the promises of reform are genuine and
these countries change the basic character of their societies as quickly as have
the Sandinistas.

The fourth alleged security threat openly introduces the critical sensibility, the commission's imagining of international politics as a vivid, global
drama: "The triumph of hostile forces in what the Soviets call the 'strategic
rear' of the United States would be read as a sign of U.S. impotence."[83]

The commission's anxiety is high, and it is fearful of global disorder: "if
wretched conditions were themselves enough to create . . . insurgencies, we
would see them in many more countries of the world."[84] Any "foreign" (i.e.,
Communist) instigators, newly emboldened by a sense of American impotence, have an alarmingly fertile field. This is the system of imagining discussed in chapter 6; from the top, alongside bold overconfidence is the para-
doxical and deep fear that everything could begin to unravel.

I want to invite the reader to reflect upon this "domino theory" of the
Report: It implicitly imagines American power to be a vivid, substantial
presence in the minds of the politically active around the globe. America's
most intimate enemy, the megalomaniacal Soviet leadership, single-mindedly
devoted to world rule, is alert for signs of impotence, and presses forward
with its diabolical schemes whenever it senses weakness. Thus the retiring
career diplomat, Undersecretary of State for Political Affairs Lawrence Eagleburger, in the spring of 1984 confidently asserted the view that "the decision
to walk away from the Angolan problem in 1975 was the beginning of our
real difficulties with the Soviet Union. That gave the Soviet leadership an impression that they could do a number of things covertly that the United States
would not be prepared to respond to . . . They are engaged—in *their* mind
at least—to our detriment."[85]

As I reviewed in chapter 6, several steps further along in this mental process
lies the total imagination entrapment of psychosis, the megalomanical and
paranoid experience that one's will is *the* determinant of events in the universe
and all of the principal evil forces in the universe are organized in hostile relationship to the self. My point is *not*, however, that such a sensibility is clinical-
ly mad. About certain Russians, the commission might be right; obviously

one can *imagine* there are men in the Kremlin whose highly dramatized sensibility mirrors the Reagan administration's and commission's own. For example, at least one Soviet propagandist has exulted that "the Sandinista revolution, being an integral part of the world revolutionary process, serves as yet one more convincing confirmation of the helplessness of imperialism to restore its lost historic initiative and to turn back the development of the modern world."[86] Soviet *public* statements not only generally endorse the commission's own interpretation but also assert there is a global drama (of falling imperialist dominoes), in which Central America, somewhat salaciously, is seen as an encouraging indicator of American helplessness.[87]

To assess political actions in a world of potentially mutual and interlocking imagination entrapments by "super" powers means that the difference between error and truth is often a matter of exaggeration, a danger to which the imagination is prone. Judgment requires calibration of the imagination by reference to the hard surfaces of local realities.[88] In this case, I believe the *Report* did get carried away by its own overdramatized imaginings. Let me suggest several observations.

First, Soviet leaders probably *are* as power-oriented — or more so — as American leaders. Richard Nixon, with an obviously different ideological and cultural content, appears a very similar personality to recent Soviet leaders: his suspicious, hardball sensibilities, and "enemies lists" kept by his staff, seem of a similar mold. Thus, too, warnings by such American leaders of Soviet orientations deserve to be treated with great seriousness.

Second, I think the commission is right that Soviet leaders *would* be encouraged if the United States did nothing, or even permitted a public victory, by people citing Marxist-Leninist ideology, in Central America.

The more important questions, however, are how such feelings of encouragement — whether permanent or transitory — would affect *actions* elsewhere, and whether the hardball power drama interpretation is, on reflection, the best interpretation on which to base an American policy.

Thus I believe the proper specific question is: What would the Soviets do, and would they be effective? I do not believe we know the answer, as even American "losses" (in Cuba and Vietnam) were permitted by America only at a high cost. There probably would be additional efforts to supply arms and encourage revolutions elsewhere. However, countries have many priorities and large-scale foreign aid has traditionally proven about as unpopular in Moscow as in Washington.[89] Moreover, the evidence suggests such victories, in the long term, do not buy the Soviet Union added influence for its own national purposes: once Americans debated who (Republicans or Democrats) lost China; today the Soviets know *they* did.[90] And the Soviet leadership, given instabilities in Eastern Europe, probably also feels extraordinarily vulnerable and could be induced to be cautious about any general escalation of such destabilization contests.

But the more important question is whether world order is effectively served by policy primarily based on the schema of East-West global drama.[91] Here I think the answer is that the commission is dangerously preoccupied by the mirror image of the opposing chess master. Except in fantasies entertained by superpowers, nations and peoples of the world are not subordinate pawns whose loyalties can be taken for granted. Revolutions in Central America have not spread in periods when there are only egregious conditions and indigenous revolutionaries hopeful of a following: the evidence is that people will prefer even odious, familiar regimes to revolution *if* there is hope for economic progress and justice. Any "contest" requires America, primarily, to assure such hope in local reality. The big-picture, East-West focus misdirects attention from this more vital basis of power: When Communists talk about the issues and American leaders become preoccupied about Communists, then Communist-linked revolution becomes the primary allegiance of those who want to choose the side with the most fervently expressed ideals. Supporting — and being strung along by — right-wing regimes for anti-Communist purposes makes America as hostile to such ideals, de facto, as Communist propaganda alleges.

Concerning whatever role America (or American "will") plays in affecting world stability (which could, after all, be unchanged if America were to disappear), it is more plausible to believe that Soviet predictions of American behavior derive from the realistic perception that genuine and vital American interests are at stake in a local reality, not upon peripheral symbolic toughness. (Thus, for example, a convincing reason the Soviets would recognize American credibility in defending oil supplies in the Middle East is that they recognize a vital American interest at stake.)

By this analysis, however, the overdramatized sensibility of foreign policy is dangerous because it abandons stability-creating interpretations, loses the intelligent discrimination between genuine vital interests and mere peripheral advantages. President Eisenhower held a different — and probably a sounder — view than the commission's: The local government of Guatemala was geopolitically unimportant, a contest worth a covert CIA operation with 110 men. No foreign statesman who shared Eisenhower's understanding of geopolitical gradation would draw an erroneous message of weakness if the CIA failed and other actions were not mounted. If the Soviets now think differently, *that* is the graver danger and would be best addressed by a *Report* which publicly rejected its present framework and sought to restore such major distinctions.[92]

There is a second good rule for international order which the commission spurns: tit for tat; that is, the evolution of norms of international conduct by which great powers agree mutually (even if privately) to respect certain conventions.[93] Since 1979, for example, 7,000 Soviet soldiers have been killed (and Soviet forces have suffered 40,000 casualties) in Afghanistan opposing rebels armed by the United States. American aid to the Afghan rebels has been $625 million. It is most unlikely the Soviet Union will reduce its own involvement in Central America under these conditions. The Kissinger Commission rejected such obvious negotiations as "unacceptable," yet acknowledged that the Soviets might agree to such discussions. It concluded: "[The Soviets] would welcome discussion of superpower spheres of influence, which would prompt Soviet assertions of . . . the need for U.S. abstention on the Soviet periphery, in such places as Eastern Europe and Afghanistan."[94] If one wanted to promote international order, this would be a straightforward, sober, and tough-minded deal.

Emotionally Organized Use of Language

I have suggested that when an American foreign policy spokesman speaks, there is — via dramatized imagining — a confused blending of emotion, language, inner reality, and outer reality, and of these, outer reality plays the lesser role. Verbal maneuvers substitute for other forms of analysis in a political world which is an arena of forces, pressures, national wills (or impotency) experienced directly in the mind of practitioner.

Three uses of language will serve as example. Like Kennedy's "plausibly deniable" construction that the Bay of Pigs project was not an aggressive policy of his administration, the plausibility of these usages carries the risk of substituting words, which are self-persuasive and comfortable for responsible American officials, for clear thinking.

"American Policy"

A first example is the commission's virtuous self-image for American policy. It disavows any direct link between American policy and the consistent pattern of morally objectionable practices of governments and ruling classes in Central America. There are (unspecific) allusions to past American omissions, errors, and insensitivities, but the matter is settled by declaring there has not been an "identity" between America and right-wing governments, a misperception "that lingers independent of the facts."[95] The commission says America cannot "associate itself with" or "condone" the brutal killings or any other objectionable feature of Central American regimes.

To be fair, the conscious intent of American policy has seldom been sinister: economic aid has been substantial; American leaders (most actively in the Carter administration) have spoken out for human rights.[96] American leaders would certainly prefer Central America to have democratic, liberal, progressive governments that treated their people well, and the *Report* is correct; there has not been full *subjective* identity or support. The radical-left charge that America fully supports dictators is a fantasy; despite their hopes, dictators of the right have been abandoned when their only rescue would be American troops (Batista, Somoza); others (Trujillo, Diem) have also been active targets for American removal plans when they did not reform quickly enough to prevent Communist advances.[97]

However, *objective* support occurs without regard to a more comfortable *subjective* dissociation regnant primarily in the mind of the policymaker. The continuing "association" of America with brutal, uncaring ruling classes is not merely fanciful. Morally (and in an American court of law) the American political system is an accessory. And the implication is important: If one wants to understand the problems of American policy, and the extraordinary difficulty of a negotiated settlement (a principal barrier to which would be fear of American treachery), one must include a de facto recognition of the objective reality of that policy in local arenas.

"Marxist-Leninist"

The commissioners used the term "Marxist-Leninist" to describe the rebel movements, too readily accepting associations with the phrase, rather than analysis of men and circumstances, as evidence that "Marxist-Leninist" revolutions in Central America will establish totalitarian dictatorships, serve the "interests" of Soviet power, be generically and implacably hostile to the United States, and yield more international aggression.

The problem of inference is genuine: the commission might be correct, and its view is not satisfactorily dismissed by a balanced and hopeful view that anyone who speaks of ideals and opposes dictators is genuinely idealistic. The Sandinistas *might* be fanatics; if not they, then the El Salvador rebels. It would be incumbent upon any national commission to warn the American people if, in its best judgment, messianic, genocidal madmen of the ilk of Hitler, Pol Pot, or the Ayatolleh Khomeni (who replaced the right-wing dictator, the Shah of Iran, but whose war with Iraq by mid-1984 had killed 250,000 people) were in power or likely to gain power. But are these Central Americans realistically imagined to be pawns of Soviet interests or megalomaniacal fanatics?

The historical record suggests it extremely unlikely that nationalist leaders who use Marxist-Leninist formulas, even out of deep commitment, will serve Soviet interests reliably. After supporting Mao's revolution, Soviet leaders lost China as an ally. After almost forty years, Soviet hegemony in Eastern Europe is still sustained only by the presence of Soviet troops and periodic threats of violence. As I noted in chapter 5, Fidel Castro himself has provided the Russians with a signal lesson: After locking in Soviet commitment and aid at the beginning of the 1960s, he turned on the growing Soviet influence in the Cuban Communist Party, purged over half its members to assure loyalty to himself and his brother, and has maintained that vigilance.[98] "Marxist-Leninist" regimes in Central America will probably afford the Soviet Union little geopolitical benefit: To power-oriented politicians, ideology is a secondary concern.

But there is a more plausible explanation of why such men and women use Marxist-Leninist, anti-American ideas for their political drama, that is, as a *reaction* to circumstances rather than because they are paranoid, megalomaniacal zealots. These are people who, in the main, have little worldly experience and know America only in their local reality. America tried to assassinate and overthrow Fidel Castro at a time when (it is now public knowledge) it knew him to be the popular choice of the majority of his people. It created the greedy Somoza regime, colluded in the removal of Allende in Chile (even though *he* was freely and democratically elected), and continues to supply the arms to the El Salvador murderers of more than 40,000 civilian noncombatants with rhetoric — which must seem grotesque in the region — that it is promoting "democracy."[99] It has created and backed the hated Somicista contras against the best government Nicaragua has ever had, and this 1980s Operation MONGOOSE has killed hundreds of young men (with CIA financing) to seek effect economic destruction and terror. On the other hand, these Central Americans know the Soviet Union and Cuba only from a distance and in the role of benefactors and supporters of their cause. Would it not be reasonable, from their point of view, to find the framework of Marxist analysis plausible?

The commissioners' imaginings that Central American revolutionaries have an implacably megalomaniacal intent appear especially odd in light of the more plausible analogy, America's experience of reactive radicalism in the 1960s. Many of these radicals were outraged idealists who supported President Kennedy enthusiastically at the beginning of the 1960s. They became radicalized in response to actions of government they considered inhumane and outrageous. The hostile, fiery rhetoric was associated with extraordinarily little antiregime violence, and the radical sentiments and commitments *subsided* when government policies ceased to incite it. Indeed, many Americans of all ages turned angry in the early 1970s and wanted to remove President Nixon when the White House kept lists, in a somewhat juvenile way, titled "enemies lists," and tried to cover up only a fumbled burglary. The better causal analysis implies that the solution to the problem of Marxist-Leninist ideology is for the United States to cease de facto policies that, at the receiving end, arouse that viewpoint.

"Our" Hemisphere

A further power-linked use of language, discussion of "our" hemisphere, is of a piece with the commission's managerial scenario. It has been traditional for (North) Americans to talk in such a proprietary way since President Monroe unilaterally formulated his doctrine (1823). Related talk of "our backyard," in the phrase of the Reagan administration (not "our neighbor's house"), reflects this imagination-based and top-down sense of power and position, as does the commission's attempt to define unilaterally whose influence in Latin America will be deemed "foreign" (i.e., non-United States).

However, such paternalistic phrases are a self-absorbed overlay which imagines America to have a greater proprietary involvement in the hemisphere than it has in reality. For example:

- American trade and comparative economic domination have diminished dramatically: in 1950 the United States bought almost half of Latin America's exports and Latin America brought 56% of its imports from the United States. Today, both numbers are less than 30% and are falling.[100]
- From World War II until 1965, Latin America did depend upon the United States for almost all of its weapons. But today, with growing military establishments, the arms sales of Germany, France, the Soviet Union, Israel, and (from within the hemisphere) Brazil approach or exceed ties to American sources.[101]
- Such indices of international power and coalitions as the voting patterns of international bodies show Latin American countries typically to be independent from — and often opposed to — U.S. positions: in 1983, on recorded votes in the United Nations, Latin American countries voted *against* the U.S. position 73.2% of the time.[102]
- Latin America's annual growth rate over the past twenty years has exceeded that of the United States (6% versus 3.5%); individual countries are impoverished but, collectively, their aggregate GNP is now greater than for Western Europe in 1950.[103]

Unrealistic Self-Prescription

Goaded by a period of perceived tension in hemispheric relations, successive administrations have announced new Latin American policies, pledged greater attention to the region, vowed their support for Latin America's economic development, and expressed their interest in the region's political evolution . . . calling [the] new approach a Good Neighbor Policy, an Alliance for Progress, a Mature Partnership, a New Dialogue, or a Caribbean Basin Initiative . . . The next phase of this historic cycle generally sees the newly announced policy toward Latin America set aside.
— A. Lowenthal[104]

Americans have had great difficulty thinking about Latin America without assigning it a lower position in a top-down system of imagining. And in this world of hardball drama, inattention (between crises) to those of lower position is their correlated fate.

The commission's official mandate included the request to address the problem of "building a national consensus."[105] Its prescription, "the best route to consensus on U.S. policy toward Central America is by exposure to the realities of Central America,"[106] echoed the limitations of Maxwell Taylor's report: It avoided a deep analysis of why the American political system has consistently failed to produce — and act on — this desired knowledge of reality.

For over twenty-five years there has been a well-validated recognition (in official studies) that America's *rationally derived* long-term policy would be to accelerate development and reform in Latin America. A deeper explanation — and, I believe, a more intelligent and effective one — is that American policy derives from strong imagination system effects. Thus, between crises, these nations (and their peoples) become invisible; they are too lacking in power and status to be noticed and to engage motivation for any long-term policy.

The understanding of American institutions and the foreign policy process I have proposed forecast, by contrast, the commission's long-range, managerial program will not be adopted and sustained by Congress. And if that long-term commitment fails, the integrity of the entire *Report* falls apart; the policy of reform and repression ("change must occur, but violence is not the way,") is a message without intellectual and moral integrity if the United States political system sets policy by a dual-track approach to thinking about the world, with primacy to imagination, and will not deliver the reforms.

This forecast is also supported by historical experience. American political institutions have generally not sustained the best instincts of the American people and its leaders in long-term foreign aid programs. The Alliance for Progress — the earlier program to contain Castro's short-term threat in the early 1960s while mounting long-term social, economic, and political development to prevent further revolutions — came apart. Crises elsewhere (especially Vietnam) diverted attention; as Latin America moved out of the headlines the take-charge consensus of the Kennedy years dissolved; competing domestic demands became more salient to the political system.

Today, there is even less basis for the commission's confidence in the effects of rational analysis. Foreign aid commitments were difficult to sustain even in the *early* 1960s when there was a mood favorable to international activism and a prosperous economy. Aid to lower status foreigners is less likely during the 1980s and 1990s with the massive, locked-in budget deficits each president and Congress will face, the mounting costs of current entitlement programs for health and the elderly, and growing pressures to meet other domestic needs. There is no evidence that rightist governments of Latin America respond constructively to handwriting on the wall, and there is little evidence to suggest the American political system has the capacity to remember it is there. The probable forecast of foreign policy created by the American system is that even if President Reagan's $8.4 billion proposal is enacted, it will substantially dissolve in three to four years; the deaths will not buy time used effectively to put a long-term solution into effect. There *will* be further revolutions and further commission reports.

In sum, my argument is that the Kissinger Report (and American policy in Central America in the 1980s) is a standard American fantasy. And as a basis for policy, such an overdramatized and oddly wired system of imagining fails (as it has since 1954) both to win the war and to win the peace.

Policy Prescriptions

It is not my intent to propose specific American policy toward Central America; the barriers to more intelligent and effective policy belong to a more intimate and basic realm than can be accessed by policy analyzing. The barriers are both systemic and belong to the knower; they are matters of self, imagination, and motivation. But there is one practical recommendation which bears directly on my thesis, judgement concerning the nature of American political institutions: if the analysis presented here is accurate, one lesson I draw is that Congress should pass President Reagan's long-term economic aid program *and* transfer its total funding, immediately, to an independent foundation so that future actions by the American political system will be unneeded to sustain the program. This rational, long-term action may be achievable. In recent years, Congress has shown wisdom in legislation to recognize features of the American political system, and especially those pressures on congressmen that need to be counterbalanced, to achieve sound long-term policies. (Both the War Powers Act and the congressional budget reforms evidence a capacity for thoughtful response to historical experience.) Such foresight and statesmanship might be used now to transfer total funding while there is still the dramatic challenge to sustain the attention and action mood.[107]

REFLECTIONS ON GOVERNMENT LEARNING

> *It won't be what we want, but we can learn to live with it.*
> —Clark Clifford (1965) in a letter to President Johnson advising a negotiated settlement, rather than escalation of the Vietnam War.[108]

Governments do learn, although primarily tactics to stay out of trouble in the press: both Presidents Kennedy and Reagan learned quickly to neutralize recurring press controversy that threatened the foreign policies they chose to pursue. But the basic motives have not been affected. Typically, beneath cloaks of secrecy and behind dust clouds of high-minded talk, initial failure has only increased motivation. Only by strong emotional impact, *in extremis* and faced by nuclear deterrence, has a lesson such as Clifford proposed (above) been accepted.

Revolutionaries also learn—perhaps more quickly because they have greater incentive to do so—and the result of their study has been to reduce the effectiveness of American repetitions. In 1954, Arbenz collapsed before a faked invasion force of 110 men; such clever, "low cost" American tactics have not succeeded again. In the early 1980s Fidel Castro openly—and successfully—

urged the Sandinistas to learn from his mistakes, avoid the public trials and executions that had given his enemies ammunition in the critical battle for American public opinion, and hold democratic elections promptly.[109]

Revolutionaries are not immune from their own mis-imaginings and hasty lessons. Implacable American hostility is not a foregone conclusion: that American governments have often pressed every advantage, including invasion and assassination, against even popularly supported regimes (Castro) or democratically elected regimes (Chile), has not meant that *every* administration will do so.[110]

CLOSING THE FEEDBACK LOOP
Lessons and American Institutions

To close the feedback loop from recent history, what lessons do we draw about our institutions and the learning potential of the American political system? How may Leviathans learn? The case material does not provide direct evidence to answer this question, but the conceptual framework we have created to understand the American foreign policy system can be used, together with the case material, to suggest several observations about the problem.

The Executive Branch

My thesis has been that repeating forms of American foreign policy express the operation of the mind engaged within an overdramatized and oddly wired sensibility of the nature of power, a sensibility inherent in the national security world. Via such a strong imagination system an inexorable policy logic (encoded within its structure) is engaged. The resulting policy syndrome includes overconfident use of countervailing aggression, disconnection of ideals and moral restraint beneath a belief in one's high-minded rhetoric, stark fears, policy discussions with categories and symbols of little genuine help to understand local realities, and lack of any rational long-term policy (among other effects). In the cases we have examined, American institutions follow a reparative (and ahistorical) logic that is neither rationally derived, nor moral, nor effective (on its own terms) in the long term.

From inside a larger-than-life drama, the decision maker's direct experience of reality appears so compelling as to dismiss as naive those whose sensibility concerning global politics is outside the system. Even good rational analysis (for example, the capacity to recognize *and* to act on the observation "this isn't working"), applied step by step as history unfolds, has not prevented recurrence.

I believe it strengthens the force of this last point (and indicates how other historical material might be understood using the framework) to discuss briefly a related case, the Vietnam War, whose unfolding was designed by most of the same men who participated in the earlier Central American decisions of the Kennedy administration.

In 1961, when Kennedy and his inner circle of advisers launched the Bay of Pigs operation, they believed they could elicit an enthusiastic response from a foreign people. Kennedy committed himself, at first ambivalently, to paramilitary action which, by its failure, strengthened the American government's commitment to resolve the Cuban problem by violence.

Yet after these events and failed policies, a decade with a similar policy sequence, increasingly terrible violence compounded with idealism, unfolded, and the men who witnessed the earlier events and helped to determine them repeated their same sequence of error. Vice President Johnson, becoming president after Kennedy's assassination, with many of the same advisers — Bundy, McNamara, Rusk, Taylor, and Rostow — began and then escalated an American war in Vietnam. Again, America faced a national liberation movement backed by Communist support and using Marxist ideology. Again, policymakers initially convinced themselves they might reform an indigenous government to win "the hearts and minds" of a foreign people. Again, a president made an initial, ambivalent commitment to resolve the problem by violence. Again it failed; initial failure engendered greater violence and more failure.

If the government learning rate could be determined by the analytical intelligence of key individuals, it would have been high during the Kennedy administration and among these men as the decade unfolded. At the cabinet table with Kennedy were men of worldly experience and unusual analytical ability: McGeorge Bundy, the National Security Adviser, was a former dean at Harvard; Dean Rusk, the secretary of state, had been president of the Rockefeller Foundation, a former assistant secretary of state for Far Eastern Affairs during the Korean War, and a college dean; Robert McNamara, secretary of defense, was formerly president of Ford Motor Company; Allen Dulles, CIA director, was the most experienced director in the history of the agency. The president himself had been educated at Harvard and had won a Pulitzer Prize.[111]

Such analytical ability, even among liberals, did not forestall the cycle of recurrence. Superbly trained analytical minds are not a sufficient condition for government learning. Presidents (who also are trapped) of both parties have followed the same policy sequence. Thus I think we must judge it fanciful to predict a remedy to be self-generated within the executive branch alone. As we have seen in chapter 5, there is a system-level logic involved, and it would take an unusual president to act outside the conventional drama.

Congress

Might Congress remedy the shortfalls in the executive branch? Perhaps, in principle, it could. But its traditional role in foreign policy has been as an emotionally expressive body. Congressional critics of hard-line policies, apprehensive of being scapegoated, typically score points yet ultimately defer the responsibility for policy to the president. Congress would likely act to block a policy were there to be prior and general change in public opinion, but any exception to the general rule of congressional impotence within this drama would depend upon the leadership of unusual individuals, not the system itself.[112]

However two American institutions – the press and the universities – do have the power, the role, and the independence to effect long-term change.

The Press

The *Times* creates the upper boundary of political system sophistication, and the principal news media are the daily guardians of truth, memory, and the standards for what will be accepted as accurate knowledge and serious discussion of foreign policy issues. In these return engagements, when an administration and the elite press offer different versions of reality, it is the journalists who have been telling the truth. The elite news media have become a vital national resource to sustain contact with reality, and they have a causal role in political system learning which extends beyond simple credibility; society "remembers" and applies the institutional memory *Times* reporters include in their stories.

There are two basic failings to be remedied to tame unrefined and overdramatized imaginings. First, the mass news media traffic in simple dramatic images and postures, simple themes of success or defeat; they create the domestic policy debate as a ritualized drama of "the administration versus its critics," assigning critics, like the chorus of a Greek tragedy, to a secondary role. The results of such self-indulgence can be misdirecting and (now, in a nuclear age) even dangerous. We have seen the results of such a sensibility when Robert McNamara observed rationally during the Cuban Missile Crisis that "a missile is a missile," and offered his conclusion that no deterioration of American security would result if Soviet missiles could be launched from Cuba as well as Russia. The president, Robert Kennedy, McGeorge Bundy, the Marine Corps commandant, and other senior advisers agreed with McNamara's point.

But, at this moment when they might have deeply wished policy *not* be trapped within the logic of a drama, they felt unable to select, and act from, a simple, rational sensibility; *others* would think in such terms.[113] They chose a response which the president believed to risk a 50% chance of nuclear war between the superpowers. Thus, at the system level, the past legacy of drama-based policy, sustained in public consciousness and expectations, blocks the rational lessons the American government may adopt, even when it wishes to so. (Decision makers *do* think in two modes; and my point is not that men are irrational per se but that even men with the ability, and preference, to be rational make consequential policy via the second – imagination – track.)

The vivid memory of McNamara's remark and Kennedy's response should be remembered by newsmen and editors: and, if they dramatize foreign policy issues less breathlessly, calmness would be a constructive, long-term contribution to learning.[114]

A second useful route to intelligent and effective policy would be to quote politicians less exclusively. Serious, purposive, and sustained discussions of foreign policy issues are badly needed, from people who are not apprehensive about reelections or selling a point of view or ideology.[115] This is true especially when the templates based on American political experience (and, too, the experience of most American politicians) awkwardly misconstrue the dynamics of foreign societies. Because of the anxieties engendered by foreign policy, and the prominent—but untrustworthy—capacity of presidents to offer reassurance, a decision to open the doors a bit wider and create what would be in the public mind a "lesser pantheon" of serious, knowledgeable, and committed people in whom confidence could grow would be a useful step.[116]

Universities

So our state will be ruled by minds which are awake, and not as now by men in a dream fighting with one another over shadows and for the power and office which in their eyes are the great good.
                                        —Plato, *The Republic*[117]

Colleges and universities play a critical role in the learning of American society. They are among the major institutions to create and sustain American standards for honesty, evidence, and what counts as serious discussion of public issues. They also have the job to codify experience and transmit its lessons to each new generation of students.

At many universities, the present curriculum in public affairs crystallized in the mid-1960s as leading universities, aided by several major foundations, drew a round of lessons about what to do next in public affairs curricula.[118] Their prescription was to design professional training programs, and specifically to develop students' ability to perform rational decision analyses using tools of microeconomic theory and scientific methods.[119]

My thesis—in part, a reflection on this lesson—has been that neither analytical brilliance nor its deficiencies have been the cause of the policies or the repeating errors in perception and judgment we have seen. Rather, an entirely separate mode of emotion-charged mental functioning now appears to be involved. Thus I derive the lesson that an appropriate public affairs education should address this mode of political knowledge and, specifically, could usefully address four orientations by which a student establishes a relationship between his or her self and the world: (a) responsibility; (b) integrity; (c) the reflective education of imagination; and (d) the developed ability to know what one wants.

Responsibility

One inference from the case material is that government learning might increase to the extent individuals (generally) come to act from a sense of personal responsibility for collective, long-term outcomes.

Technical rationality itself is irrelevant to the selection of *whose* costs and benefits, weighted in what degree, will affect a foreign policy decision. When the death and economic destruction visited upon a foreign people are counted as "nothing to lose," the cause is not "irrationality" in a technical sense but a refusal to be responsible to (and for) anything wider than one's own nation-state. As we have seen, no one in American government can be depended upon (by assignment to any conventional role) to act responsibly (and consistently) for long-term collective outcomes of the international political system, not even an American president.

Personal responsibility, however, needs to be *chosen*. American society, like the federal bureaucracy, engenders its own self-limiting definitions and divisions of responsibility.[120] Ritualized acts of criticism, whether from Congress or citizens, still defer responsibility to the executive branch and a presidential "over-mind," with the typical outcome that substantive criticism becomes merely a domestic political problem for the executive branch, addressed primarily tactically, as an imagery and press relations problem. Yet government learning is a dependent variable, and committed individuals — anywhere — willing to be responsible to effect policy outcomes and government learning would be an improvement.

Honesty and Integrity

By contrast with behavior characteristic of the hardball political imagination system, honesty is a good basis for effective long-term foreign policy. There is nothing Pollyannish about the recommendation: in the long term, there is no sequence in the case material for which lying or dissembling for short-term tactical advantage effected a net American benefit. More typically (chapter 4), this type of individual "sophistication" systematically snarled the executive branch.

Nations develop reputations, and the reputation for sophisticated lying weakens the international power of the United States more consequentially than any of the hostile, external forces actually encountered in these return engagements. A high-minded *Report* by a commission whose chairman (Dr. Kissinger) was responsible for secret policies of bombing Cambodia and "dual-track" (in another sense of the term) operations to destroy Allende in Chile (behind a public facade of "noninterventionism") can scarcely be credible to revolutionaries in foreign countries (of whom there will continue to be many in the world, in the years ahead, with whom the United States will wish to deal). To mount covert operations behind a pretense of high-minded rhetoric undercuts the credibility — hence the power — of the words of a nation's leaders: ultimately, when the words of a nation's leaders cannot be trusted, there is no basis for either power or international order left, save violence and the threat of violence.[121]

The ability of anyone in American government to make an important, truthful statement rests on more than individual honesty. It requires collective intellectual integrity, that is, a coherent and consistent policy.[122] In principle, presidential leadership should integrate American foreign policy, but between crises inattention has been the rule instead. Eisenhower's separate instincts were not bureaucratically integrated, and America's sudden Dr. Jekyll/Mr. Hyde switch occurred because State Department moderates initially set policy but did not personally embody the full range of Eisenhower's instincts. (They were strung along, too.) Whether the hawks or the "moderates" within the Reagan administration reflect the president's views, perhaps not even he has decided.[123]

Improved Imagination Ability

My argument has been that two separate faculties of the mind operate in political life and policy formation. Thus I have presented a brief, in part, for education of the imagination, and with it (I would argue) the development of the capacity for realistic empathy, maturity of motivation, well-calibrated judgment, and genuine learning.[124]

This entire section reflects the implications of this framework, which are perhaps especially strong for universities whose students' imaginations lead them to desire upward mobility in a literal (and psychological) sense. But I want to emphasize that while I have judged standard theories of American foreign policy to be overintellectualized portrayals, my conclusion is *not* that "rational" policy is the prescription for intelligence and effectiveness. Rationality has little to do with policy, one way or the other, and maximum technical rationality would not change a great deal.[125] One *needs* the "hardball" system — rather than dismissing it — to understand the world (and *other* actors): The prescription is to recalibrate the overdramatizations and reconnect (in a more healthy way) the oddly wired connections.

But there is a further area which would be useful to address from a different angle: the problem that systems are not single individuals and cannot always be usefully imagined in this way.

First, a caveat: To some extent, as we have seen, systems *do* operate as people. The archetypal drama of American relations with Central American revolutionaries is, in part, a battle of impulses and motives based on the model of interpersonal (and intrapsychic) relations, tense dramas of the self for dominance and control extended across thousands of miles to a hemispheric — and global — scale.[126]

But it is also true that systems do not function as single individuals. Their behavior is a compound of institutions, recruitment and selection procedures, electoral risks, the penchant for drama, and the standards of truth reflected in the mass media; they reflect the curricula of universities and the sense of personal responsibility, knowledge, and sustained commitment of unofficial establishments. And much else.[127] There are, then, many processes, and many entry points, where changes may spin out their effects to support learning. And thus it follows that it would also be useful to discuss with students the nature of the political sophistication that is required for constructive effect. Now often what passes for "sophistication" is only recognition that unprincipled and selfish behavior may lie behind idealistic pretenses. Yet, while the sentence "the patient is ill because germs are pursuing their self-interest" is not wrong, neither is it scientifically sophisticated. If a patient's symptom is low energy, a well-trained physician might think of 1,200 or more possible diagnoses, each linked to appropriate, well-targeted remedies. Similarly, the capacity to appraise — and remedy — failures of government learning requires understandings of political systems which are more intelligent and effective than simple domestic dramas of moral and political criticism have been.

What One Really Wants America to Contribute to the World

A final lesson from the case material: The American foreign policy system, in its 1980s dealing with Central America, is not "on track." The political system was never designed to learn or to create foreign policy in a complex world. Behaving naturally, by its current design, its return engagements unfold in the same way as in the past, to produce the same results. What one learns from Europe's political history, an historian once observed, is how little of it one would care to repeat, and the same, I think, is true of American policies towards the impoverished peoples of Central America and their revolutions.

If the basis for learning is caring (motivation), the question to pose for students, or anyone, is: what does one really want to contribute to the world? Connected to the answer to this question, historical memory becomes useful and suggests a final observation. Specifically, the radical-left image of American policymakers has been incomplete and wrong; no past American decision maker has wanted Latin American policy to work out this badly. There is, to be sure, the standard perpetual short-term preoccupation of each administration with its simple images, anxious apprehensions, breathless activism, and obsessions to restore a challenged sense of control over world events. But each return engagement with Central American radicals, beginning with the Arbenz overthrow in 1954, has found contemporary American leaders to recognize the now-standard two problems (short-term: revolution; long-term: development and improved governments). Each generation of policymakers has wanted solution to the long-term problem to be among its legacies: in historical perspective, the performance of the American political system has not been satisfactory to its leaders, either. That the American political system, given its design, does not yet naturally embody this second purpose and hope of the individuals who serve as its leaders is one of the lessons of history.

NOTES

1. By this model of dual-track information processing I do not intend to reject the model that rational decision processing also occurs. The case material shows ample evidence that there is a *zone* of strategic and rational calculation, primarily tactical. My argument is that almost all of the *consequential* inputs into such rational calculations derive from understandings of the nature of power, assessments of reality, motivations, and designations of costs and benefits which are produced via the strong imagination operating of the mind. For example, Bueno de Mesquita, *The War Trap* (New Haven, CT: Yale Univ. Press, 1981) shows an "expected utility" model may be useful, *provided* one assumes almost all of the *important* variables as "givens" (e.g., what is worth going to war about, how much the cost of human life is considered a "cost" by the decision maker, etc.). M. Howard, "The Causes of Wars," *The Wilson Quarterly* 8 (1984): 90–103, provides a similar view by an historian, endorsing the applicability of a "rational calculation" model, that is, if one does not also seek to explain (as the current model does) the source of motivations.

   I do not intend to single out the United States. There have been many further examples of the intellectual vulnerability of instinctive, power-motivated thinking. (The British and French actions against Nasser of Egypt, for example, a failure which did not dissuade Kennedy in the early 1960s.) If one surveys the conduct of international relations, it is surprising how frequently erroneous and self-defeating the decisions of major powers have been. In Karl Deutsch's summary: "When a hungry cat concentrates his attention on a mousehole, there usually is a mouse in it; but when the government of some great country has concentrated its attention and efforts on some particular foreign-policy objective, the outcome remarkably often has been unrewarding. . . . During the half century from 1914 to 1964, the decisions of major powers to go to war or to expand a war, and their judgments of the relevant intentions and capabilities of other nations, seem to have involved major errors of fact, perhaps in more than 50% of all cases." Cited in L. Etheredge, *A World of Men: The Private Sources of American Foreign Policy* (Cambridge, MA: MIT Press, 1978), p. 1. A recent discussion that would suggest application of a theory of larger-than-life drama to the American Civil War is J. McPherson, "The Confederacy as a Pre-Emptive Counterrevolution" (Photocopy, 1981).

2. Etheredge, *A World of Men* presents quantitative evidence for these motivational patterns in the American national security world and reviews cross-cultural evidence that the causes of war are linked to competition and power motivation. I should emphasize that we lack evidence of how widespread such encoding might be throughout American society, potentially a crucial problem for the analysis of political economy and blockages to learning in economic growth policy. See the discussion in Lloyd Etheredge, "Dual-Track Information Processing in Public Policy Decision Making: Models of Strong Imagination Systems." Symposium paper presented to the American Psychological Association Meetings, Toronto, 1984; Lloyd Etheredge, "President Reagan's Counseling," *Political Psychology* (in press, 1985).

3. M. Halperin, P. Clapp, and A. Kanter, *Bureaucratic Behavior and Foreign Pol-*

icy, (Washington, DC: Brookings Institution, 1974); C. Argyris, *Some Causes of Organizational Ineffectiveness Within the Department of State* (Washington, DC: Department of State Center for International Systems Research, 1967); L. Bloomfield, "Planning Foreign Policy" *Political Science Quarterly* 93 (1978): 369–391.

4. See, for example, Murray Edelman, *The Symbolic Uses of Politics* (Urbana, IL: Univ. of Illinois Press, 1964) and *Political Language: Words That Succeed and Policies That Fail* (New York: Academic Press, 1977); Doris Graber, *Verbal Behavior and Politics* (Urbana, IL: Univ. of Illinois Press, 1976).

5. See, for example, Karl Deutsch, *The Nerves of Government: Models of Communication and Control* (New York: Free Press, 1963). For a brief discussion of the possible learning superiority of democracies—undercut by national security secrecy—see the comparative perspective of David Apter, "Letter to the Editor," *New York Times.* October 23, 1983.

6. See R. Packenham, *Liberal America and the Third World: Political Development Ideas in Foreign Aid and Social Science* (Princeton, NJ: Princeton Univ. Press, 1973); S. Eisenstadt, "Interactions Between Organizations and Societal Stratification" in P. Nystrom and W. Starbuck, eds. *Handbook of Organizational Design,* vol. 1. (New York: Oxford University Press, 1981), pp. 309–322.

7. National Bipartisan Commission (hereinafter NBC), *Appendix to the Report of the National Bipartisan Commission on Central America* (Washington, DC: Government Printing Office, 1984), pp. 29, 50.

8. Ibid., p. 31. A useful collection of relevant documents is P. Rosset and J. Vandermeer, eds., *The Nicaraguan Reader: Documents of a Revolution Under Fire* (New York: Grove Press, 1983).

9. NBC, *Appendix,* p. 31.

10. NBC, *The Report of the President's National Bipartisan Commission on Central America* (New York: Macmillan, 1984), p. 26.

11. NBC, *Appendix,* pp. 31–32.

12. NBC, *Report,* pp. 49–53.

13. NBC, *Appendix,* pp. 32–33.

14. Ibid., p. 32.

15. Ibid., pp. 32–33. This same type of last-minute search occurred 20 years ago as Castro's movement spread.

16. Ibid., p. 33.

17. Ibid., pp. 33–35.

18. Ibid., p. 34.

19. Ibid., pp. 34, 798.

20. R. Fagen "Revolution and Crisis in Nicaragua" in M. Diskin, ed., *Trouble in Our Backyard: Central America and the United States in the Eighties* (New York: Pantheon 1983), pp. 125–154; NBC, *Appendix* (1984), pp. 39. See also pp. 482–490, however, for specific discussion of relations with the Miskito Indian population by Americas Watch and Helsinki Watch.

21. The aid package ran into trouble in Congress where the reality of uncontrolled leftist revolutionaries again (as in 1959–60) produced fervent debate, demands and conditions far exceeding those applied to right wing governments, and delay; it was almost 11 months before the Carter bill, encumbered with amendments, was approved. See I. Destler "The Elusive Consensus: Congress and Central America" in R. Leiken, ed., *Central America: Anatomy of Conflict* (New York: Pergamon, 1984), pp. 319–335, p. 320.

22. NBC, *Appendix,* p. 45.

23. A useful review of learning by the revolutionaries is provided by E. Evans, "Revolutionary Movements in Central America: The Development of a New Strategy" in H. Wiarda (ed.), *Rift and Revolution* (Washington, DC: American Enterprise Institute, 1984), pp. 167–193.

24. U.S. Department of State, *Background Paper: Nicaragua's Military Build-up and Support for Central American Subversion* (Washington, DC: Department of State, 1984), p. 8–11; NBC, *Appendix*, pp. 40–41; J. Cirincione and L. Hunter, "Military Threats, Actual and Potential" in R. Leiken, ed., *Central America*, pp. 176–177, 181.

25. U.S. Department of State, *Background Paper*, pp. 8–11. There is a tacit arms control process involving the Soviet Union and American limitations for the level and amount of weaponry it supplies to Afghanistan rebels. The Soviet buildup has given Nicaragua a solid defensive capability against any combination of its immediate neighbors but probably does not allow it to defeat Honduras. See Cirincione and Hunter, "Military Threats," p. 177. This refined appraisal is absent from the Kissinger (NBC) *Report* discussed below.

26. For a discussion of the Honduran military, see NBC, *Appendix*, p. 41. The commission's estimates are more dire than those of Cirincione and Hunter, *op. cit.*, pp. 177–178.

27. This is one, defensive, reason for American forces now to be stationed in Honduras, although this emplacement has been officially described as simply a result of Big Pine II (and other training exercises), thus not requiring congressional approval.

28. NBC, *Appendix*, pp. 50–56.

29. Packenham, *Liberal America*, provides a critique.

30. American policy beginning in the mid-1960s intentionally strengthened the military in these countries with the opposite expectation. See W. LaFeber, *Inevitable Revolutions: The United States in Central America* (New York: Norton, 1983) for a general discussion. In evaluating his thesis it should be noted that military coups and repression also occur at a non-zero rate in underdeveloped countries not penetrated and managed so extensively by the U.S.

31. NBC, *Appendix*, p. 51.

32. For discussions of the El Salvador military and the *tanda* system of organization see R. Millett, "Praetorians or Patriots: The Central American Military" in R. Leiken, ed., *Central America*, pp. 73–75; R. Bonner, *Weakness and Deceit: U.S. Policy and El Salvador* (New York: Times Books, 1984), pp. 44–64, 290–321. Millett emphasizes that the El Salvador military does *not* have defeat of the revolutionaries as its top priority: institutional protection and promotion of one's own *tanda* are more salient. Thus motivation and combat effectiveness of the El Salvador military are probably only modestly affected by American material aid.

33. R. Meislin, "Duarte Could Win at Polls, Lose a Nation," *New York Times* (April 1, 1984), p. 1 discusses the problem of interpretation.

34. The tabulation is an underestimate: the Archdiocese requires firsthand testimony which is more difficult to obtain from rural areas distant from San Salvador. These figures do not include "abductions by government security forces" after which the victim does not reappear: approximately 2,300 were in this category between October 1979 and mid-1983. Bonner, *Weakness and Deceit*, p. 62; R. White, *The Morass: United States Intervention in Central America* (New York: Harper and Row, 1984), p. 44, gives monthly statistics.

35. R. White, *The Morass* details the terror campaign. Comparing overt press cen-

sorship between Nicaragua and El Salvador, it is important to note that only arch-conservative newspapers have survived in El Salvador since 1983 and there is little need for further overt acts of censorship. See Bonner, *Weakness and Deceit*, p. 360.

36. Department of State, *Background Paper*, p. 18 admits that the flow of arms was "heavy" from November 1980 until January 1981 and since has "varied," i.e., not been consistently heavy. The evidence provided by the department would not support the conclusion that such arms shipments now play a vital role in the El Salvador fighting. An alert Sandinista government, however, might have shipped such massive amounts of arms in the early period as to leave little need for further external support. See also Evans, "Revolutionary Movements."

37. The continuing argument about arms shipments, primarily a symbolic argument (I have suggested) rather than a motivating concern of the Reagan administration, is discussed in T. Buckley. *Violent Neighbors: El Salvador, Central America, and the United States* (New York: Times Books, 1984), p. 307 who records that the Honduran "contra" forces, officially funded by the United States to interdict the flow of arms, have not captured any weapons in 3 years. See also D. Oberdorfer and J. Goshko, "Ex-CIA Analyst Disputes U.S. Aides on Nicaragua," *Washington Post* (June 13, 1984), p. 1; S. Kinzer, "Salvador Rebels Still Said to Get Nicaraguan Aid," *New York Times* (April 11, 1984), pp. 1, 8. For a discussion of international clandestine arms trade and the indigenous black market, see Bonner, *Weakness and Deceit*, pp. 267–268. Bonner's statistics suggest about 250 government weapons are captured each month by the revolutionaries. Ibid., p. 268.

38. U.S. Department of State, *Background Paper*.

39. H. Smith, "Salvador Vote Settles Little at Home or in Washington," *New York Times* (April 1, 1984), IV; p. 1.

40. For discussions of popular support, see Bonner, *Weakness and Deceit*, pp. 134–141; White, *The Morass*, p. 40–42 estimates an infrastructure of 100,000 and a popular base of one million: the source of his estimates is not provided.

41. Official American estimates must be used with caution because, from a range of estimates and definitions, they could be understated to imply success or overstated to urge the need for prompt, massive aid. By February 1984 the American embassy said there were 9,000 to 12,000 guerrillas. Note that, by official estimates, this number had grown from about 2,000 three years earlier and 6,000 in mid-1983. See Bonner, *Weakness and Deceit*, pp. 137–138.

42. Buckley, *Violent Neighbors*, p. 299 discusses the casualty rate reported by the El Salvador military. The military reporting of the war has not been as complete as for Vietnam and it is difficult to derive an accurate, independent military assessment from public sources. A brief discussion of guerrilla military advances is provided in Bonner, *Weakness and Deceit*, p. 138.

43. Bonner, *Weakness and Deceit*, p. 139.

44. NBC, *Appendix*, p. 463.

45. Haig's approach is reviewed in B. Rubin, "Reagan Administration Policymaking and Central America," in R. Leiken, ed., *Central America*, pp. 302–308. See also W. Smith, "Dateline Havana: Myopic Diplomacy," *Foreign Policy* 48 (Fall 1982): 157–174; Destler, "Elusive Consensus."

46. From October 1979 until early 1984 American military aid to El Salvador was about $300 million through open official channels. See Bonner, *Weakness and Deceit*, p. 63. But this number depends heavily upon definition: by a broader definition White, *The Morass*, pp. 232–244, estimates $280 million of American

"security aid" to El Salvador in 1983 and $216 million in 1982.

47. For a review of Reagan Administration policymaking, see Rubin, "Reagan Administration Policymaking"; V. Vaky, "Reagan's Central American Policy: An Isthmus Restored," in Leiken, ed., *Central America*, pp. 237–257. Concerning the "secret war" see White, *The Morass*, pp. 52–74, which also contains an especially good account of the role of *Newsweek's* November 1982 special report: J. Brecher, J. Walcott, D. Martin, and B. Nissen, "A Secret War for Nicaragua," *Newsweek* (November 8, 1982), also reprinted in Rosset and Vandermeer, ed., *Nicaragua Reader*, pp. 208–215. Bonner, *Weakness and Deceit*, reflects the stories he wrote while the *New York Times* correspondent in El Salvador.

48. Concerning the Argentine connection, see White, *The Morass*, p. 54–55 and references to the original reporting in the *New York Times, Washington Post*, and *Newsweek*.

49. Destler, "Elusive Consensus," p. 321.

50. Shultz's soporific style and personal decency aided the administration's public relations. As Shultz was interpreted as a moderating influence in Soviet-American relations, and this influence was greatly desired by potential critics of Central American policy, Shultz (and the administration) has probably, for this reason as well, been the subject of fewer attacks. Substantially overconfident, fanciful, and — on the part of some Reagan Administration officials — deceitful comments with respect to human rights "progress" in El Salvador are reviewed by a *New York Times* correspondent in Bonner, *Weakness and Deceit*.

51. In a novel move against the press, the Reagan Administration forbade press coverage when it invaded Grenada in 1983. The maneuver worked surprisingly well, from its point of view, and thus is likely to be repeated.

52. The Israeli connection is more "known" than documented. See, for example, R. White, *The Morass*, p. 59; S. Kinzer, "Anti-Sandinista Rebels Fail in New Attempt to Unite," *New York Times* (April 26, 1984), p. A10; Associated Press, "Salvadorans Talk of More Israeli Aid," *New York Times* (April 21, 1984), p. 4; P. Taubman, "Nicaragua Rebels Reported to Raise Millions in Gifts" *New York Times* (September 8, 1984), pp. 1, 14. Israel's involvement in Honduras has also effected a double-level cut-out operation, with aid to Honduras, offset by American aid to Israel, then diverted to contra forces. It would be a very difficult channel for congressional opponents to stop. These press stories can be considered timely "alert" messages to an elite audience (especially to Congress) that such sophisticated channels should be known about. The Israeli connection began when the Carter administration officially cut off aid to Somoza. Israel and Argentina served as "cut-outs" to sell Somoza the arms he wanted while the administration, symbolically, expressed toughness about human rights violations and distanced America from Somoza's regime, in anticipation of its downfall. See, for example, Buckley, *Violent Neighbors*, p. 200.

53. See P. Taubman, "Private Groups in U.S. Aid Managua's Foes" *New York Times* (July 15, 1984), p. 1. Taubman, "Rebels Raise Millions." American leftist groups also supply money to the El Salvador rebels and to the Nicaraguan government.

54. The pattern continues within the policy process as well: " . . . the State Department is generally reluctant to oppose military escalation for fear of losing influence." H. Smith, "Ambiguities on Goals" *New York Times* (April 11, 1984), p. 8. The self-perceived political vulnerability of those whose counsel might lead to "defeat" or be stylistically "soft" can probably be accepted as a rule of the foreign policy process: Destler, "Elusive Consensus," p. 334, astutely notes the historical, self-blocking pattern that the congressional critics of hard-line policies

operate to score points but also maneuver to assure their own ineffectiveness, so that blame for the consequences lies with the president.

55. For example, see L. Chavez, "Salvador Military Questions the U.S. Role" *New York Times* (August 19, 1984), p. 1.

56. For example, Smith, "Ambiguities."

57. A review of American military preparations, with reference to the ineffectual congressional criticism, is H. Smith, "U.S. Latin Force in Place if Needed, Officials Report" *New York Times* (April 23, 1984), pp. 1, 8. A detailed, professional assessment of military planning is Cirincione and Hunter, "Military Threats," pp. 178–182. A review of the role of Congress through late 1983 is provided in Destler, "Elusive Consensus."

58. A large sum, even by American standards, and massive in such a poor country. The original report in the *New York Times* was later confirmed by the Reagan administration. See also J. Kelly, "The CIA's 'Free' Elections" *Counterspy* 8 (June–August, 1984): 33.

59. For a review of the CIA mining see L. Cannon and D. Oberdorfer, "The Mines, the CIA, and Shultz's Dissent" *Washington Post National Weekly Edition* (April 23, 1984), p. 16.

60. Ibid.; J. Brinkley, "Threats by CIA Said to Influence Anti-Sandinistas" *New York Times* (April 22, 1984), p. 1. An unusually candid interview by a former contra leader, dismissed after criticism of a CIA-authored manual discussing assassination, is J. Brinkley, "A Rebel Says CIA Pledged Help in War Against Sandinistas" *New York Times* (November 1, 1984), p. 1. (The CIA has regularly counseled contra leaders concerning their public statements and effects of American public opinion and briefed them prior to meetings with congressmen and senators.) Major aggressive activity directly commanded by the CIA occurred on October 10, 1983, when a devastating raid on the port of Corinto blew up 3,000,000 gallons of fuel. The columnist Anthony Lewis, "Fear of Change" *New York Times* (April 19, 1983), p. A19 has suggested the raid's timing, several days before an "unwitting" Kissinger Commission arrived to discuss the possibility of a negotiated settlement, may have been intended by the Reagan Administration and helped to produce a "bristling," uncompromising meeting.

Note, too, the "surfacing," of Mr. Llovio, a former Cuban official and defector. As Mr. Llovio defected in 1982, and he was not a highly ranked Cuban official (he had been the chief adviser to the Minister of Culture from 1980 to 1982), his sudden appearance on the front page of the *New York Times* (with a photograph) in 1984, soon after President Reagan's re-election, suggests CIA contingency planning against Castro. L. Maitland-Werner, "High Cuban Defector Speaks Out, Denouncing Castro as 'Impulsive'" *New York Times* (November 19, 1984), p. 1.

61. For example, H. Smith, "Ambiguities", p. 8; J. Goshko and J. Omang, "The Secret War Inside the White House Over Peace with Nicaragua" *Washington Post National Weekly Edition* (July 23, 1984), p. 16. A general review is Rubin, "Reagan Administration Policymaking," pp. 313–315.

62. The other members of the commission were: Nicholas F. Brady, former Republican senator from New Jersey; Henry G. Cisneros, Democratic mayor of San Antonio; William P. Clements, former Republican governor of Texas; Carlos F. Diaz-Alejandro, professor of economics at Yale; Wilson S. Johnson, president of the National Federation of Independent Business; Richard Scammon, a political scientist and public opinion specialist; John Silber, president of Boston University; Potter Stewart, a retired associate justice of the Supreme Court; Dr.

William Walsh, president of Project HOPE, an international medical care and education organization with major programs in the underdeveloped world. There were six Democrats and six Republicans.

63. Details are provided in NBC, *Report, Appendix*, pp. 10–24.

64. The theory that a "hardball politics" system of imagination produces the outcome of the foreign policy process was published in 1979; its application to the Reagan administration and the Kissinger *Report* is also a prediction. See L. Etheredge, "Hardball Politics: A Model" *Political Psychology* 1 (1979): 3–26.

65. J. Chace, "Deeper into the Mire" *New York Review of Books* (March 1, 1984), pp. 40–48 reviews this history. For reasons of space I have omitted the Rockefeller Report of 1969, which helped to codify the theory (adopted earlier) that the military forces in Central America would be agents of modernization and stability.

66. NBC, *Report*, p. 104.

67. Ibid., p. 5.

68. Ibid.

69. Ibid.

70. Ibid.

71. Ibid., p. 5.

72. Ibid., pp. 116–118, 120–123. Aid was also to be linked specifically to human rights "progress": unfortunately the commission did not specify requirements, probably a serious mistake in dealing with an administration that has ignored past requirements. See Buckley, *Violent Neighbors*.

73. Primarily, then, my methodology will be to cite the commission's own report, the analyses of its own staff, and the testimony presented to it and published in its *Appendix* to assure that I am not relying upon sources they might inadvertently have overlooked or excluded without the knowledge of some of the commissioners.

74. A checklist useful to inventory ethnocentric errors in American policy is Eisenstadt, "Interactions."

75. NBC, *Report*, p. 113.

76. See Arthur Schlesinger's reflections on his own learning over 20 years: "The counter-insurgency delusion began in the Kennedy years and expanded in the years thereafter. The trouble is that regimes that call for military shields to defend themselves against their own people don't care a damn about their own dispossessed. . . . .As soon as we insert our marvelous shield, moreover, we lose most of our leverage . . . we become the client's prisoners . . . Most of the time the military-shield approach only nourishes the folly and arrogance of the regime." Schlesinger in NBC, *Appendix*, pp. 791–792.

77. Also the left: Evans, "Revolutionary Movements."

78. See Howard Wiarda's testimony in NBC *Appendix*, pp. 207–209 et passim. LaFeber, *Inevitable Revolutions*, also reviews this feature of these societies.

79. Schlesinger in NBC, *Appendix*, pp. 789–793. See also the discussion by M. Greenfield, "A Lesson in Futility" *Newsweek* (March 5, 1984), p. 92.

80. NBC, *Report*, p. 111. Vaky, "Reagan's Policy" and W. LeoGrande, "Through the Looking Glass: The Report of the National Bipartisan Commission on Central America" *World Policy Journal* 1 (Winter 1984): 251–284 also provide trenchant critiques of the security threat hypothesis.

81. Mexico would then be America's major line of defense.

82. Funding will probably continue via indirect routes if direct congressional appropriations are not obtained.

83. NBC, *Report*, p. 111.

84. Ibid., p. 104.
85. L. Eagleburger, "Interview" *New York Times* (April 22, 1984), p. E2. Underlining added.
86. Cited in M. Rothenberg, "The Soviets in Central America" in Leiken, *Central America*, p. 133.
87. Ibid.
88. For a further discussion of the problem of realistic empathy in Soviet-American relations, see R. White, *Fearful Warriors: A Psychological Profile of U.S.-Soviet Relations* (New York: Free Press, 1984).
89. Schlesinger, "Testimony" in NBC, *Appendix*, p. 793.
90. See the discussion, below, of Castro's stringing along of the Soviet Union and purge of the Cuban Communist Party in 1962–1963 after the Soviet Union was publicly committed to his support.
91. This reflective issue — of perspective on how one thinks about a problem and its effect on efficacy — is raised in K. Weick and R. Daft, "The Effectiveness of Interpretation Systems" in K. Cameron and D. Whetten, eds., *Organizational Effectiveness: A Comparison of Multiple Models* (New York: Academic Press, 1983) and illustrates why I have included efficacy, along with intelligence, in my definition in chapter 2.
92. Yet as American power has extended worldwide, the imagination of American leaders has extended to encompass the globe: The commissioners are in the good company of recent American presidents who have publicly perceived "vital" American security interests in every part of the globe with the exceptions of Antarctica and most of Africa. See Vaky, "Reagan's Policy."
93. See J. Nye, ed., *The Making of America's Soviet Policy* (New Haven, CT: Yale Univ. Press, 1984); A. George, ed., *Managing U.S.-Soviet Rivalry: Problems of Crisis Prevention* (Boulder, CO: Westview Press, 1983); R. Axelrod, *The Evolution of Cooperation* (New York: Basic Books, 1984) for extended discussions of this and other approaches.
94. U.S. "covert" aid to Afghanistan, and Soviet casualties, are discussed in L. Gelb, "U.S. Aides Put '85 Arms Supplies to Afghan Rebels at $280 Million" *New York Times* (November 28, 1984), pp. 1, 9. Saudi, Israeli, Chinese, and other Arab aid was about $100 million per year in 1984. NBC, *Report*, p. 146. Gelb, ibid., and M. Erulkar, "CIA is Less Than Top-Notch in Afghanistan" *New York Times* (November 26, 1984), p. A23 discuss evidence of waste, corruption, and poor management.
95. Ibid., pp. 41, 42.
96. Ibid., pp. 42–44.
97. U.S. Senate. Select Committee to Study Governmental Operations with Respect to Intelligence Activities, *Alleged Assassination Plots Involving Foreign Leaders*. Senate Report 94: 465. November 20, 1975. (Washington, DC: Government Printing Office, 1975), pp. 191–223.
98. See Jorge Dominguez, *Cuba: Order and Revolution* (Cambridge, MA: Harvard Univ. Press, 1978), pp. 212–213.
99. For example, Robert White, President Carter's second ambassador to El Salvador, testified to a congressional subcommittee: "The guerrilla groups [in El Salvador], the revolutionary groups, almost without exception, began as associations of teachers, associations of labor unions, *campesino* unions, or parish organizations which were organized for the definite purpose of getting a schoolhouse up on the market road. When they tried to use their power of association to gain their ends, first they were warned and then they were persecuted and tortured

and shot. . . . So the leadership of the groups gradually became discouraged and, of course, the Soviet Union – at least Cuba was there to give them understanding and support. So . . . the large majority of the leaders of the Salvadoran guerrillas are Marxist or Marxist oriented . . . I would also add that I do not really believe that the ideological roots of these people go all that deep. I think it is more a response to persecution than anything else." Quoted in Bonner, *Weakness and Deceit*, p. 88.

100. A. Lowenthal, "Latin America and the Caribbean: Toward a New U. S. Policy" in J. Lewis and V. Kallab, ed., *U.S. Foreign Policy and the Third World Agenda* (New York: Praeger, 1983), pp. 53–57.

101. Ibid.

102. P. Fromuth, "U.S. Now More Isolated in U.N. Votes" *The Interdependent* 10 (March/April, 1984): 4, discusses these statistics and their interpretation. The percentage is computed for all recorded votes, disregarding abstentions.

103. Lowenthal, "Latin America," pp. 53–57.

104. Lowenthal, "Latin America," p. 51.

105. NBC, *Appendix*, p. 3.

106. NBC, *Report*, p. i.

107. If the American political system is willing for regimes whose leaders use Marxist-Leninist rhetoric to survive in Central America, then many alternatives become possible. As a practical matter, two guidelines might be suggested by the case material, each of them directed in opposition to the instincts of current power-drama sensibility.

　　1. A barrier to any settlement with the Sandinistas is their fear – partly derived from recent history – of American treachery. If there is misperception on this account it is urgent that it be credibly addressed, preferably in a dramatic way.

　　2. As a basis for an internal settlement in El Salvador (as well as Guatemala and Honduras), the successful policies adopted by the British in India and by the Japanese during the early Meiji restoration might be considered more hopeful than complex American-managed policies built around crucial American symbolisms, such as buying out the relatively small ruling classes with reimbursements or pensions to allow them to resettle in other countries and live out their lives peacefully in the style to which they have become accustomed. Such a financial solution might violate American moralism, but if the day of the oligarchs is to pass, it is self-indulgent to force all participants locked into the process to effect the change at a cost of blood and terror.

108. Clifford's letter is reprinted in L. Gelb and R. Betts, *The Irony of Vietnam: The System Worked* (Washington, DC: Brookings Institution, 1979), p. 371.

109. Buckley, *Violent Neighbors*, p. 206. Rothenberg, "Soviets in Central America," p. 143. See Evans, "Revolutionary Movements" for a general discussion of leftist revolutionary learning.

110. However, if it did not wish to be treacherous, that is, seek to eliminate the Sandinista government behind the lulling guise of negotiations, the Regan administration would need to correct a common misperception in Nicaragua. Given their past learning, America's self-conception is not an accurate guide to the perceptions of leftist revolutionaries.

111. Too, the Kennedy and Johnson administrations shared, in significant measure, a liberal ideology. Justifiably or not, the political right is typically judged to have settled upon simple lessons to guide its policies. The Kennedy and Johnson administrations had a more open style; they attracted men who knew the difference between hypotheses and evidence, men practiced and sophisticated in the

discernment of other viewpoints, men who could articulate their assumptions and then step back to examine them.

112. See for example Gelb and Betts, *Irony of Vietnam*; Destler, "Elusive Consensus."

113. H. Parmet, *JFK: The Presidency of John F. Kennedy* (New York: Dial Press, 1983), p. 278 et passim; N. Lebow, "The Cuban Missile Crisis: Reading the Lessons Correctly" *Political Science Quarterly* 98 (1983): 431–458.

114. Research at the *New York Times* by C. Argyris, *Behind the Front Page: Organizational Self-Renewal in a Metropolitan Newspaper* (San Francisco: Jossey-Bass, 1974) suggests newsmen may instinctively bias the news toward power drama themes. See H. Gans, *Deciding What's News: A Study of CBS Evening News, NBC Nightly News, Newsweek and Time* (New York: Pantheon, 1979) for a general discussion of the creation of political reality and, for a theoretical statement, P. Berger and T. Luckmann, *The Social Construction of Reality* (Garden City, NY: Doubleday, 1967).

115. George Kennan has provided a steady, thoughtful alternative view in discussions of Soviet-American relations, but in sustaining and developing thinking about other areas of the world, policy discussions in American society are remarkably insular.

116. The founding fathers thought the Senate would be such a body, but those hopes have not been fulfilled. Syndicated columnists have not filled the gap, and none has achieved major stature in foreign affairs since the death of Walter Lippman.

117. Plato, *The Republic* in E. Hamilton and H. Cairns, eds., *The Collected Dialogues of Plato* (New York: Pantheon, 1966), VII, p. 128. Translation is from Richards. Models of strong imagination systems suggest a refinement of the theory of upward-mobility entrapment he had in mind. The issue is not a preference for "rational" over "irrational" forms of thought but of ego-integration of diverse imaginative capacities and impulses. See L. Etheredge, "Larger Than Life Problems: The Citizen, the State, and Policy" Photocopy, 1983; L. Etheredge, "Dual-Track Information Processing in Public Policy Decision Making: Models of Strong Imagination Systems." Symposium paper presented to the American Psychological Association Meetings, Toronto, 1984) and, for a related discussion, J. Loevinger with A. Blasi, *Ego Development* (San Francisco, CA: Jossey-Bass, 1976).

118. For example, one might consider the Harvard/M.I.T. Arms Control Program, funded by foundations, which has had extraordinary benefit in producing analysts of defense and strategic issues. The program has made for well-informed critics, certain of their technical grounding, in the nuclear freeze movement and elsewhere — but these assessments are not in the same universe of thought — of global drama — in which national policy has been made.

119. For reflective essays in this tradition see J. March, "Bounded Rationality, Ambiguity, and the Engineering of Choice," *Bell Journal of Economics* 9 (1978): 587–608; J. March and Z. Shapira, "Behavior Decision Theory and Organizational Decision Theory" mimeo, 1982.

120. Responsibility also activates learning because it raises new questions and concerns. A university with a limited responsibility (e.g., bureaucratized) will have a different character, and have less civic value, than a university where the sense of collective responsibility expands to include a society, a domestic political system, even an international political system that, through its students, learns well.

121. One of the tricks of the mind is that the hardball politics practitioner, experiencing himself to be "sophisticated" about power, in long-term practice acts naively and increases the impotence he strives to overcome.

122. For example, as I discussed in chapter 5, the Eisenhower administration had only a general rule: Any "regime dominated by international Communism" would be eliminated. But it did not communicate clearly — because it did not decide beforehand — what would trigger such a judgment. American economic warfare, beginning with a terminated sugar quota, was unexpected by Castro. The threat had not been used as a bargaining tool, and the abrupt cancellation undoubtedly scared him and provided desperate moments. When the axe fell, there was no Soviet agreement to buy Cuba's sugar, and the Soviet Union apparently had not decided to commit its prestige in Castro's support. Castro undoubtedly was testing limits and angling for what he could get. He needed to know the limits. Why should Washington conclude there was Communist *domination* at a $100 million threshold? If trade patterns and aid were Washington's test of "domination" then — at the $100 million mark — America retained massive domination of Cuba.

123. Presidential inconsistency, even when not duplicitous, reduces power. Eisenhower's ambassador, Philip Bonsal, presented a liberal American self-image: Castro was gracious to the ambassador; understandably he seldom bothered to talk with him. Carter's ambassador, a "kindly Dutch uncle" in his treatment of Nicaraguan Sandinistas, was also treated graciously, while the Nicaraguans speeded their arms shipments and military build-ups in anticipation of the Reagan administration. See NBC, *Appendix*, p. 45.

124. In the case of domestic policy as well, evidence is mounting that the repetition of simple ideological themes similarly reflects operations of the imagination in need of refinement. See Etheredge, "Larger Than Life Problems," "Dual-Track Information Processing," and "Strong Imaginative Systems: The Liberal Activist Case" (Photocopy, 1983) for discussions of the role of larger-than-life dramas and strong imagination systems in American domestic policy learning. R. White, *Fearful Warriors*, provides an excellent discussion of the problems of developing realistic empathy in international relations and basic elements of what might become a general algorithm.

We might contrast the traditional university education in politics and public policy with another field where the welfare of others is eventually to be affected and a practitioner must also use personal judgment. To become a clinical psychologist a student is expected to enlarge his sense of self: his own rigidities, anxieties, instinctive imaginings, personal ideals, ambivalences, and other barriers to empathy and realism are on the agenda of his (or her) education — and in part with the purpose that he be able to understand others who are *not* like his (initially restricted) sense of self. By contrast, political education was (and is) the exception, with the implication that if people are "good enough" (i.e., smart enough) they will make good choices, their right to self-expression should be honored, and they should not be intruded upon in the area of their political styles and beliefs. The traditional university education in politics and public policy can be a license for arrogance which universities, including elite universities, still have not developed a dialogue fully to engage.

125. A. Meltsner, *Policy Analysts in the Bureaucracy* (Berkeley, CA: Univ. of California Press, 1976) gives an extended and perceptive description: in these cases, "political" analysis and "policy" analysis merge and his discussion of individuals with joint expertise is a useful direction.

126. These are zero-sum, or intra-psychic, battles. In a sense American political leaders are practicing (albeit crude) psychoanalytic theorists: The attitudes and impulses beneath the surface generalize and authority everywhere may suffer a common fate which should not be encouraged by the wrong messages.

127. See L. Etheredge, "Government Learning: An Overview" in S. Long, ed., *Handbook of Political Behavior*, vol. 2, (New York: Plenum Press, 1981), pp. 73–161 for a general discussion; L. Etheredge and J. Short, "Thinking About Government Learning" *Journal of Management Studies* 20 (1983): 41–58 for an extended discussion of definitions. They are also a function of the a priori nature of predictable beginner errors: being instinctive and encoded a priori, the hardball sensibility is too plausible; each new generation of policymakers will begin with the same lessons to learn, and will learn them too late; subsequent administrations will repeat the cycle.

 INDEX

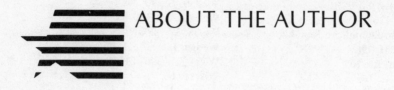# ABOUT THE AUTHOR

Lloyd F. Etheredge received his Ph.D. in political science from Yale University. During the past ten years he has taught at MIT, Yale, and the University of California at Berkeley. He is a specialist in political psychology and the study of government learning. Etheredge is presently visiting professor and Senior Research Fellow at the Rockefeller Institute of Government, SUNY.